Linux Email

Set up and Run a Small Office Email Server

Magnus Bäck

Patrick Ben Koetter

Ralf Hilderbrandt

Alistair McDonald

David Rusenko

Carl Taylor

PUBLISHING

Birmingham - Mumbai

Linux Email
Set up and Run a Small Office Email Server

First edition: June 2005

Published by Packt Publishing Ltd.
32 Lincoln Road
Olton
Birmingham, B27 6PA, UK.

ISBN 1-904811-37-X

www.packtpub.com

Cover Design by www.visionwt.com

Credits

Authors
Magnus Bäck
Patrick Ben Koetter
Ralf Hilderbrandt
Alistair McDonald
David Rusenko
Carl Taylor

Commissioning Editor
David Barnes

Technical Reviewers
Konstantin Ryabitsev
Cami Sardinha

Technical Editor
Nanda Padmanabhan

Layouts
Niranjan Jahagirdar
Nanda Padmanabhan

Indexer
Niranjan Jahagirdar

Proofreader
Chris Smith

Cover Designer
Helen Wood

Illustrator
Dinesh Kandalgaonkar

About the Authors

Magnus Bäck has been playing with computers right since he was a kid, and is interested in everything from digital typography and compilers to relational databases and UNIX. His interests also include e-mail services, and he is an active contributor to the Postfix mailing list. Magnus holds a master's degree in computer science and engineering from Lund Institute of Technology, Sweden, and currently works with software configuration management and tools development for GSM/UMTS phones at Sony Ericsson Mobile Communications.

Patrick Ben Koetter is an active and well-known figure in the Postfix community and works as an information architect. Patrick Koetter runs his own company consulting and developing corporate communication for customers in Europe and Africa.

He speaks about Postfix at industry conferences and hacker conventions and contributes regularly to a number of open-source mailing lists. Patrick Koetter has also co-authored *The Book of Postfix* (ISBN: 1-59327-001-1).

Ralf Hildebrandt is an active and well-known figure in the Postfix community and works as a systems engineer for T-Systems, a German telecommunications company.

He speaks about Postfix at industry conferences and hacker conventions and contributes regularly to a number of open-source mailing lists. Ralf Hildebrandt has also co-authored *The Book of Postfix* (ISBN: 1-59327-001-1).

Alistair McDonald is a freelance IT consultant based in the UK. He has worked in the IT industry for over 15 years and specializes in C++, Perl development, and IT infrastructure management. He is a strong advocate of open source, and has strong cross-platform skills. He prefers vim over vi, emacs over xemacs or vim, and bash over ksh or csh. He is very much a family man and spends as much time as possible with his family enjoying life.

David Rusenko was born in Paris in France, but spent most of his childhood overseas. He began working as a freelance web designer in 1996 and shortly after, in 1999, had his first experience with open source—a box copy of RedHat 5.2. After six years and as many versions of RedHat, he now creates appealing web pages and devises solutions implementing high availability through clustering and alternative security models.

He founded Aderes (www.aderes.net) in 2001, a company that provides e-mail and web-based security solutions. His search for an appropriate webmail platform for the company led him to SquirrelMail. Managing all aspects of the business initially—from the technical concerns to customer support—gave him the experience he now shares with the readers in the webmail chapter of this book.

David has studied both **Information Sciences and Technology (IST)** and **Management Information Systems (MIS)** at the Pennsylvania State University. He speaks both English and French fluently, and is conversational in Arabic. During his free time and vacations, he enjoys scuba diving, backpacking, playing racquetball, and playing electronic music records.

I'd like to take this opportunity to acknowledge my wonderful family, including my parents, Jack and Kathy, and my two sisters, Sarah and Rachel. I'd also like to thank my grandparents, John and Helen, for all they have done. Finally, my good friends, Zac, Jack, Chris, Rachel, Jordan, Diana, Dan, Ryan (both of them), Dana, Kevin, Nick, Lauren, Esteban, and many more.

Carl Taylor has worked over 20 years in the IT industry and has spent the majority of that time working on UNIX-type systems, mainly communications or office automation projects. He was an early user of the UseNet network and taught himself to program in C by working on a variety of open-source software. His experience covers roles including pre- and post-sales support, product development, end-user training, and management.

Carl now runs his own Web Solutions development company **Adepteo** where they specialize in intranet and workflow products building on the best open-source applications available. While not working or looking after his children, Carl is something of a dance addict and is currently learning Latin and Ballroom and Salsa.

I would like to thank my parents and my children Robert, Jack and Harry for their support and understanding whilst I have been working on this project.

Table of Contents

Introduction

If you want an internal mail server for your business then Linux is an excellent choice. For a start, it's free. Not only the operating system but also the essential software components that make up an e-mail server can be acquired without expense.

For most purposes, e-mail is a mature technology. Your server requirements are unlikely to change significantly over time. While commercial servers make their money by introducing new features and forcing customers onto an upgrade path, Linux gives you no such pressure. Once the server is set up, it only needs to be maintained. Sweeping upgrades to the operating system and other software should not be necessary.

On the other hand, setting up a Linux e-mail server can be bewildering. There are many different components to consider, all of them with a wide variety of configuration options and their own unique approaches and terminologies. Which components should you choose, and how can they be made to work together?

This book provides you with one way to set up a fully working e-mail server. There are many other possible ways, and the options can be bewildering. The purpose of this book is to provide you with a path that will work, without bewildering you (too much!) with a massive array of confusing alternatives.

What This Book Covers

As you work your way through this book, your e-mail server will take shape. We'll start with the essentials—building an e-mail server that can send and receive messages using SMTP, POP, and IMAP. From then on, we'll supplement your configuration with extra features: webmail, anti-virus, anti-spam, and setting up e-mail processing rules. We'll also see how to protect an e-mail server from misuse, and finally learn how to develop and implement an e-mail server backup strategy.

Specifically, here's what we will cover in each chapter:

Chapter 1 takes you through the essential elements on a Linux e-mail server, and the network protocols that make e-mail possible. Like it or not, running a Linux e-mail server does require some understanding of the underlying networking—and this chapter is where you will start to get that understanding.

In *Chapter 2*, you'll learn about basic Postfix setup. Postfix is our chosen **mail transfer agent (MTA)**, which forms the heart of any e-mail server. The MTA is responsible, among other things, for moving messages between the various mail servers on the Internet.

Chapter 3 covers what to do with incoming e-mail. It will show you how to setup IMAP and POP access to mailboxes. This means that users will be able to send and receive messages using their familiar e-mail clients.

Now the basics are covered, we can add some more advanced features. *Chapter 4* shows how to set up webmail access using SquirrelMail. This will give users easy out-of-office access to their e-mail.

Chapter 5 looks at how your installation can be secured to prevent misuse of your users' data and the e-mail facility itself.

Chapter 6 and *Chapter 7* introduce Procmail, an application for processing e-mail messages. For example, you can set up forwarding rules, so that messages meeting particular criteria can be forwarded to another user, or handled in some other way. You'll also see how to use Procmail to set up automatic replies to certain messages.

In *Chapter 8* we'll use SpamAssassin in conjunction with Procmail to filter out the wide range of spam that afflicts the modern e-mail user. Then in *Chapter 9* you'll see another way to protect users from rogue e-mail—this time the spread of e-mail viruses.

Finally in *Chapter 10* you'll see how to protect all your hard work by backing up not only the e-mail itself, but also all of the configuration options that make up your e-mail server. Of course, you'll also learn how to restore data from these backups.

Conventions

In this book you will find a number of text styles that distinguish between different kinds of information. Here are some examples of these styles and an explanation of their meanings.

Code words in text are shown as follows: "The `vacation.cache` file is maintained by formail"

New terms and **important words** are introduced in a bold-type font. Words that you see on the screen—in menus or dialog boxes, for example—appear in the text as follows: Dragons are mystical monsters.

Tips, suggestions, or important notes appear in a box like this.

Reader Feedback

Feedback from our readers is always welcome. Let us know what you think about this book, what you liked, or may have disliked. Reader feedback is important for us to develop titles that you really get the most out of.

To send us general feedback, simply drop an e-mail to feedback@packtpub.com, making sure to mention the book title in the subject of your message.

If there is a book that you need and would like to see us publish, please send us a note in the Suggest a title form on www.packtpub.com or e-mail suggest@packtpub.com.

If there is a topic that you have expertise in and you are interested in either writing or contributing to a book, see our author guide on www.packtpub.com/authors.

Customer Support

Now that you are the proud owner of a Packt book, we have a number of things to help you to get the most from your purchase.

Errata

Although we have taken every care to ensure the accuracy of our contents, mistakes do happen. If you find a mistake in one of our books—maybe a mistake in text or code—we would be grateful if you would report this to us. By doing this you can save other readers from frustration, and also help to improve subsequent versions of this book.

If you find any errata, report them by visiting http://www.packtpub.com/support, selecting your book, clicking on the Submit Errata link, and entering the details of your errata. Once your errata have been verified, your submission will be accepted and the errata added to the list of existing errata. The existing errata can be viewed by selecting your title from http://www.packtpub.com/support.

Questions

You can contact us at questions@packtpub.com if you are having a problem with some aspect of the book, and we will do our best to address it.

1

Linux and E-Mail Basics

If you are one of those thousands of system administrators who manage the networks and computers of small to medium-sized companies thinking of hosting their own e-mail service, this book is for you.

We will start with the most basic components of an e-mail system. Together they will allow your users to receive mail from each other and from other people on the Internet, and send messages to whomever they want. This might be all you need, but many companies also want to provide their users with an accessible webmail service that people can use from home or when they are on the road. Another feature that many people unfortunately cannot be without today is proper protection against viruses spread via e-mail as well as filtering of spam messages.

This book will not cover all aspects of the software in question, but it will give you a solid ground to stand on and from there you will be able to delve into the more detailed descriptions of more advanced setups found elsewhere.

As the technical platform for our endeavor, we have chosen the GNU/Linux operating system and a proven selection of free software tools that will help us achieve the goal of a reliable e-mail server for the smaller company. The tools we have chosen are widely known and accepted, written by software professionals, and are supported by a large community of users.

In this very first chapter of the book, we start with what you need to know before you even start working on your server. Questions such as what kind of server hardware and network connection you need will be answered. We will also give you a brief introduction to internet e-mail and its working.

Why Manage your own E-Mail Server?

Why have your own e-mail server and manage it by yourself? Is that not why there are Internet Providers? Since you are, after all, reading this book you may already have your reasons, but let us anyway discuss these questions and some possible answers to them.

The most important reason for hosting and managing your own e-mail server is *control*. For many organizations, e-mail is an important part of the IS/IT infrastructure. Keeping the control over your e-mail has many advantages:

- If your company has offices in multiple places, you have full freedom when choosing how to connect them. Virtual private network between the offices, TLS-secured connections between the offices, a single server for all offices, one server per office, etc.

- By keeping your own messaging in-house, you can send messages to each other without having them travel across the line to and from your provider. This gives a more reliable service if your Internet connection fails, and it avoids unnecessary latencies.

- You are not dependent on the competence of the provider's staff. If you manage your own server and need to solve a difficult problem or implement a custom solution for something, just hire a consultant to help you.

- If the provider goes bankrupt, all your data resides safely in your server room and on your backup media.

- You are not subject to the limitations that your provider may set regarding, say, use of disk space or the maximum size of messages.

- You can implement any policies for anti-spam or anti-virus that you choose.

More control requires more responsibility and more knowledge, and that is where this book comes in.

These hopefully compelling arguments aside, there are also downsides to hosting your own e-mail server. This is a task that requires a certain level of knowledge and commitment and so should not be undertaken be everyone. With your own server, you are not only responsible for the service you provide to your users, but you also have a responsibility towards the whole Internet community. An ill-configured e-mail server can help worms and spam to spread, which not only is a disservice to the community but can also get your server blacklisted. Even though a properly set up server can run for years without requiring much maintenance, you must keep yourself reasonably updated and be prepared to act upon new threats that may arise. Now this is not meant to scare you off, but just to make you think twice.

What you need to Host an E-Mail Server

Your server needs to be available through a permanent Internet connection with a fixed IP address. SMTP does provide an option to let you have your messages delivered to your provider's server, and then have those messages delivered to your own server upon request. The request can be automated and placed every time your connection is up. You can also retrieve new messages to your own server via the **Post Office Protocol**,

(**POP**), normally used by end-user mail application. Neither of these solutions is especially good and they largely defeat the whole purpose of managing your own e-mail server.

In theory, it is possible to run an e-mail server with a non-fixed (dynamic) IP address, but it will not be reliable when the IP address is changed and you will risk losing messages. With a dynamic IP address, you will also face a bigger risk of being put on one of the blacklists for dynamic IP address ranges.

If you are serious about running an e-mail server, get a decent business-class Internet connection. These are inexpensive to come by these days, and investing in one may save you a lot of trouble later on. E-mail traffic does not depend on high bandwidth, so the capacity of a simple DSL line will do fine.

Even though you will need a fixed IP address, you do not necessarily need a public IP address dedicated to the mail server. If you only have a few external IP addresses and use private RFC 1918 addresses (192.168.x.y) on the inside with a **Network Address Translation (NAT)** router connecting your private network to the rest of the world, you can set up your router to forward the ports required by your e-mail services to your internal e-mail server. The table below shows which TCP ports are most likely to come in question for this:

Port	Service
25	SMTP
110	POP
143	IMAP
993	IMAP over TLS

If your employees want to access their messages from home or from the road, all you really have to do is make sure that no firewall is blocking access to the required ports and that your NAT router (if any) forwards these ports correctly. If your users want to send messages via your SMTP server, some extra configuration will be necessary to allow your server to authenticate to the SMTP server.

Sizing the Hardware of your E-Mail Server

When sizing a computer to use as an e-mail server, a lot of people have misconceptions regarding the hardware required to perform this task well. The constantly increasing performance of computers seems to lead people into thinking that they really need the latest and most buzzword-compliant stuff, even if they only want to handle a few thousand messages per day.

Although a certain expertise is required to assess the hardware needs for an organization closely, common sense goes a long way. For a company with 100 users, a reasonably high upper limit for the number of messages per day would be 5,000. That would allow each user to send or receive 50 messages every day. Even if we say that each and every message is sent within the eight hours of the working day, on an average, the system will not have to cope with more than 10 messages per minute. Is it reasonable that a modern computer needs more than six seconds to receive and act upon a single e-mail message, often only a few kilobytes in size? No, it is not.

This little back-of-the-envelope exercise is obviously very rough and does not, for example, take into account the fact that messages typically do not arrive uniformly distributed in time, but it is still a pretty good way of estimating.

Let us now take a little deeper look into what to think about when sizing your server. For an SMTP server that does not perform any content scanning (viruses, spam, etc.), the performance is typically not bound by the CPU but by the I/O performance, specifically the seek time of the hard disk(s) and the quality and configuration of the I/O controller. Throwing more CPU horsepower at the problem will not help. Modern computers are relatively better equipped CPU-wise than I/O-wise, so investing in a multiple gigahertz dual-CPU configuration is probably useless. For any reasonably modern 1 GHz-class PC a handful of messages per second is no problem. That load equates to almost 20,000 messages every hour.

Adding content scanning will probably increase the CPU load quite a lot, and the I/O system will also require more power to keep up. Still, one or two messages per second should not place a noticeable load on the system.

What we have been discussing so far is just the SMTP server. All it does is receive messages and deliver them to other hosts or to local mailboxes. When sizing a server, do not forget that people are going to want to read their e-mail too. This service is provided by server software for POP, IMAP, or both. Just like SMTP software, the key requirement is I/O and not CPU. The number of users of the system is by itself an irrelevant figure; what are important are the usage patterns. How often will the users poll their mailboxes? If 100 users poll their mailboxes once every five minutes, on an average there will be one every three seconds. Checking if a mailbox has any new messages takes a fraction of a second, so the burden will not be significant.

These guidelines may appear vague and non-specific, but it is impossible to give exact figures. The performance you can get from a given piece of hardware depends on so many factors that trying to give anything but general guidelines would be misleading. Use common sense and simple back-of-the-envelope calculations; do not buy the fanciest server you can find unless you are sure you really need it, but also do not use any old abandoned desktop machine you can find. Even if the performance of the old desktop machine may suffice, the components may be old and the service agreement or warranty may be out of date.

Main E-Mail Protocols—SMTP, POP, and IMAP

Why are we discussing basic network communication protocols in this book? Are we not running advanced software? Indeed we are, but knowing one's way around the protocols can not only assist debugging a possibly non-working system but also increase the understanding of a mail system's behavior. We will start with a rather non-technical bird's-eye view of the protocols, after which we will dwell upon the protocol details.

Overview

In the UNIX environment, traditional mail applications have not used any network protocol at all. They have instead accessed the locally stored mailbox files directly through the file system. Typically, the inbox of each user is stored in a single file in either the /var/mail or the /var/spool/mail directory with the same name as that of the user (for example, /var/spool/mail/joe). The focus of this book is to discuss Linux-based e-mail solutions for the small office where users do not wish to log on to a central server with a terminal application in order to access their mail, so local mail storage will only be covered briefly on a need-to-know basis.

The most important protocol in Internet mailing is the **Simple Mail Transfer Protocol (SMTP)**. Its simple purpose is to transport e-mail messages between two computers. These computers may either both be servers, or one of them may be a client machine on which the user runs the mail application—Outlook, Thunderbird, Eudora, or whatever. To collect new messages, the end user does not utilize SMTP. This is where the **Post Office Protocol (POP)**, and the **Internet Message Access Protocol**, **(IMAP)**, come in.

Some proprietary systems such as Microsoft Exchange and Lotus Notes use their own protocols to access messages, and we will not discuss them here.

POP Protocol

POP is the older and more widely used protocol of the two. It focuses on giving the users access to their inboxes, from which the users can download the new messages to their local computers and then delete them from the server. POP servers are not meant to be used for permanent storage of messages and the POP services of some Internet providers even prohibit users from leaving messages on the server after they have been downloaded once. The chief disadvantage of POP is that it only provides access to an intermediary storage medium and the users must store their messages permanently someplace else (for example, on their local hard drives). This is not only impractical for users who want to access their e-mail messages from multiple locations, but it is also a hassle for the system administrator who has to implement a backup solution for the users' messages. POP also does not have any notion of providing multiple folders for every user; with POP a user can access his or her inbox, period.

IMAP Protocol

IMAP is meant as an access method to a first-class mailstore, that is, it is designed to allow the user to store the messages permanently on the server. This solves the system administrator's backup problem and allows the user to access all messages from any place in the world (firewall restrictions aside). IMAP also has a more widespread implementation of TLS-secured connections, making IMAP safe to use in hostile environments. To improve performance and allow users to work with their mailboxes while not being connected to the mail server, most mail applications with IMAP support cache the downloaded mailboxes and messages in the local hard drive.

The SMTP Protocol

SMTP is a line-oriented text protocol that runs over TCP, which makes it trivial to decode SMTP transcripts and to initiate SMTP sessions using the regular Telnet client found on just about any computer. An SMTP client starts a session by connecting to port 25 on the SMTP server. After the server has greeted the client, the client must respond by saying hello, or actually HELO or EHLO, followed by the client's hostname. If the server accepts the cordial greeting, the client may begin the first mail transaction.

An SMTP mail transaction consists of three parts: a sender, one or more recipients, and the actual message contents. The sender is specified with the MAIL FROM command, each recipient with an RCPT TO command, and the start of the message contents with a DATA command. If the server accepts the message then the client may continue with additional transactions or issue the QUIT command to terminate the SMTP session.

Let us be less abstract and look at an actual SMTP session to give you a better idea. The bold face print represents what the client sends to the server.

```
220 mail.example.com ESMTP Postfix (2.2.3)
EHLO gw.example.net
250-mail.example.com
250-PIPELINING
250-SIZE
250-VRFY
250-ETRN
250 8BITMIME
MAIL FROM:<jack@example.net> SIZE=112
250 Ok
RCPT TO:<jill@example.com>
250 Ok
RCPT TO:<jack@example.com>
250 Ok
RCPT TO:<joe@example.com>
550 <joe@example.com>: Recipient address rejected: User unknown in local
recipient table
DATA
354 End data with <CR><LF>.<CR><LF>
Subject: Test mail
To: <root@example.com>
Date: Sun, 15 May 2005 20:23:22 +0200 (CEST)
```

```
This is a test message.
.
250 Ok: queued as B059D3C2B
QUIT
221 Bye
```

This example shows a host that claims to be named `gw.example.net` connects to an SMTP server that calls itself `mail.example.com`. Because the server's first response contains **ESMTP**, the client decides to try **Enhanced SMTP (ESMTP)** and greets the server with `EHLO` instead of `HELO`. The server accepts this greeting and responds with a list of the supported ESMTP extensions.

Together with the sender address, the client sends the `SIZE` attribute to indicate the size of the message to the server. This is allowed because the server has stated that it supports the `SIZE` extension. If the size specified by the client exceeds the message size limit set by the server, the message can be rejected at once rather than after the whole message has been received and the server can assess the size.

An SMTP message can obviously have more than one recipient. This has a few consequences that must be remembered while implementing a mail system and inventing policies. In the example above, the mail server accepts the first two recipients but rejects the third one. Since two recipients have been accepted by the server, the client will try to send the message contents. Here the message is accepted by the server and queued for delivery (`250 Ok: queued as B059D3C2B`), which means that the SMTP server has taken over the responsibility for the delivery of the message to the accepted recipients. If the message cannot be delivered, the server will send a **non-delivery message (bounce)** back to the sender. The server could also have chosen to reject the whole message. If so, it would have rejected it for all recipients and not delivered it at all. In other words, in response to the message contents the server must either reject the message for all recipients or accept it for all recipients.

It is vital to understand the difference between the envelope and the header. The envelope of a message consists of the information given in the `MAIL FROM` and `RCPT TO` commands, that is, the sender and recipient information that is used to deliver the message. An SMTP server pays no attention what so ever to the `From`, `To`, and `Cc` message headers. In our example the `To` header contains just a single address with no other relation to the actual recipient addresses than the domain, but that is just a coincidence. Bounces are always sent to the envelope sender address, in this case `jack@example.net`. The sender address of bounce messages is the empty sender address, often called the **null sender**. However tempting it may be for some people, the null sender address must not be blocked.

So far we have not commented on the numerical codes given by the server at the beginning of each line. Each number has a specific meaning and it is important to learn the correct interpretation of the first digit.

Digit	Meaning
2	Server has accepted the previous command and is awaiting your next command.
3	Used only in response to the DATA command, and means that the server is ready to accept the message contents.
4	Temporary error: the request cannot be performed at the moment, but it may be successfully serviced later.
5	Permanent error: the request will never be accepted.

In SMTP, error conditions can be either **temporary** or **permanent**. Both 4 and 5 are used to signal errors. A client that receives a temporary error designated by 4 should disconnect, keep the message in the queue, and retry at a later time. Typical temporary error conditions include a full mail queue disk, a server configuration error that must be resolved before messages can be accepted, or a temporary DNS lookup error. Permanent errors are indicated by the first digit being 5 and mean that the request will never be accepted, so a client will have to remove the message from the queue and send a bounce to the sender telling him or her that the message could not be delivered.

There is a lot more to SMTP than this quick introduction has covered, but this should get your started. A number of **RFC** documents cover SMTP related topics, but the probably most important ones are **RFC 821 (Simple Mail Transfer Protocol)** and **RFC 822 (Standard for the format of ARPA Internet text messages)**.

E-Mail and DNS

The **Domain Name System**, or **DNS**, plays an important role in e-mailing. The DNS is used by both e-mail clients and e-mail servers. Even if you do not intend to maintain your own DNS server, a thorough understanding of DNS's role in e-mailing is a necessity for the mail server operator. This section assumes that the reader has basic knowledge of how DNS works in general.

DNS Record Types Used by E-Mail Applications

In many networking scenarios, only two DNS record types are used: A and PTR. These map hostnames to IP addresses and IP addresses to hostnames, respectively. These record types are also used for e-mail, but there is also a third DNS record type that is uniquely available for e-mail.

How does an SMTP server discover to which host a message for a certain domain should be delivered? The recipient domain is, not surprisingly, used as the key in one or more DNS lookups. The first lookup that is made is for the mail-specific MX record—the **mail**

exchanger record type that allows the DNS operator to specify the hostname or hostnames of servers that receive mail for a certain domain. For example, MX records can be used to specify that messages to someone at example.com should be sent to mail.example.com. If the recipient domain does not have an MX record, an attempt is made to find an A record for the recipient domain. If the A record lookup succeeds, the mail will be delivered to the host. If both the MX and A lookups do not return any results, the message is deemed undeliverable and is returned to the sender.

What is the point of having these MX records? There are two good reasons:

First, it might not be desirable to be forced to map the A record of a domain to the mail server. What if Example, Inc. with the WWW address http://www.example.com/ wants to allow visitors to use the shorter http://example.com/ URL, but does not want to run the web server application on the mail server (or vice versa)?

The more important reason is that the result of an MX lookup does not only contain a list of hostnames, but rather a list of (hostname, priority) tuples. The priority field is an integer describing the priority of the hostname within the list. The absolute magnitude of the priority number does not matter, but it is used in relation to the priority of any other hostnames to create an ordered list of hostnames to try when delivering a message. The list is in ascending order, so the hostname with the lowest priority number will be contacted first. If two hostnames have equal priority, they will be tried in random order.

Equal-priority MX records can be used as a very crude form of load balancing between two or more servers, but this is also possible with A records that map to multiple IP addresses. The hierarchy of backup mail servers with different priorities that can be set up for a domain using MX records cannot be made to happen with A records. Let us look at a constructed example of an organization that uses a lot of mail servers:

Priority	Hostname
10	mx1.example.com
10	mx2.example.com
20	mx3.example.com
30	mx4.example.com

If this DNS configuration is set for the domain example.com, SMTP servers are expected to try to deliver messages for example.com to mx1.example.com or mx2.example.com first. If both connections fail, mx3.example.com should be tried, and if even that server does not respond in a timely way, mx4.example.com is the last resort. Should that fail too, the message is kept and delivery is retried at a later time.

Backup Mail Servers

Having a backup server that can receive your messages if your own server is unavailable sounds like a really good idea, but today's reliable Internet connections together with spam, worms, and other rubbish have for the most part made backup mail servers unnecessary and often even harmful. The rationale for having a backup server is that it can receive messages while your primary server is down, and then deliver them to the primary server when it is up again. The advantage of this is, however, very small since all SMTP servers are required to queue undeliverable messages anyway for at least five days before they are returned to the sender. Granted, by having a backup server you can choose to store unavailable messages for longer time than five days, but if your main SMTP server is unavailable longer than five days at a stretch you probably have bigger problems than a few lost messages.

But how does the spam fit in? Because a backup mail server typically does not have the same spam-thwarting configuration as the primary server, spammers often specifically target backup servers in order to bypass the stricter rules of the primary server.

Another strong reason to avoid backup mail servers is that they typically do not perform **recipient validation**. This means that they do not know which recipient addresses are valid for the domains they act as a backup servers for. This requires a backup server to accept all messages for the backed-up domains and attempt to deliver them to the primary server. The primary server will reject invalid recipients, causing the backup server to bounce such message back to the sender. This is known as **backscatter** and is bad for two reasons; sender addresses are often spoofed, so the bounces may be sent to an innocent bystander, and it may fill your mail queue with bounced messages that cannot be delivered because the receiving server is unavailable. A busy server that does not perform recipient validation and is hit heavily with spam may have thousands or tens of thousands of undeliverable messages residing in the queue.

Summary

In this chapter, we started by discussing why you should even consider hosting your own e-mail server. Then, we looked at some questions that need to be answered before you can start working with your server—the kind of network connection and computer power you can expect to need for your server. To manage an e-mail server successfully, an understanding of the network communication protocols used is important. We gave an overview of POP and IMAP, and delved more deeply into the most important of them all, SMTP. Finally, we looked at the vital role that the DNS plays in e-mailing.

2

Setting Up Postfix

The **Mail Transfer Agent (MTA)** is perhaps the most important part of a mail system. It is responsible for receiving messages from the Internet or from your own users and making sure that the messages safely arrive at their destinations—the other mail servers or mailboxes of your users.

Postfix has been chosen as the mail transfer agent to be covered in this book. Postfix has a large feature set, it has an excellent security track record, it is fast, easy to configure, and under active development.

This book assumes that you run Postfix 2.0 or later. Any feature or behavior of Postfix that is specific to later releases will be noted.

> If you still run Postfix 1.x it is highly recommended that you upgrade. Even though Postfix did not change dramatically between version 1.x and 2.0, several configuration parameters covered in this book have changed or were added since 1.x. So reading this book when using Postfix 1.x may be rather confusing.

Introduction to Postfix

This first section gives a brief introduction to how Postfix works and describes how its behavior can be controlled.

What is Postfix?

Postfix is a modular mail transfer agent developed by IBM researcher and physics Ph.D. Wietse Venema. It is free software and was released publicly for the first time in 1998 under the name **VMailer**. It is written in C and currently consists of about 70,000 lines of code (comments excluded) and works on most non-historic variants of UNIX and Linux.

As a pure mail transfer agent, Postfix does not provide any service for allowing users to collect their mail via **POP**, **IMAP**, and so on. That task must be carried out by some other piece of software, the e-mail client. The software discussed in this book for retrieving the e-mail from the host is **Courier**.

All current Postfix documentation as well as the source code and links to third-party software and archives of the very active mailing list can be found at the Postfix web site at `http://www.postfix.org/`.

Postfix Architecture: An Overview

This section will describe the different parts of the Postfix mail transfer agent and explain what really goes on when you send a message through the system. Although this might not be the most exciting text you have ever read, understanding the basics of how Postfix works is essential to successfully manage a Postfix server.

Postfix is divided into a number of separate **daemons** that communicate with each other. These daemons all have distinct areas of responsibility, may run in different security contexts, and may have different rules for the number of processes of their type that may be created. All daemon processes are created as needed and are supervised by a mother daemon, the `master`. Some daemons are rarely or never restarted, but most of them will commit suicide after having served a configurable number of requests or after they have been idle for a configurable duration in time. The following figure shows how messages flow through a Postfix system, and can be used to accompany the text that follows. The solid lines show the path of the message content while dotted lines show other forms of communication:

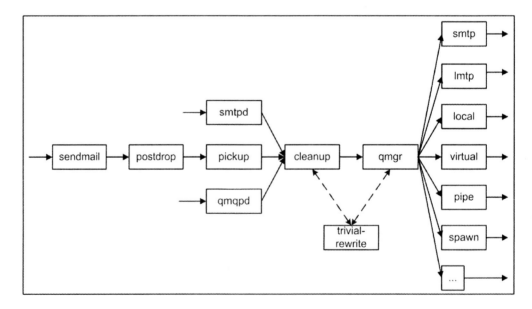

Not all Postfix daemons will be described here, just the important ones. A complete run-down of all daemons can be found in the **Postfix Architecture Overview** document at http://www.postfix.org/OVERVIEW.html.

New Message Arrival

New messages can arrive into the Postfix system in three ways. The most common way is, of course, via **SMTP** and the responsible daemon is named smtpd. The uncommon **QMQP Submission Protocol**, introduced in Dan J. Bernstein's **qmail**, is also supported with the qmqpd daemon.

The third way a message can arrive is via local submission with the sendmail program. This is the standard way to submit mail messages from programs and scripts running on a host. Postfix provides a sendmail program that in most regards is compatible with the sendmail program of the **sendmail** mail transfer agent (http://www.sendmail.org/). Many UNIX mail user agents such as Mail, Pine, and Mutt use the sendmail interface to submit new messages. The sendmail program hands messages on to the **postdrop** program, which places a message file in the maildrop directory within the Postfix queue directory. This does not require Postfix to be running. The pickup daemon waits for messages to arrive into the maildrop directory, and passes them on to the cleanup daemon. From there on, sendmail-submitted messages take the same road as messages submitted via SMTP or QMQP.

When smtpd, qmqpd, or pickup has received a new message, it hands it to the cleanup daemon. This daemon enforces restrictions on the message size, acts on any content restrictions configured by the user, rewrites sender and/or recipient addresses as required by the configuration, adds any required headers that are missing, and a few other things. The cleanup daemon uses the trivial-rewrite daemon for some address rewriting operations. When done with its business, cleanup puts the queue file in the incoming queue and notifies the queue manager.

Scheduling Message Deliveries

The **queue manager**, qmgr, is responsible for scheduling the delivery of messages. To decide how a message should be delivered to each recipient (namely the delivery method and the next destination), qmgr gets help from trivial-rewrite. The queue manager requests delivery agent processes from the master daemon and collects the results of the deliveries.

The queue manager is responsible for all messages from the point when the cleanup daemon hands them over until they are removed from the queue. This can be either because they have been successfully delivered to all recipients or because they have been in the queue so long (by default, messages will remain in the queue for five days) that

Postfix decides that they are undeliverable. It uses the bounce daemon to send a bounce message to the sender.

The queue manager uses a number of directories for different purposes. The incoming queue is monitored for new messages, and the next stop is the **active queue**. The active queue contains the messages that are ready for delivery. If a delivery attempt fails, the message is moved to the **deferred queue**. That queue will be scanned now and then, and if it is time to retry the delivery of a message, the queue file for the message will once more be moved into the active queue. Whether a delivery of a message should be reattempted when the queue is scanned depends on two factors; how much time has passed since the message arrived and the two configuration parameters that set a minimum and maximum time interval between the reattempts.

The different queues used by Postfix are described in detail in the QSHAPE_README document (http://www.postfix.org/QSHAPE_README.html).

Message Delivery

Postfix comes with a number of delivery agents that are used to deliver messages using various means and protocol. The delivery agents are the last daemons that touch the messages before they leave your system.

The Postfix SMTP client, smtp (not to be confused with the SMTP server, smtpd), is used to deliver messages to other hosts via the SMTP protocol. It is very similar to the LMTP client, lmtp, which delivers messages via the LMTP protocol.

The **local delivery agent**, local, delivers messages to users with normal accounts on the system. It supports aliases for simple mailing lists or role addresses as well as .forward files so users themselves can set up forwarding of their messages.

If you have virtual mailbox users—that is users that do not have real accounts (shell accounts, if you will) on the system—their messages are delivered with virtual.

If Postfix's standard delivery agents should not suffice, you can write your own delivery agent and have Postfix invoke it for some (or all) messages. In that case you can either use the pipe daemon to have the message bodies given to your delivery agent via the standard input stream, or you can use the spawn daemon if you want to write a delivery agent that accepts messages via some network protocol.

Supporting Programs

Postfix contains a number of supporting programs that you can use to control, test, and debug your Postfix system. This list is not exhaustive and only gives a brief description of each program, but some of the programs will be used later on in the chapter. It is a good idea to get acquainted with them so you at least know what sort of problems they can help you solve.

Program	Description
mailq	Views the current contents of the Postfix queue. Includes the size, time of arrival, sender address, and recipient address(es) of each message. Internally just invokes the postqueue command and exists only for backwards compatibility with the sendmail mail transfer agent.
Newaliases	Uses the postalias command to rebuild all local alias files. Local aliases will be covered in the *Virtual Alias Domains and Local Alias* section.
Postalias	Rebuilds a single alias file, or queries an alias lookup table.
postcat	Shows the contents of a binary queue file residing in the Postfix queue.
postconf	Shows the current or default values of Postfix's configuration parameters. Can also modify the main configuration file, which can be useful in scripts.
postmap	Rebuilds an indexed database file used for table lookups, or queries any lookup table. The *Troubleshooting Lookup Tables with Postmap* section discusses how this can be used to debug a Postfix setup.
postqueue	Apart from carrying out the work for the mailq program, can also be used to flush the queue. Flushing a queue means moving all messages in the deferred queue to the active queue. This can be useful to schedule immediate message delivery, but be careful. If your server is heavily loaded and performing badly, flushing the queue will only make matters worse. The sendmail program can also be used to flush the queue, once more for compatibility reasons.
postsuper	Allows you to take actions on already queued messages, for example deleting or re-queuing them. Can also perform a structural check on the queue directories and fix problems such as queue files having the wrong names. Such a check is for example necessary if the whole queue directory has been moved or restored from a backup.

Installation and Basic Configuration

In this section, we will take a look at how to obtain and install Postfix as well as how to make the first and most basic configuration changes. By the end of this section you will be able to use Postfix to send and receive e-mail messages.

Choosing the Postfix Version

There are two separate branches of Postfix development; the official release and the experimental release. The official release is sometimes referred to as the stable release, but that is somewhat misleading as it implies that the experimental release is unstable.

That is not the case. The experimental release is used to introduce all new Postfix features. When the implementations of the features and their interfaces (for example, their configuration parameters) have stabilized sufficiently, they are brought into the official release. The only changes made to the official release are bugfixes and fixes for portability problems.

The experimental release is fully usable in production environments, but the code is of course less tested and configuration parameters and their semantics may change between releases. If you choose to use the experimental release you should build and install Postfix from source code instead of using some package management system (say RPMs). This will allow you to easily apply any patches for newly discovered problems.

The experimental release has a version number that indicates the number of the upcoming official release together with the release date of the experimental release in question. For example, at the time of writing the current official release was 2.1 and the current experimental release was 2.2-20041215.

Installing from a Package

Probably all current Linux distributions include Postfix as a package that can easily be installed. You are better off with the distribution's package unless you are comfortable building software from source and, if required, debugging any build problems that might occur. Most packages come pre-built with some extra features that would otherwise require a more complicated build process.

Because there are many different packaging systems, the actual process of installing the Postfix package(s) will not be covered here. Please consult the documentation of your package management system for details.

> A word of caution for users of distributions that allow multiple mail transfer agents to be installed at the same time: If you are installing Postfix to replace another mail transfer agent you should make sure the previous software is properly removed from your system. Since probably all mail transfer agents provide a sendmail program, this file is installed with a name such as sendmail.postfix, and a symbolic link points from sendmail to sendmail.postfix or whatever mail transfer agent's sendmail program is chosen to be the main one. If that symbolic link does not point to Postfix's sendmail program, you might get surprised when you attempt to send a message.

Installing from Source Code

Installing Postfix from the original source code is not very difficult and enables you to run any version you want and not just the version chosen by the package maintainer of your Linux distribution. The Postfix source code can be downloaded from a number of mirrors accessible from the main Postfix web site (http://www.postfix.org/download.html).

Once you have downloaded and unpacked the archive in a suitable directory (/usr/local/src is typical), you will notice that the Postfix build system does not use GNU autotools and does therefore not have the configure script that one normally finds in the root directory of the unpacked archive. The Postfix build system will automatically take care of this step. Do not worry if you want to install Postfix in some non-standard location, you will get an opportunity to set various installation directories later.

If you need to enable non-standard features such as support for MySQL or LDAP lookups, you must inform the build system about this and where to find the libraries and include files for the feature. For exact instructions and details about each non-standard feature, please review the README file for each and every one of them. For example, the MySQL instructions found in README_FILES/MYSQL_README tell you to run the following command to enable MySQL support when building Postfix:

```
$ make -f Makefile.init makefiles \
        'CCARGS=-DHAS_MYSQL -I/usr/local/mysql/include' \
        'AUXLIBS=-L/usr/local/mysql/lib -lmysqlclient -lz -lm'
```

Adjust the paths to where the MySQL include files and shared libraries are located on your system. You must have the development libraries for MySQL installed. If you need more than one extra feature you will have to combine the commands given in each of the README files.

After this, you are all set to build Postfix:

```
$ make
```

When the build is completed (hopefully without errors), it is time to create a user and groups that Postfix uses for many of its daemons. Start by adding two groups, postfix and postdrop. You can for example use the groupadd tool, which probably is available in your Linux distribution:

```
$ groupadd postfix
$ groupadd postdrop
```

The next step is to create a user named postfix. This user requires no shell access, nor a valid home directory. The primary group of this new user should be the newly created postfix group. Here is how to do it using the useradd tool:

```
$ useradd -c postfix -d /tmp -g postfix -s /bin/false postfix
```

Now, you should add something similar to the following to /etc/passwd:

```
    postfix:x:12345:123:postfix:/tmp:/bin/false
```

And something like the following to /etc/group:

```
postfix:x:123:
postdrop:x:321:
```

The next and final step is to install your newly built Postfix. If you are installing Postfix for the first time in this particular Linux installation, run the following command:

$ make install

This command will guide you through an interactive installation procedure where you get to choose various installation directories and file locations.

If you are upgrading Postfix from a previous release, run the following command instead:

$ make upgrade

All right! Postfix is now installed on your system, and you will soon be ready to use it.

To make sure that Postfix starts when your system boots, some extra measures are needed. Most Linux systems have a SysV-style init, so you to construct an init script and make proper links in the runlevel directories.

The Postfix Configuration

Like most UNIX software, Postfix reads its configuration from text files stored under the /etc directory. Postfix configuration files are usually stored in /etc/postfix, but you can configure Postfix to use any other directory. Postfix uses two main configuration files, master.cf and main.cf, and any auxiliary files that you set up yourself.

After a change to any of these files, Postfix must be reloaded. This can be done with the same program that started Postfix, via the init scripts, or via some other service management tool that your distribution provides:

```
postfix reload
/etc/init.d/postfix reload
/etc/rc.d/init.d/postfix reload
```

> **Postfix restart required after changing inet_interfaces:**
>
> If the inet_interfaces parameter is changed, a reload is not enough. Postfix must be stopped and restarted for the changes to take effect. This is also true for the inet_protocols parameter introduced in Postfix 2.2.

main.cf

The file you will be editing most frequently is `main.cf`. That file defines the parameters
that control the behavior of Postfix's daemon processes. Each line has the following form:

```
parameter = value
```

This simply means that the parameter named `parameter` is given the value `value`. A
parameter may only be specified once in `main.cf`. If you by mistake give the same
parameter different values at different places in `main.cf`, the last occurrence will be the
one used by Postfix. Apart from this, the order in which parameters are listed in `main.cf`
is insignificant. However, *within* a parameter value the order of the keywords may matter.
For example, the following two parameters are not necessarily equivalent:

```
parameter = A, B
parameter = B, A
```

If the value of a parameter is not specified in `main.cf`, Postfix will use the default value.
The default value for most parameters is hard-wired in the source code, but some default
values are determined at build time, and a few of them at run time.

Lines in `main.cf` can be marked as comments by starting them with #.

```
# These two lines are comments. They can be used to temporarily
# disable parameters, or to explain the configuration.
mydomain = example.com
mydestination = $mydomain, localhost
```

This short example also shows how the current value of another parameter can be
inserted when setting a parameter value; simply type a dollar sign directly followed by
the name of the parameter whose value you wish to obtain. The last line above is
equivalent to the following:

```
mydestination = example.com, localhost
```

Sometimes it is not convenient to have everything on one line. By starting a line with
whitespace, you tell Postfix that the line is a continuation of the previous line. For
example, the following two are equivalent (the first example is a single line, and has
wrapped here because of page constraints):

```
smtpd_recipient_restrictions = permit_mynetworks,
reject_unauth_destination
```

```
smtpd_recipient_restrictions =
        permit_mynetworks,
        reject_unauth_destination
```

In Postfix 2.1 and later, the format of the `main.cf` configuration file is documented in the
`postconf(5)` manual page, which also describes all available configuration parameters.

The `postconf` program is very useful for examining the current and default value of `main.cf` parameters. Start the program with one or more parameter names as options and it will report the values that Postfix would use. If you use the -d option, `postconf` will report the default value of the parameter(s) you list.

For example, here is how to compare the current value of `mydestination` with its default value:

```
$ postconf mydestination
mydestination = $mydomain, localhost.$mydomain
$ postconf -d mydestination
mydestination = $myhostname, localhost.$mydomain, localhost
```

Using this method is often quicker than looking in `main.cf` or wading through a huge manual page to find the default value. It also reveals the actual value Postfix thinks a parameter has, making it easier to spot mistypes.

master.cf

The `master.cf` file configures the Postfix master daemon that we discussed earlier. Each line in `master.cf` defines a service that a certain program carries out. For example, the daemon that receives and processes SMTP connections, `smtpd`, is one service. The program that delivers messages to the local users, `local`, is another service. In addition to the 15–20 services that Postfix defines from the start, you can add your own services.

The fifth column in `master.cf` controls whether each service should be run in a `chroot` environment. `chroot` is a UNIX feature that changes the root of the file system, making it impossible to access a file outside the new root directory even if a running process is compromised by an evildoer with root privileges. The source distribution of Postfix disables `chroot` completely by default, but some Linux distributions have it enabled. Although `chroot` is a security feature that can be quite useful as an extra safety net, it makes Postfix more difficult to maintain and is more or less useless unless the rest of your system is really tight.

In Postfix 2.2 and later, the format of the `master.cf` configuration file is documented in the `master(5)` manual page. In earlier releases, most of that information can be found in comments in the `master.cf` file itself.

For most simple Postfix setups, `master.cf` does not need to be touched at all.

Lookup Tables

Some information cannot be conveniently represented in `main.cf` or `master.cf`. Postfix's concept of lookup tables allows information to be stored in external files, relational databases, or LDAP directories.

To Postfix, a lookup table is an abstract entity that maps one string, the **lookup key**, to another string, the **lookup result**. Those who are mathematically inclined may look upon it as a function or as a collection of (key, value) tuples and programmers may recognize it as a 'hashtable'. Basically it is like a phonebook; you look up a name and get a phone number back.

In most cases, the simple indexed lookup table types will often be the most convenient ones. An indexed lookup table is nothing more than a text file that you can edit using your favorite text editor. The first part of each line, up to the first whitespace, will be taken as a lookup key and the rest of the line will be taken as the corresponding value.

```
key                         value
```

The term 'indexed' is used because Postfix does not read these text files directly. That would be too slow. Instead, the text files are built to indexed binary files that simple database libraries can read. In the Linux environment, the lookup table type 'hash' is the most commonly used one. It uses the Berkeley DB library, as does the 'btree' type. To build the indexed file, the postmap program is used. You do not have to reload or restart Postfix after having updated an indexed file with postmap. Postfix will discover the updated file itself and restart its daemon processes as required.

The topic of lookup tables can fill a whole chapter by itself, so this section will just mention them briefly. We will use lookup tables in a few places later in this chapter, for example, when we set up policies for spam control.

For a more elaborated discussion of lookup tables and a list of all available lookup table types, see DATABASE_README (http://www.postfix.org/DATABASE_README.html) and the manual pages that document the use of some of the more complex lookup table types.

Getting Postfix Up and Running

Now that you have installed Postfix, let us make some basic configuration changes, fire it up and take it for a test drive. If you installed Postfix from a package you may already have answered some configuration questions and have had Postfix started for you.

Domains and Hostnames

Before starting Postfix, let us review some fundamental settings in main.cf. The first ones concern the names of your domain and your mailhost. The mydomain parameter should be set to your main Internet domain. If you run Example, Inc. having the domain http://www.example.com/, the following setting would be reasonable:

```
mydomain = example.com
```

The value of mydomain will affect how Postfix transforms hostnames that are not fully qualified. This means that all bare hostnames encountered in places like sender and recipient addresses will be qualified with this domain—a hostname such as jeeves will in this case be turned into jeeves.example.com. We will also refer to mydomain in other parameters using the $parameter notation described earlier. Note that the feature of appending mydomain can be disabled by setting the append_dot_mydomain parameter to NO, and some Linux distributions make this modification by default. In general, the value should be left as YES.

A related parameter is myhostname, which incidentally tells Postfix the hostname of the machine. The hostname is among other things used as default when the Postfix SMTP server greets a client and when the SMTP client says HELO to a server. Postfix is normally able to determine this by itself, but sometimes you want to override this. Use the postconf command to see if the current value looks good:

```
$ postconf myhostname
myhostname = jeeves
```

Yes, this looks fine. Note that this hostname is not fully qualified, so the actual hostname used in various places will include mydomain.

A parameter that is related to mydomain is myorigin. This parameter specifies the domain that should be used to qualify e-mail addresses that have no domain part at all. This may seem highly irregular but it is actually pretty common. Messages submitted with the sendmail program will by default get the current username as the sender address, and because usernames do not have domains the username will be qualified with myorigin before the message is delivered anywhere. By default, myorigin is set to the same value as myhostname:

```
$ postconf -d myorigin
myorigin = $myhostname
```

This should be OK, but you might want to set it to mydomain instead:

```
    myorigin = $mydomain
```

The next parameter we will give attention is mydestination. That parameter is quite important because it tells Postfix which domains are considered local, that is, which domains should be delivered to UNIX accounts on this machine. Unlike mydomain and myorigin, mydestination may contain multiple domains separated by space or commas. By listing example.com here, Postfix will accept messages addressed to joe@example.com and deliver them to the UNIX user 'joe'.

One important property of local domains is that they are all considered equal. If example.com and example.net are both listed in mydestination, joe@example.com will be equivalent to joe@example.net. If you need additional domains where the users are not equal you need to implement virtual alias domains, described in the *Virtual Alias Domains* section.

Returning to Example, Inc., you will want to have example.com listed in mydestination since it is your primary domain. The old domain, example.net, should also work for the time being so that one should be included too. Additionally, it is wise to list the value of myhostname in mydestination as well as making sure that mail addressed to localhost gets delivered properly. This yields the following complete list of local domains for Example, Inc.:

```
mydestination = $mydomain, example.net, $myhostname,
localhost.$mydomain
```

So why localhost.$mydomain instead of just localhost if we want messages to root@localhost to be delivered locally? Remember that mydomain is used to qualify all hostnames that are not already fully qualified (one may argue that localhost in fact already is a fully qualified hostname, but Postfix does not make a special case for that hostname). The address root@localhost will be rewritten to root@localhost.example.com.

Two very important Postfix parameters, mynetworks and mynetworks_style, control which hosts are allowed to use your server as a relay. Setting these incorrectly may allow your server to be abused by spammers and the likes, so it is important that you get them right. By default, all hosts on the subnets that your server is directly connected to will be allowed access. This should be secure in most cases. These parameters and other methods of allowing relay access will be discussed in depth in Chapter 5.

Indirect Mail Delivery through Your ISP

Some Internet service providers do not allow their customers to directly access remote mail servers via the standard SMTP port (25). Instead they provide a relay server that all outbound messages must go through. This policy is common for residential cable or DSL connections, but some providers have the same policy for commercial-grade connections. If such is that case, you need to configure Postfix to deliver all outbound messages indirectly via your ISP's relay server.

This is done with the relayhost parameter, which contains the hostname or IP address of the relay server to use. The following forms are allowed:

```
relayhost = example.com
relayhost = [mail.example.com]
relayhost = [1.2.3.4]
```

The first form will cause Postfix to perform an MX lookup on the hostname, just as it would do for a normal message delivery. Enclosing the hostname in square brackets as in the second example suppresses the MX lookup. The square brackets are also required in the third case when an IP address is specified.

Optionally, the hostname or address can be followed by :port to specify an alternative TCP port. Note that you cannot specify multiple hostnames or addresses to achieve fallback or load balancing behavior. If you need fallback hosts if the normal relay server is unreachable, take a look at the fallback_relay parameter. Refer the *Other Useful Configuration Parameters* section for additional information on other parameters.

Choosing Network Interfaces

The inet_interfaces parameter decides the network interfaces that Postfix will use for both listening to new connections and sending out messages. If you have multiple network interfaces and you do not want Postfix to use all of them, you can adjust this parameter to list the addresses or hostnames of the interfaces you do want Postfix to use.

Some Linux distributions set inet_interfaces to localhost by default, which means that Postfix will only listen on the loopback interface. This makes at least some sense for workstations, but it is obviously completely unusable for servers that need to receive messages from foreign hosts. If the Postfix packaging of your Linux distribution has this feature, just delete or comment the inet_interfaces line from main.cf to disable it. Postfix will then use the default value of all, which of course means that all interfaces should be used.

Again, note that changing inet_interfaces requires Postfix to be restarted. A reload is not enough.

Choosing Mailbox Format for Local Deliveries

By default, Postfix delivers local messages (messages to domains listed in mydestination) into files in mbox format. The mbox format for mailboxes stores all messages of a mailbox in a single text file. These files are named after the user and go into the directory specified by mail_spool_directory (normally /var/mail or /var/spool/mail). If the user desires additional mailboxes to store messages, those files are stored somewhere in the user's home directory (often in $HOME/mail or $HOME/Mail).

The mbox format has a few flaws that make it rather undesirable. The single-file format makes message deletion expensive since the whole file must be rewritten completely unless the message deleted is the last one, in which case the file can just be truncated. Mbox also puts up hurdles when multiple processes need to access the same mailbox concurrently, which for example, happens when a user uses a POP server to retrieve and delete messages while new mail is being delivered. This requires that some method of exclusive locking is used to avoid the concurrent access that might corrupt the files. Such locking is not a big problem if all software run on the same machine, access the same local file system, and agree on which locking method to use, but it is a royal pain if mailboxes need to be accessed over the network via, say, NFS.

To avoid these problems, D. J. Bernstein, the author of software such as qmail and djbdns, designed the `maildir` format for mailboxes. As the name implies, `maildir` uses directories and one file per message. Deletion of messages is always very fast, but on the other hand it takes longer to scan a mailbox and produce a list of all messages since all message files have to be opened and read. `Maildir` is safe to use with NFS. In the `maildir` delivery format, the inbox of a user is typically found in $HOME/Maildir.

To configure Postfix to deliver new messages to local users to $HOME/Maildir, set the `home_mailbox` parameter like this:

```
home_mailbox = Maildir/
```

Note the slash at the end of the line; it is important! Postfix follows the convention used by many other programs that a mailbox location ending with a slash denotes `maildir`. If you omit the slash, Postfix will try to deliver messages to the mbox file $HOME/Maildir.

The `home_mailbox` parameter is only effective for local domains when Postfix performs the delivery itself. If delivery is made by some other delivery agent such as Procmail or Maildrop, you have to configure that software for `maildir` delivery.

The rest of this book assumes that you have chosen `maildir` delivery. The IMAP/POP server you will be introduced to later, Courier, does not support the mbox format at all. Converting mailboxes between mbox and `maildir` is not difficult, so if you want to switch format later that is not a problem.

Error Reporting

The final step is to make sure that Postfix and real people around the world can notify you as a postmaster about error conditions. Internet standards require all domains to have a postmaster address, but you do not need to create an account with that name. Instead you can use the aliasing feature of Postfix to redirect messages addressed to the postmaster address to yourself and any other people that manage the mail system. Also, you should redirect messages to the root account.

Aliases will be discussed in more detail in the *Local Aliases* section, but this step should be done right now so we will take a quick look anyway. To make Postfix redirect root's messages and accept messages addressed to postmaster even though no such user account exists, the local alias table must be modified. The configuration parameter `alias_maps` controls the location of the lookup tables that define such mappings:

```
$ postconf alias_maps
alias_maps = hash:/etc/aliases, nis:mail.aliases
```

Here the local aliases are stored in the file /etc/aliases (additionally, Postfix will look for aliases in the NIS map mail.aliases). Edit that file so that it contains two lines similar to these:

```
postmaster: root
root: jack, jill
```

This means that messages addressed to the postmaster will be sent to the root user, and messages to the root user will be redirected to the users, 'jack' and 'jill'. Save the file and run the newaliases command so that Postfix will pick up the changes to the file.

The type of problems that Postfix will report to the postmaster is configurable with the notify_classes parameter. By default, only resource problems such as out-of-disk-space problems and software problems will be reported, but you may configure Postfix to report more types of problems. For example, you might also want to know about SMTP protocol violations:

```
noticy_classes = resource, software, protocol
```

When Postfix reports a problem, a transcript of the SMTP session is included. This can be a valuable debugging aid.

Opt for more extensive error reporting rather than too terse reporting. If you receive too many error reports, see if you can use the filtering features of your delivery agent or your mail client to remove the error reports that are not interesting reading. Protocol violations by badly written spam software can typically be ignored, but if one of your own computers behaves badly you will want to know about it.

Other Useful Configuration Parameters

In addition to the configuration parameters covered so far, I will mention a few others that can be useful to know about. You will most likely do fine using their default values. If you want more information about them please consult the documentation that came with your version or Postfix, or read the documentation online from http://www.postfix.org/documentation.html.

Parameter	Description
always_bcc	Sends a copy of each message to a specified recipient. This can be used for e-mail archiving. If you need more fine-grained control over which messages are copied, take a look at sender_bcc_maps and recipient_bcc_maps. The latter two parameters require Postfix 2.1 or later.
defer_transports	Contains names of transports (delivery agents, more or less) whose deliveries should be temporarily deferred. This allows you to suspend local message deliveries if the file system for the home directories is broken or unavailable but the rest of the system works fine.
delay_warning_time	By default, Postfix does not send a warning if a message cannot be delivered for some time. Setting this parameter to a particular duration, say 5h for five hours, will cause Postfix to send a single warning message when messages

Parameter	Description
	have been undeliverable for that period of time.
	A word of caution, though: Your users may not be able to interpret this warning message correctly. Even though Postfix clearly states that it is only a warning and that the message *does not* need to be resent, many users do not understand this and resend their delayed message.
mailbox_size_limit	This parameter controls the maximum size of a local mailbox, or maximum size of a message when using maildir mailboxes. The default of 50 MB may be too low especially if you are using the default mbox format for mailboxes.
maximal_queue_lifetime	Specifies how long Postfix will retry failed deliveries of messages before they are returned to the sender. The default of five days is reasonable.
message_size_limit	This parameter controls the maximum size of a message. The default value of 10 MB is reasonable (mail is not the best transport method for large files), but may need to be adjusted. Remember that messages are only sent using 7 bits, so if you want to allow 20 MB binary files you must add about 35% to compensate for the overhead of the 7-bit encoding of the file.
proxy_interfaces	If your server is connected to the Internet via a proxy or NAT device so that Postfix cannot determine all network addresses that can be used to reach the server, add those addresses to this parameter.

Starting Postfix and Sending the First Message

With these settings in place, it is time to start Postfix. Use the following Postfix command to do this:

```
$ postfix start
postfix/postfix-script: starting the Postfix mail system
```

To verify that Postfix is running, take a look in the log file. Postfix logs via the standard syslog interface, and the exact location of the log files depends on the syslog daemon configuration. The mail logs will typically be named /var/log/maillog, /var/log/mail.info, or something similar.

```
Jan  3 21:03:28 jeeves postfix/postfix-script: starting the Postfix
mail system
Jan  3 21:03:29 jeeves postfix/master[22429]: daemon started --
version 2.1.5
```

Postfix is now ready to receive and deliver messages. To try it out, use your favorite mail client and send a test mail to yourself. If your mail client uses SMTP, remember to reconfigure it to use your server.

If you get an error message from your mail client when you try to send the test message, read your log again. Does it show any traces of a connection from the host on which you run your mail client? If so, is any error message logged? To get hints on how to debug Postfix problems, see the *Troubleshooting Postfix Problems* section.

Once you have sent the message successfully you will also want to check that it is delivered properly. Since you have not yet configured a POP or IMAP server that road is not an option, but if you fancy a mail client that reads mail directly from the file system (mail, Pine, Mutt, and many more) things should work fine as long as your mail client is configured to look for new messages in the same place as Postfix delivers them. If you have chosen maildir delivery, the default settings of your mail client probably won't do.

In any case, reading the mailbox directly from the file system is always an option. With normal mbox delivery, the mailbox file has the same name as the user and resides in the directory pointed to by the mail_spool_directory configuration parameter. With maildir delivery, the message will typically be found in a file of its own in the $HOME/Maildir/new directory.

If all has gone well, the message was delivered to the expected place.

Stopping Spam and Other Unwanted Messages

This section will discuss the various methods Postfix provides to help stop unwanted messages. Spam, or unsolicited commercial e-mail, is perhaps the biggest problem that e-mail server administrators face but there may also be other kinds of messages that one does not want to receive.

Postfix by itself will not stop all spam, but it can catch many spam messages. For some people this may be adequate, but if you need to fight large volumes of spam you additionally need a tool such as SpamAssassin, described in Chapter 8. Even if you use SpamAssassin, Postfix's own lightweight methods can help reduce the load on the server by rejecting the messages before they even reach SpamAssassin.

Postfix's Anti-Spam Methods: An Overview

There is no silver bullet to stop all spam, but Postfix provides a number of methods that you can use to help the situation:

- **SMTP restrictions**: SMTP restrictions let you define rules for which messages should be accepted. The rules cannot take into account the content of the message, just the envelope information. The SMTP restrictions are not merely a tool for stopping spam, but a general way of defining policies for the usage of the mail system.

- **DNS blocklists**: DNS blocklists are globally published blocklists containing IP addresses of known spammers and other likely sources of junk mail. Postfix lets you use this information to reject messages.

- **Matching header expressions**: The header fields and message bodies can be matched against regular expressions, allowing you to reject certain types of e-mail.

Additionally, Postfix provides the following methods for filtering spam:

- **After-queue content filtering**: After Postfix has accepted a message, it will not be delivered to the destination right away. Instead, it will be fed to a content filter that can do anything with the message; delete it, scan it for viruses, strip unwanted attachments, and so on.

- **Before-queue content filtering**: The drawback with after-queue content filtering is that Postfix always accepts the message before the message is sent to the content filter. This means that Postfix cannot reject a message based on the verdict of the content filter. Before-queue content filters receive the messages during the SMTP session and can choose to reject them. Notice that one before-queue content filter connection is required for each open SMTP session, so this type of content filter does not scale and is not suitable for high-traffic sites. This feature requires Postfix 2.1 or later.

- **Access policy delegation**: If the SMTP restrictions are not sufficiently expressive, you can construct your own access policy server that Postfix can contact during each SMTP session. Using this tool, you can enforce just about any specialized policy you want. Postfix comes with a very simple policy daemon for use to implement greylisting, but several other policy daemons have been made by other people. Links to these daemons and other Postfix add-on software can be found at `http://www.postfix.org/addon.html`.

Understanding SMTP Restrictions

Postfix has a simple but still pretty expressive notation for defining rules that will be applied to messages that arrive via SMTP. For example, you can express a policy to reject messages sent from certain networks, clients who say HELO with certain hostnames, or clients that have no reverse records in DNS unless they are one of your own clients.

Postfix defines a number of parameters that contain lists of restrictions. Each restriction list may contain zero or more restrictions, and each restriction may or may not return something when evaluated. As in a few other places in Postfix, the "first match wins" principle reigns here too. This means that the restrictions are evaluated in the order they are specified, and the first restriction that returns something terminates the evaluation of the current restriction list.

The restriction lists get evaluated during the SMTP session. The following table contains the restriction lists that Postfix uses, and shows at what stage in an SMTP session they are evaluated:

Parameter	Point of evaluation
smtpd_client_restrictions	Directly upon connection.
smtpd_data_restrictions	When the client has sent the DATA command.
smtpd_end_of_data_restrictions	When the client has sent the complete message. This restriction list is available in Postfix 2.2 and later.
smtpd_etrn_restrictions	When the client has sent the ETRN command. This command is not used in a normal SMTP session.
smtpd_helo_restrictions	When the client has sent its greeting with HELO or EHLO.
smtpd_recipient_restrictions	When the client has sent a recipient address with RCPT TO.
smtpd_sender_restrictions	When the client has sent the sender address with MAIL FROM.

Having said that, the default value of the smtpd_delay_reject parameter is yes. This means that all rejections will be postponed until after RCPT TO. The reason for this is that some client software do not like being rejected before RCPT TO, so it will disconnect and try again. A common misunderstanding is believing that, say, only restrictions on the recipient address can be placed in smtpd_recipient_restrictions. The name of the restriction list only tells at what stage in the SMTP session the listed restrictions will be applied, but because of smtpd_delay_reject that is not strictly true.

Let us dig in by using the postconf command to inspect the default values of the most commonly used restriction lists:

```
$ postconf -d smtpd_client_restrictions smtpd_helo_restrictions \
        smtpd_sender_restrictions smtpd_recipient_restrictions
smtpd_client_restrictions =
smtpd_helo_restrictions =
smtpd_sender_restrictions =
smtpd_recipient_restrictions = permit_mynetworks,
reject_unauth_destination
```

This tells us that Postfix by default does not have any client, HELO, or sender restrictions. It does, however, have two recipient restrictions. The first one, permit_mynetworks, permits the current recipient if the connecting client is within the networks specified by mynetworks. It is this restriction that gives your own clients relay access. If the connecting client is not within mynetworks, the next item in the restriction list will be evaluated. reject_unauth_destination will reject recipients whose domain is not one of the domains that Postfix will accept mail for. In other words, reject_unauth_destination rejects relay attempts. If no rejection takes place here, the end of the restriction list has been reached. If that happens, Postfix accepts the message.

A permit result in one restriction list will not cause the message as a whole to be accepted. Only the remaining restrictions in the same list will be bypassed. This is not true for restrictions that return reject—that result is always terminal and stops the evaluation of all restriction lists.

There are more than 50 standard SMTP restrictions to choose from, and there is no room to cover them all here. This table will present a little smorgasbord with useful restrictions.

Restriction	Description
permit_mynetworks	Permit if the connecting client is listed in mynetworks.
permit_sasl_authenticated	Permit if connecting client has authenticated itself. (SMTP authentication is covered in Chapter 5.)
reject	Reject the request, unconditionally.
reject_invalid_hostname	Reject if the syntax of the HELO/EHLO hostname given by the client is incorrect.
reject_non_fqdn_hostname	Reject if the HELO/EHLO hostname given by the client is not a fully qualified domain name.
reject_non_fqdn_recipient	Reject if the domain part of the recipient address is not a fully qualified domain name.
reject_non_fqdn_sender	Reject if the domain part of the sender address is not a fully qualified domain name.
reject_unauth_destination	Reject the request unless the recipient domain is one of the domains that the Postfix server hosts, or for some reason, will accept mail for.
reject_unknown_recipient_domain	Reject if the domain part of the recipient address has no A or MX record in DNS.

Restriction	Description
reject_unknown_sender_domain	Reject if the domain part of the sender address has no A or MX record in DNS.
reject_unlisted_recipient	Reject if the domain part of the recipient address is a domain hosted by Postfix and the complete address is not a valid recipient address. By default, this restriction is implicitly evaluated at the end of smtpd_recipient_restrictions. This behavior is controlled by the smtpd_reject_unlisted_recipient parameter. By using reject_unlisted_recipient, you can put the restriction into effect earlier on. This restriction is available in Postfix 2.1 and later. Previous versions of Postfix can use the check_recipient_maps parameter.
reject_unlisted_sender	Reject if the domain part of the sender address is a domain hosted by Postfix and the complete address would not be acceptable as a recipient address. The idea behind this feature is that there is no reason to accept messages with sender addresses known to be incorrect. This restriction is available in Postfix 2.1 and later. See also the smtpd_reject_unlisted_sender parameter.

Access Maps

In addition to the restrictions already discussed, Postfix defines a number of restrictions that look up information in **access maps**. An access map is a lookup table with contents that affects whether a message will be accepted. The name of the restriction controls what information is used as the lookup key.

For example, the check_client_access restriction looks up the client IP address and hostname in a lookup table, allowing you to, say, ban certain clients that are known to send spam. Together with the restriction name you also state the type and name of the lookup table:

```
smtpd_client_restrictions =
        check_client_access hash:/etc/postfix/client_access
```

Although not an exhaustive list, the following are the most important restrictions that use access maps:

Restriction name	Lookup key
check_client_access	Client IP address and hostname.
check_sender_access	The message sender address. Just like check_recipient_address, the parts of the address are looked up separately.
check_recipient_access	A recipient address. The whole address, the domain part, and the part before the @ (the local part) are looked up separately.
check_helo_access	The HELO/EHLO hostname.

The following results are recognized for a given lookup key (this is again not an exhaustive list):

Result	Description
OK	Permit the request.
REJECT [optional text]	Reject the request with a permanent error code and either the specified error message or a generic message.
DISCARD [optional text]	If the message eventually gets accepted, it will be discarded and not delivered.
HOLD [optional text]	Place the message in the hold queue. Messages that are held will not be delivered and can be inspected with the postcat program and subsequently released for delivery or deleted. This can be used as a simple way of quarantining messages that might be unwanted.
WARN [optional text]	Places a warning message in the log file. Only available in Postfix 2.1 and later.
restriction, restriction, ...	Apply one or more restrictions and use their result. Only simple restrictions that do not refer to any lookup tables are allowed here unless you use restriction classes. Those are not covered in this book, but you can read about them in RESTRICTION_CLASS_README (http://www.postfix.org/RESTRICTION_CLASS_README.html).

Full details about the lookup keys and possible results can be found in the access(5) manual page.

Examples

We will now use a series of examples with access maps to discuss how they can be used, both alone and along with other restrictions in order to form pretty expressive policies:

```
smtpd_client_restrictions =
        check_client_access hash:/etc/postfix/client_access
```

In this first example, the lookups will be made against the hash-type lookup table /etc/postfix/client_access. This file is not created by Postfix, and you may give it any name. From the *Lookup Tables* section we recall that 'hash'-type lookup tables are just text files from which binary files (in this case with the file extension .db) should be built with the postmap command whenever the source file changes:

postmap hash:/etc/postfix/client_access

Let us take a look at the client_access file:

```
# Block RFC 1918 networks
10                      REJECT RFC 1918 address not allowed here
192.168                 REJECT RFC 1918 address not allowed here

# Known spammers
12.34.56.78             REJECT
evil-spammer.example.com  REJECT
```

What does all this mean? The first two non-comment lines are used to reject clients that appear to connect from the networks 10.0.0.0/8 and 192.168.0.0/16. These are not valid Internet addresses, so no legitimate client will connect from any of these addresses. The rejection will be made with the error message RFC 1918 address not allowed here. If your own clients have such RFC 1918 address you need to place a permit_mynetworks restriction before the check_client_access. Otherwise you will reject your own clients.

Indexed access maps support network block matching on even octet boundaries, but CIDR notation (as in 10.0.0.0/8) is not supported. If you need to specify network blocks with CIDR notation, consider the CIDR lookup table type available in Postfix 2.1 and later. Earlier releases can use a script such as cidr2access by Rahul Dhesi (http://www.rahul.net/dhesi/software/cidr2access) that expands CIDR blocks to a notation that is acceptable for indexed access maps.

Note how comments are used to explain why and when entries were added. This can be valuable if more than one person is maintaining the files.

The last lines are used to match a couple of notorious spammers (fictional, of course) and demonstrate that both complete IP addresses and hostnames are acceptable here. These rejections will be made with a generic error message.

Let us continue with another example:

```
smtpd_sender_restrictions =
        check_sender_access hash:/etc/postfix/sender_access
```

Contents of /etc/postfix/sender_access:

```
hotmail.com                    reject_unknown_client
example.com                    permit_mynetworks, reject
```

If someone attempts to send a message with a hotmail.com sender address, the client attempting to deliver the message will be subject to the reject_unknown_client restriction which, as you might recall, rejects client that do not have a valid mapping between IP address and hostname.

The second line exemplifies a useful policy that only allows clients from your networks to use your domain in the sender address.

Finally, if you only use Postfix internally within your network and you have no need to allow anyone else to connect, the following two restrictions enforce this policy:

```
smtpd_recipient_restrictions = permit_mynetworks, reject
```

Implementing New Policies

Be careful when you implement new policies. Some of Postfix's restrictions are far too strict for general use and may reject significant amounts of legitimate e-mail. For each new restriction you plan to implement, examine the conditions under which messages are rejected and try to come up with cases where legitimate messages fulfill these conditions. To help you determine whether a restriction is safe to use, the warn_if_reject restriction can be used. This restriction affects the restriction that immediately follows it in the restriction list, and if the following restriction should have resulted in a rejection, it will be converted to a rejection warning. A rejection warning places a line in the mail log, but does not reject the message.

For example, you may want to evaluate the reject_unknown_client restriction because you have noticed that many spam messages are received from clients that do not have a reverse pointer in DNS, that is, there is no mapping from their IP address to a name that maps back to the IP address in question.

Here is one way of doing it:

```
smtpd_client_restrictions = warn_if_reject reject_unknown_client
```

This will result in log messages like this one:

```
Dec 31 16:39:31 jeeves postfix/smtpd[28478]: NOQUEUE: reject_warning:
RCPT from unknown[222.101.15.127]: 450 Client host rejected: cannot
find your hostname, [222.101.15.127]; from=<jdoe@example.com>
to=<me@example.com> proto=SMTP helo=<222.101.15.127>
```

This log messages contains all known information about the envelope of the message, and this should hopefully be enough for you to decide whether a message was legitimate or not. After a few days, inspect your mail logs and try to determine whether the ratio between would-be rejected unwanted messages and would-be rejected legitimate messages is acceptable.

Using DNS Blacklists

Since 1997, the **Domain Name System (DNS)** has been used to thwart spam. The method, **DNS-based Blackhole List (DNSBL)** or **Real-time Blackhole List (RBL)**, also known as **blacklist** or **blocklist,** uses the DNS to publish information about certain clients or sender domains. When a mail server such as your own is contacted by a client, your server can combine the client's IP address or the given sender address with the domain of one or more DNSBLs and perform a DNS lookup. If the address is listed by the DNSBL the lookup succeeds, and your server may choose to for example reject the client.

For example, let us say that you have configured Postfix to use the widely used `relays.ordb.org` blacklist. If a client with the address `1.2.3.4` connects, Postfix will look in DNS for an A record for the address `4.3.2.1.relays.ordb.org`. If such a record exists, Postfix will not accept a message from the client.

Postfix supports three types of DNSBL lookups; client host address, client hostname, and sender domain. Each lookup type has a restriction of its own, and they all require that you specify the name of the DNSBL domain after the restriction name:

DNSBL type	Syntax	Description
Client host address	`reject_rbl_client rbl_domain`	The IP address of the connecting client is looked up. This is the original and by far most common DNSBL type.
Client hostname	`reject_rhsbl_client rbl_domain`	The hostname of the connecting client is looked up.
Sender address domain	`reject_rhsbl_sender rbl_domain`	The domain of the given sender address is looked up.

Feel free to list multiple DNSBL restrictions. Make sure you use the restriction that corresponds to the DNSBL type—using `reject_rbl_client` with a sender address domain DNSBL does not make sense.

The following code shows one way of configuring Postfix to use the `relays.ordb.org` standard-type DNSBL and the `dsn.rfc-ignorant.org` sender domain-DNSBL:

```
smtpd_recipient_restrictions =
        permit_mynetworks,
        reject_unauth_destination,
        reject_rbl_client relays.ordb.org,
        reject_rhsbl_sender dsn.rfc-ignorant.org
```

Notice how these restrictions are listed after both `permit_mynetworks` and `reject_unauth_destination`. This is because DNSBL lookups are comparatively expensive, and there is no use in wasting time on such lookups for your own clients or for clients that might get rejected anyway. To avoid unnecessary delays, be sure to list the DNSBLs that block the most messages first among your DNSBL restrictions.

Choosing DNS Blacklists

In the beginning, the DNSBLs only listed **open relays**, that is, SMTP servers that accept all messages from all clients to all destinations. Open relays once were the primary source of spam, but this has changed in recent years. Today, a lot of spam is sent from hijacked home computers of innocent and unknowing people.

Different block lists have different policies for listing hosts and removing listed hosts. Naturally, the bigger the blacklist, the more legitimate messages are you likely to reject. Before starting to use a particular DNSBL to reject messages, you should examine these policies carefully and preferably also try them out for a while without actually rejecting any messages. The `warn_if_reject` restriction can help you with this.

There is no single authoritative list of the best DNSBLs. The blocklists that work great for some people and reject huge amounts of spam but no legitimate messages may have little value for other people and may actually reject more legitimate messages than spam. Do not blindly copy allegedly good sets of DNSBLs from other sites.

Still, some general advice on a few useful client address DNSBLs (`reject_rbl_client`) is in order.

Client Addresses	Description
`relays.ordb.org`	Lists only open relays. Will not block that much spam nowadays, but will not block many legitimate messages either. Currently blocks about 225,000 addresses.
`list.dsbl.org`	Lists open relays and open proxies. More aggressive than `relays.ordb.org`, but should be OK for most people. Currently blocks about 700,000 addresses.

Client Addresses	Description
sbl.spamhaus.org	Does not list open relays or open proxies, but does list known spam sources. This includes IP addresses used by known spammers, or Internet Providers that are known to support spammers.
xbl.spamhaus.org	Lists open proxies, spam-sending worms on hijacked machines, and hosts that are in other ways exploited by spammers. This blocklist contains all entries in the cbl.abuseat.org and opm.blitzed.org DNSBLs, so you should not use xbl.spamhaus.org in conjunction with either of those two.
sbl-xbl.spamhaus.org	This DNSBL combines the contents of the sbl.spamhaus.org and xbl.spamhaus.org zones. If you want to use both blocklists, using just this one will save you DNS lookups.

Before implementing any DNSBL at all, make sure you know how to exempt certain clients or domains from rejections. Sooner or later and no matter which DNSBL you choose to use you will have cases with legitimate messages being blocked. When that happens, it is too late to start digging in the documentation trying to find out what you can do about it.

The solution to the problem is to have whitelisting access maps before your DNSBL restrictions. Which type of access map you should use depends on the DNSBL type, but in most cases check_client_access will be suitable, although check_sender_access is more appropriate if you use reject_rhsbl_sender.

Continuing our previous example, this is what you can do to exempt certain clients and sender addresses from rejection by any following restrictions:

```
smtpd_recipient_restrictions =
        permit_mynetworks,
        reject_unauth_destination,
        check_client_access hash:/etc/postfix/rbl_client_exceptions,
        check_sender_access
hash:/etc/postfix/rhsbl_sender_exceptions,
        reject_rbl_client relays.ordb.org,
        reject_rhsbl_sender dsn.rfc-ignorant.org
```

In /etc/postfix/rbl_client_exceptions:

```
# Added 2005-01-10 to avoid blocking legitimate mail. /jdoe
1.2.3.4                         OK
example.net                     OK
```

In /etc/postfix/rhsbl_client_exceptions:

```
mybusinesspartner.com           OK
```

Stopping Messages Based on Contents

Sometimes, unwanted messages cannot be spotted without looking at their contents. Postfix provides some unsophisticated but still very useful tools for this purpose. The idea is that the lines in a message are matched against a set of regular expressions that you supply, and if there is a match an action will be carried out. Most often you use header and body checks to reject messages, but they can also be discarded or redirected to another recipient. Header and body checks can help you solve the following problems, all of which will be discussed in the following sections:

- Reacting to messages containing attachments with forbidden filenames
- Quickly stopping big virus outbreaks
- Custom logging of certain header fields
- Removing certain message headers

An introduction to regular expressions is beyond the scope of this book. If you do not have that knowledge already, there are many regular expression resources and tutorials on the net. If you are looking for a book on the topic, Jeffrey E. F. Friedl's *Mastering Regular Expressions* (O'Reilly, 2002) is quite comprehensive.

Configuring Header and Body Checks

The main.cf parameters—body_checks, header_checks, mime_header_checks, and nested_header_checks—can contain references to regular expression lookup tables (regexp or pcre), which will be considered when a message is being received. These parameters are used for different parts of the message:

Parameter	Part of message it applies to
body_checks	The body of each message part.
header_checks	All non-MIME top-level headers.
mime_header_checks	All MIME headers found in any message part. The following headers are considered to be MIME headers: Content-Description Content-Disposition Content-ID Content-Transfer-Encoding Content-Type MIME-Version
nested_header_checks	All non-MIME message headers in messages that are attached to the received message.

This means that for each header line, a lookup will be made against the lookup tables specified in header_checks, each line in the message body will cause a lookup against the lookup tables in body_checks, and so on.

As we will see soon, the format of regular expression lookup tables is very similar to ordinary indexed ones. One big difference is that these are not indexed and should not be run through the postmap program. Postfix will reread regular expression lookup tables when the daemons are restarted, which in many cases is often enough. If you want an immediate update, you must reload Postfix.

Regular expression lookup tables are not exclusively for header and body checks. They can be used wherever Postfix expects a lookup table.

The right-hand side of lookup tables used for header and body checks can contain many of the previously described actions allowed in access maps, but one action, IGNORE, is only available here. The IGNORE action simply removes the matched line from the message.

Message headers—like the ones in the following example—that are wrapped to form multiple physical lines will be joined together before being used as a lookup key.

```
Received: by jeeves.example.com (Postfix, from userid 100)
        id 2BB044302; Sat,  1 Jan 2005 20:29:43 +0100 (CET)
```

If possible, make sure your Postfix has support for the PCRE lookup table type. Regular expressions of the **PCRE (Perl-Compatible Regular Expression)** flavor have a richer syntax that allows some shortcuts. Another reason to use PCRE is that the PCRE library generally is faster than the standard regular expression library that the operating system provides. To check whether your Postfix supports the PCRE lookup table type, use the postconf command:

```
$ postconf -m
static
cidr
nis
regexp
environ
proxy
btree
unix
hash
pcre
ldap
sdbm
```

Great! This Postfix supports PCRE tables.

Most pre-built packages have PCRE support built in, but if you build Postfix yourself you will have to make sure you have the PCRE library installed before you build Postfix. Read http://www.postfix.org/PCRE_README.html for details.

Examples

Now, let us get concrete and take a look at how header and body checks can be used. Unless otherwise noted, these examples all work with both the regexp and the PCRE lookup table type. Many computer viruses spread by e-mail, and most of them through programs or scripts attached to the messages. Although reacting to messages containing attachments with forbidden filenames is a blunt and inexact tool, it is a simple way to take care of these unwanted messages even before they reach any antivirus scanner. By avoiding large-overhead scanning, your server can cope with much larger virus outbreaks. There is no complete list of the filenames that can be banned, but just blocking .exe, .scr, .pif, .bat, and a few more will probably suffice for most people. To implement this in Postfix, we need to recognize that the filename of an attachment is found in Content-Disposition or Content-Type headers. These are MIME headers, so the expression needs to go in mime_header_checks. In this example, the message is rejected with a message that indicates the offending filename. If a legitimate mail is rejected the sender will hopefully be able to interpret the error message and resend the message.

```
/^Content-(Disposition|Type).*name\s*=\s*"?(.*\.(
    ade|adp|bas|bat|chm|cmd|com|cpl|crt|dll|exe|hlp|hta|
    inf|ins|isp|js|jse|lnk|mdb|mde|mdt|mdw|ms[cipt]|nws|
    ops|pcd|pif|prf|reg|sc[frt]|sh[bsm]|swf|
    vb[esx]?|vxd|ws[cfh]))(\?=)?"?\s*(;|$)/x
    REJECT Attachment not allowed. Filename "$2" may not end with
".$3".
```

Note the indentation on all but the first line. It is needed to have the lines be treated as a single line. Lookup tables work in the same way as the main.cf and master.cf configuration files in this respect. The /x modifier will cause all whitespace to be ignored. This expression, originally constructed by Russell Mosemann and further refined by Noel Jones, requires a PCRE lookup table, but it is possible to rewrite the expression to use regexp.

body_checks can be a useful tool in quickly stopping big virus outbreaks. A number of the previous virus outbreaks have had messages with certain characteristics that made them pretty easy to block. If filename blocking is not an option, you can try to find lines that are unique to these messages and construct suitable expressions.

```
/^Hi! How are you=3F$/          REJECT SirCam virus detected.
/^ I don't bite, weah!$/        REJECT Bagle.H virus
detected.
```

If you are unsure whether an expression will be too broad and catch legitimate messages, you can use HOLD or WARN instead of REJECT. HOLD will put the messages on hold, allowing you to examine them and either release the messages or delete them. WARN will accept the message but log the incident.

This method of blocking viruses can also be useful when a new virus is just starting to spread and the antivirus software you are using has not yet been updated to catch it.

The WARN action can also be used to get custom logging of certain header fields:

```
/^Subject: /                                    WARN
```

Having this expression in header_checks will result in all subject headers being logged as a warning message similar to this:

```
Jan  2 00:59:51 jeeves postfix/cleanup[6715]: 6F8184302: warning:
header Subject: Re: Lunch? from local; from=<jack@example.com>
to=<jill@example.com>
```

Sometimes it can be useful to remove certain message headers. For example, some programming libraries that provide SMTP clients add an X-Library header to all messages sent. Apparently, many spammers use these libraries and therefore SpamAssassin gives a pretty high score for messages that contain this header. If you need to use such a library and you cannot or will not modify the source code to avoid having the header added in the first place, Postfix can help you remove it. This header_checks expression will remove all X-Library headers in messages passing through Postfix:

```
/^X-Library: /                                  IGNORE
```

Caveats

Header and body checks are simple and blunt tools for inspecting message contents. They are useful for a number of things, but do not attempt to use them for general-purpose spam fighting. Many people try to use these tools incorrectly, and I will try to straighten out some common misconceptions.

Header and body checks will only inspect one line at a time, and no state is kept between different lines. This means that you cannot reject messages that contain one bad word on one line *and* another bad word elsewhere in the message. Do not be fooled by the if...endif construct allowed in regular expression lookup tables! You cannot use them in this way:

```
if /^From: spammer@example.com/
/^Subject: Best mortgage rates/         REJECT
endif
```

Remember, lookups are made one line at a time. Obviously, a line that starts with From cannot possibly start with Subject.

Many spam messages have the mail body in **Base64** encoding. Because of how Base64 works, a word has many possible Base64 representations. Postfix does not perform any decoding before the message contents is fed to the header and body checks.

This means that using `body_checks` to block messages containing bad words doesn't work universally. If `body_checks` is your only tool to fight spam, you will spend a couple of hours every day maintaining your regular expressions so they will catch the spam of the day, but you will still not reach a very high accuracy.

Header and body checks apply to *all* messages. You cannot whitelist a certain sender or a certain client. If you host multiple domains you have the option of using different header and body checks for your hosted domains by running multiple `cleanup` daemons and multiple `smtpd` daemons listening on different IP addresses.

You cannot use header and body checks to check for the nonexistence of something, so you cannot reject messages that have an empty body or messages that do *not* contain a secret password.

Having a large number of regular expressions in `body_checks` is not only a maintenance nightmare but may also seriously degrade the performance of your server. A reasonable configuration should not need more than, say, 10–20 expressions. If you have too many expressions, Postfix's `cleanup` processes will use a lot of CPU.

Virtual Alias Domains and Local Aliases

In this section we will use some of Postfix's features for address rewriting to allow hosting multiple domains and implementing group addresses (distribution lists, if you will).

Additionally, we will take a look at how to find information in MySQL databases using Postfix. The goal of the exercise will be to use MySQL lookups for alias lookups, but the knowledge you can gain will be applicable for all other situations where you might want to use MySQL together with Postfix. It will be assumed that you have basic SQL knowledge and that you are able to set up and operate a MySQL server.

Virtual Alias Domains

As was explained earlier, even though you can have several local domains (several domains listed in `mydestination`) they will always be equivalent—they share a single localpart namespace. In other words, `joe@localdomain1.com` is `joe@localdomain2.com` is `joe@localdomain3.com`. Obviously, this is not good enough. In order to host multiple domains with distinct localpart namespaces, you need **Virtual Alias Domains**.

A virtual alias domain is a domain where each valid address maps to one more other e-mail addresses, possibly in other domains. Compare this to local domains where an address typically maps directly to a UNIX system account. `joe@virtualdomain1` and `joe@virtualdomain2` can lead to completely different mailboxes.

> Virtual alias domains are sometimes called just virtual domains, but to avoid confusion with virtual mailbox domains, which sometimes also are called virtual domains, the full term will be used.

To show how virtual alias domains work in Postfix, let us return to our friends at Example, Inc. for a couple of examples of how they can enhance their mail system by using virtual alias domains.

Many Virtual Alias Domains Mapping to One Local Domain

The directors of Example, Inc. have now expanded their business significantly and want to have subdomains for their branch offices to avoid name clashes when two people in different offices share the same name. For their offices in London, Paris, and Berlin they want the domains, `gb.example.com`, `fr.example.com`, and `de.example.com`, respectively. They have a single Postfix server that receives all messages.

The solution to Example, Inc's problem is to let `gb.example.com`, `fr.example.com`, and `de.example.com` all be virtual alias domains. The original `example.com` domain should remain a local domain. Postfix looks for virtual alias domains in the `virtual_alias_domains` parameter:

```
virtual_alias_domains = gb.example.com, fr.example.com,
de.example.com
```

Make sure that you do not list any of these domains in `mydestination`. The next step is to tell Postfix which addresses in the virtual alias domains map to which addresses in the `example.com` domain. This is done by specifying one or more lookup tables in the `virtual_alias_maps` parameter. For starters, we will just use a simple hash-type lookup table. When things work as we expect them to, we will create an equivalent configuration that looks up data in a MySQL database.

```
virtual_alias_maps = hash:/etc/postfix/virtual
```

Now, Postfix will use the virtual aliases you put in `/etc/postfix/virtual`. The format of a virtual alias lookup table is very simple; the recipient address is the lookup key and the address(es) to which the recipient address should be rewritten is the result.

```
joe@gb.example.com          joe1@example.com
joe@de.example.com          joe2@example.com
jane@fr.example.com         jane@example.com
```

After editing the `/etc/postfix/virtual` file, do not forget to run postmap to transform the file into `/etc/postfix/virtual.db`.

```
# postmap /etc/postfix/virtual
```

The format of virtual alias lookup tables is described in the `virtual(5)` manual page.

In the above example, all messages to joe@gb.example.com will end up in the mailbox of the user 'joe1', all messages to joe@de.example.com will end up in the mailbox of the user 'joe2', and all messages to jane@fr.example.com will end up in the mailbox of the user 'jane'.Note that introducing virtual alias domains does not cause the original local domain to stop accepting messages. Jane and our two Joes will also receive messages addressed to their actual usernames at example.com.

One Virtual Alias Domain Mapping to Many Local Domains

After running the previous setup for a while, the staff at Example Inc. decide that they want to return to the old setup with a single domain for all employees. The name clashes can be resolved by including the users' last names in the address. They also want to have one mail server per branch office to avoid latency and network load when the users are accessing their mailboxes. All London users will have their accounts residing on the London server, Paris users on the Paris server, and Berlin users on the Berlin server. This problem gives us an opportunity to look at a different way of using virtual alias domains.

The idea in this setup is that example.com will be the virtual domain and that each Postfix server will have a local domain of its own. The server at the London office will have gb.example.com listed as a local domain. Virtual aliasing will be used to map from the example.com addresses to the office-specific subdomains. This mapping can either be done exclusively on a master server, or it can be done on the servers for each of the branch offices. Having a single master server introduces the problem of synchronizing the data between the servers, but that problem can be solved easily be storing the data in a relational database. We will take a look at how to use MySQL for alias lookups in the *Introducing MySQL Lookups* section later in the chapter.

To implement this, start by removing example.com from mydestination and add it to virtual_alias_domains instead. This needs to be done on all servers. The branch office servers—one of which could easily be the master server—should have their own domain (gb.example.com etc) listed in mydestination. Do not forget to set up DNS so that messages to the branch office domains will be routed to the branch office servers. Finally, the virtual alias table should look like this:

```
joe.smith@example.com          joe1@gb.example.com
joe.schmidt@example.com        joe2@de.example.com
jane.doe@example.com           jane@fr.example.com
```

This problem illustrates an important point; the address or addresses in the right-hand side of a virtual alias table do not have to be local. Any domain can be put there. This is what happens when the master server receives a mail to joe.smith@example.com:

1. Postfix looks in virtual_alias_domains to see if example.com is a virtual alias domain. It is.

2. Next, it looks up `joe.smith@example.com` in `virtual_alias_maps`. The lookup returns `joe1@gb.example.com`.

3. Postfix on the master server decides that `gb.example.com` is not a domain that it hosts, and uses DNS to resolve the destination of the message and finally delivers it to the London branch office server.

Group Addresses

This third and final virtual alias example will do little more than state that the right-hand side of virtual alias tables may contain several addresses, which can be the names of other aliases rather than actual account names.

```
everyone@example.com          management@example.com,
accounting@example.com
management@example.com         joe.smith@example.com,
joe.schmidt@example.com
accounting@example.com         jane.doe@example.com,
jack.black@example.com
```

In this example, a message sent to `everyone@example.com` will be sent to all in management and all in accounting, which in turn means Joe Smith, Joe Schmidt, Jane Doe, and Jack Black.

It may not be desirable to let anyone send messages to large distribution lists. Luckily, you can use Postfix's SMTP restrictions to restrict the access to the sensitive addresses. If you only want your own users (clients within `mynetworks`) to be allowed to send messages to an address, the solution is very simple. In `main.cf`, use the `check_recipient_access` restriction to disallow access to the address, but use `permit_mynetworks` to exempt your own clients.

```
smtpd_recipient_restrictions =
        permit_mynetworks,
        check_recipient_access
hash:/etc/postfix/restricted_recipients,
        reject_unauth_destination
```

If you already use `smtpd_recipient_restrictions` in your `main.cf` you will have to modify that parameter rather than just adding what is listed in the example above. The key feature is to list the `check_recipient_access` restriction after the `permit_mynetworks` restriction.

Contents of `/etc/postfix/restricted_recipients`:

```
everyone@example.com                    REJECT
```

In more complex scenarios, you may need to use Postfix's restriction class feature. It is described in `RESTRICTION_CLASS_README` (`http://www.postfix.org/ RESTRICTION_CLASS_README .html`) along with an example for this particular case.

Introducing MySQL Lookups

If your organization is large, maintaining a flat text file with aliases can be tedious. Storing the data in a real database comes with many advantages; many users can edit the data simultaneously, the users themselves can be allowed to perform some tasks via web interfaces, the data can easily be shared over the network, and so on.

Postfix supports looking up data in a number of *complex* lookup table types. These include MySQL, PostgreSQL, and LDAP. I say 'complex' not because it is very difficult to set up, but because there are inherently more things that can go wrong and, yes, simple indexed files (hash, dbm, btree, cdb) are easier to get right. If you want to solve a problem with a lookup table, always start with an indexed file. When you get things working and you understand why and how they work, try to transform the same idea to the complex lookup table type.

Postfix does not require you to conform to some specific database schema. For each lookup table where you use MySQL you can use a separate configuration that, given whatever schema you have chosen to use (more or less—the current version of Postfix does not quite allow arbitrary MySQL queries), returns the desired result. Each configuration is stored in a separate file, which can have restrictive permissions since they contain database passwords. To use MySQL for looking up virtual aliases, the following setting in main.cf will do:

```
virtual_alias_maps = mysql:/etc/postfix/mysql-virtual.cf
```

The configuration file follows the same format as main.cf and contains all information required to make a lookup—in this case, a virtual alias lookup. The following table describes the parameters that you can put in the configuration file. The parameters will be used to construct the SELECT query. In Postfix 2.1 and later, the format of such configuration files can be found in the mysql_table(5) manual page.

Parameter	Description
hosts	A list of the MySQL hosts that Postfix will contact to perform the query. Can contain either IP addresses, hostnames, or when prefixed with unix:, the path to a local UNIX domain socket. If you specify multiple hosts, they will be tried in random order. Any UNIX domain socket hosts will be tried first.
user	The username that should be used to login to the MySQL server.
password	The password that should be used to login to the MySQL server.
dbname	The name of the database to use.

Parameter	Description
select_field	The name of the column from which the lookup result will be taken.
table	The table that will be searched for the data.
where_field	The table column with which the lookup key will be compared.
additional_conditions	If you require some additional conditions to be tacked on at the end of the constructed query, you can put them here.

Let us start with a simple example. You have a table alias with two columns—alias and address. The alias column is the left-hand side of the virtual lookup table (the address with the virtual alias domain) and the address column contains the right-hand side (the new address).

```
mysql> SELECT * FROM aliases;
+--------------------+------------------+
| alias              | address          |
+--------------------+------------------+
| joe@gb.example.com | joe1@example.com |
| joe@de.example.com | joe1@example.com |
| jane@fr.example.com | jane@example.com |
+--------------------+------------------+
3 rows in set (0.00 sec)
```

The following simple SQL query is needed to find out whether an address in one of the virtual domains exists and should be rewritten to some other address:

```
SELECT address FROM aliases WHERE alias = 'lookup key'
```

Translating this into a Postfix MySQL lookup table configuration yields the following:

```
hosts = localhost
user = postfix
password = secret
dbname = mail
select_field = address
table = aliases
where_field = alias
additional_conditions =
```

For brevity, the hosts, user, password, and dbname parameters will henceforth be omitted from the example configurations.

Sometimes reality is a bit more complicated than this trivial example, so we will move on to something a bit more difficult.

The `select_field`, `table`, `where_field`, and `additional_conditions` parameters are really just inserted directly into the following SELECT query template, together with the lookup string:

```
SELECT select_field FROM table WHERE where_field = 'lookup key'
additional_conditions
```

This means that `select_field` does not have to be a single column; it could specify multiple columns combined to one value, and `table` could be multiple tables with the join conditions in `additional_conditions`. For example, construct the complex query:

```
SELECT CONCAT(aliases.user, '@example.com') FROM aliases, domains
WHERE CONCAT(aliases.name, '@', domains.name) = 'lookup key'
AND aliases.domain = domains.id
```

The following lookup table configuration would be required to do it:

```
select_field = CONCAT(aliases.user, '@example.com')
table = aliases, domains
where_field = CONCAT(aliases.name, '@', domains.name)
additional_conditions = AND aliases.domain = domains.id
```

Before putting a new MySQL lookup table configuration to work, you should make sure that it returns the desired result for all lookup keys. This can be done with the `postmap` program, and the procedure is described in the *Troubleshooting Lookup Tables with Postmap* section.

Local Aliases

Local aliases are an alternative to virtual aliases. Local aliases pretty much work in the same way, but they only apply to local domains. Local alias tables also provide a couple of extra features. We took a brief look at local aliases even before we started Postfix the first time in the *Error Reporting* section.

Lookup tables for local aliases are specified in the `alias_maps` parameter. These lookup tables have a slightly different format than virtual aliases, and the reason is to stay compatible with the file format of the `sendmail` mail transfer agent. Because of this, you should not use the `postmap` command to rebuild the alias file but `postalias` instead. You may also find the `newaliases` command to be convenient.

Many people are confused by the two similar parameters `alias_maps` and `alias_database`. The difference between the two of them is that `alias_maps` contains the lookup tables that Postfix will use to do local alias rewriting, and `alias_database` contains the lookup tables that the `newaliases` command will rebuild when invoked. Only indexed lookup tables (hash, btree, dbm, cdb) need to be rebuilt, so it does not make sense to list for example MySQL lookup tables there.

53

Often, you will want `alias_maps` and `alias_database` to refer to the same lookup table(s):

```
alias_maps = hash:/etc/aliases
alias_database = $alias_maps
```

Compared to virtual alias tables, the lookup key in local alias tables does not include the domain part. That information would be useless since all local domains have the same localpart namespaces. When indexed files are used for local aliases, the lookup key must end with a colon. For example:

```
$ cat /etc/aliases
postmaster:         jack, jill
$ postalias /etc/aliases
```

This will send messages addressed to the postmaster address in any local domain to the two users, jack and jill, assuming that the domain in `myorigin` is local. The next section explains why this assumption is important.

The right-hand side of alias tables does not necessarily have to point to local users. In fact they may point to any valid address in any domain. The format of local alias tables is described in the `aliases(5)` manual page.

Command Deliveries

Up until now, everything that could have been done with a local alias could just as well have been done with a virtual alias. So what is the point of local aliases? One big difference is that local aliases support delivering messages to commands. This is typically required by mailing list manager software. Postfix delivers messages to commands by passing the contents of the messages on the standard input stream.

To run a command when a message is delivered, the following syntax is used:

```
mylist:                    |"/usr/local/mailman/bin/wrapper post mylist"
```

The double quotes are only necessary if the command, as in this case, contains spaces.

But what if you want to run a mailing list on a virtual domain? You will have to use virtual aliases to rewrite the addresses in the virtual domain to local aliases. Say you want messages sent to the address `mylist@virtual.example.com` to be posted to the `mylist` mailing list, which accepts messages via command delivery. To enable this you will need a virtual alias such as:

```
mylist@virtual.example.com              mylist@localhost
```

Pay attention to what user the programs will run as. Postfix normally uses the owner of the alias file, but not if the owner is the root user. In that case the user in the `default_privs` parameter (typically 'nobody') will be used to run the program.

If you write your own program that you want Postfix to deliver messages to, make sure you return an appropriate exit status when errors occur. Postfix uses the error status constants in sysexits.h to determine what to do if the program exits with a non-zero exit status. Depending on the exit status, Postfix will either return the message to the sender or let it remain in the queue and retry delivery later.

Common Pitfalls

Virtual aliases do not only apply to virtual alias domains, they apply to all messages that pass through Postfix. Not recognizing this may lead to surprises. For example, if you host many virtual alias domains that all should have some aliases in common—say, root, postmaster, and abuse—you might be tempted to use a regular expression lookup table (regexp or PCRE) to alias these addresses for all of your virtual alias domains to yourself:

```
# Warning! Does not work!
/^abuse@/                         abuse@example.com
```

Do not do this! Since virtual aliases apply to all messages, any messages that you or your users send to, for instance, abuse@aol.com or abuse@mindspring.com will be sent to you instead of to the intended recipient.

A very common pitfall is believing that a non-qualified address in the right-hand side implicitly refers to a local user. For example, that joe would always mean the local user joe. This is equally untrue for both virtual aliases and local aliases. Recall from the beginning of this chapter when we discussed the myorigin parameter. Just as in all other places, Postfix will qualify bare usernames with myorigin. If your value of myorigin happens to be a local domain listed in mydestination, which it probably is, joe will indeed refer to the local user joe. To avoid surprises if you at some time set myorigin to a non-local domain, it is a good idea to always qualify the right-hand side addresses with a local domain. Since localhost.$mydomain almost always is listed in mydestination, a good candidate might be localhost:

```
postmaster@example.com :          jack@localhost, jill@localhost
```
need colon? ——— ?

Other Address Rewriting Mechanisms

Virtual and local aliases are not the only mechanisms for address rewriting that Postfix provides. Most notably, canonical rewriting can be used to rewrite sender and/or recipient addresses in both the envelope and the headers. This type of rewriting is provided by the parameters canonical_maps, sender_canonical_maps, and recipient_canonical_maps and can among other things be useful to rewrite sender addresses like joe@example.com to Joe.User@example.com if you do not want to expose the actual usernames of the users.

How Postfix rewrites addresses and in what order rewriting happens is described in
ADDRESS_REWRITING_README (`http://www.postfix.org/`
`ADDRESS_REWRITING_README.html`).

Troubleshooting Postfix Problems

I realize having a whole section devoted to troubleshooting Postfix might look bad. Is
Postfix really so hard to get right? No, it is not; quite the opposite in fact. Postfix
provides many tools to simplify problem solving and these tools need a section of their
own. While implementing new features in your Postfix mail system, do it step by step.
The more insecure you are in what you are doing, the smaller steps you should take. If
you run into problems, you will discover them early and it will be easier to figure out
what went wrong. This is especially true when implementing complex lookup tables
using MySQL databases. To reiterate what was said before: if you are even slightly
uncomfortable with complex lookup tables, never introduce a new feature *and* a complex
lookup table configuration at the same time. If something breaks, you will have much
more trouble figuring out where to start.

When trying out new configurations, it does not hurt to be on the defensive side until the
configuration is fully tested. By setting the following feature all permanent errors will be
turned into temporary errors:

    soft_bounce = yes

This means that the transmission of any messages rejected by your server will be retried,
and that Postfix will retry sending any messages that get rejected by a remote server.
With this setting in effect, closely monitor the logs and look for rejections that do not
seem normal. Do not forget to turn this feature off when your configuration is tested!

Reading and Interpreting the Log Files

One key element in troubleshooting Postfix problems is being able to read and interpret
the log messages that Postfix produces. Because they are plain text files with one log
message per line, they do not require any special programs for inspection. We have
looked at the logs a few times before, but this section will explain the messages and give
examples of both successful mail deliveries and failures. When reading the examples,
refer to the figure in the *Postfix Architecture: An Overview* section and note how the
order of the log entries closely follows the path of the mail through Postfix.

The topic of understanding Postfix's logging is also discussed in Kyle Dent's article
Troubleshooting with Postfix Logs (`http://www.onlamp.com/pub/a/onlamp/`
`2004/01/22/postfix.html`).

Message Queue ID

An important property of each message, received and processed, is the **queue ID**. The queue ID is a hexadecimal number of varying lengths that identifies a message. Log messages that have a message context will also log the queue ID. This makes it easy for you to find all log messages that pertain to a message if you have the queue ID (the path to the log file needs to be adjusted for your system):

```
$ grep 92AFD4302 /var/log/maillog
```

The queue ID is assigned when the cleanup daemon creates a queue file in one of the Postfix queue directories. The queue file remains in the system until all recipients have been delivered to or the message expires, after which the qmgr daemon removes the queue file. In recent releases of Postfix this removal event is logged, as we will see in the examples.

Sometimes you will find that there is no queue ID but instead the word NOQUEUE in the log, as in this example that we have seen before:

```
Dec 31 16:39:31 jeeves postfix/smtpd[28478]: NOQUEUE: reject_warning:
RCPT from unknown[222.101.15.127]: 450 Client host rejected: cannot
find your hostname, [222.101.15.127]; from=<jdoe@example.com>
to=<me@example.com> proto=SMTP helo=<222.101.15.127>
```

The reason is that this message has not yet been given a queue file and thus has not been assigned a queue ID. The queue file is created by the cleanup daemon when the first recipient has been accepted. This is a performance optimization.

Do not confuse the queue ID with the message ID. The latter is contained in the Message-ID header of each message and is normally added by the mail client before the message is handed over to Postfix. If no such header field is present, Postfix' cleanup daemon will add one for you. The cleanup daemon will always log the message ID of received messages:

```
Jan  5 23:49:13 jeeves postfix/cleanup[12547]: 92AFD4302:
message-id=<20041214021903.243BE2D4CF@mail.example.com>
```

The Message-ID header contains the hostname of the computer and typically the current date and time, and it will be unique for each message. Do not fall in the trap of thinking that the queue IDs also are unique. Queue IDs can and will be reused for different messages, theoretically as often as every second (but that would have to be on an incredibly busy system).

Example: SMTP Submission, Local Delivery

Let us start by looking at two examples of successful mail transactions. The first one shows a message being received by SMTP and delivered to a local mailbox, and the second example will show a locally submitted message that is delivered to a foreign mailbox via SMTP.

Our first example shows what the logs contain after a message has been received via SMTP and delivered to a local user.

```
Jan  5 23:49:13 jeeves postfix/smtpd[12546]:
connect from mail.example.com[1.2.3.4]
```

The smtpd daemon has received a connection from a client.

```
Jan  5 23:49:13 jeeves postfix/smtpd[12546]: 92AFD4302:
client=mail.example.com[1.2.3.4]
```

Postfix has now accepted the first recipient of this message and requested a queue file from the cleanup daemon. This is the first log message for this message that contains the queue ID:

```
Jan  5 23:49:13 jeeves postfix/cleanup[12547]: 92AFD4302:
message-id=<20041214021903.243BE2D4CF@mail.example.com>
```

The cleanup daemon has received the whole message from the smtpd daemon and logs the message ID:

```
Jan  5 23:49:13 jeeves postfix/smtpd[12546]:
disconnect from mail.example.com[1.2.3.4]
```

The client disconnected from the SMTP server:

```
Jan  5 23:49:13 jeeves postfix/qmgr[22431]: 92AFD4302:
from=<joe@example.com>, size=4258, nrcpt=1 (queue active)
```

The message has entered the active queue and is thus eligible for delivery (unless the queue is congested, delivery will start more or less immediately). The queue manager logs the sender address, the message size in bytes, and the total number of recipients. The reported size will be slightly larger than the actual number of bytes in the message and the size of the message when stored on disk. This is because the reported size is the total size of the message content records in the queue file, and this gives a little overhead:

```
Jan  5 23:49:14 jeeves postfix/local[12653]: 3C21A4305:
to=<jack@example.net>, orig_to=<postmaster@example.net>,
relay=local, delay=1, status=sent (delivered to maildir)
```

The local delivery agent successfully delivered the message to the maildir of the local user 'jack'. The message was originally addressed to postmaster@example.net, but some address rewriting mechanism (typically a local or virtual alias) rewrote the recipient address. Finally, the message was delivered about one second after it was received.

Note that this message is logged when the delivery is completed. If the delivery agent invokes another program during the delivery and that program logs messages if its own, these will end up in the log before this delivery completion message.

Each recipient delivered to will emit a log message:

```
Jan  5 23:49:26 jeeves postfix/qmgr[22431]: 92AFD4302: removed
```

All recipients have been delivered to so the queue file can be removed.

Example: Local Submission, SMTP Delivery

Our next example is somewhat the opposite if the previous example. Here, a message is submitted via the sendmail command is delivered to another host via SMTP:

```
Jan  6 01:41:29 jeeves postfix/pickup[12659]:
CBA844305: uid=100 from=<jack>
```

The submitted message has been taken care of by the pickup daemon. The message was submitted by the user having user ID 100, and the sender was the unqualified address, jack:

```
Jan  6 01:41:30 jeeves postfix/cleanup[13190]: CBA844305:
message-id=<20050106004129.CBA844305@example.net>
```

Again, the message has been read by the cleanup daemon and the message ID is logged:

```
Jan  6 01:41:30 jeeves postfix/qmgr[12661]: CBA844305:
from=<jack@example.net>, size=1309, nrcpt=1 (queue active)
```

Note how the previously unqualified sender address has now been rewritten to a fully qualified address, probably because the myorigin parameter is equal to example.net.

```
Jan  6 01:41:31 jeeves postfix/smtp[13214]: CBA844305:
to=<joe@example.com>, relay=mail.example.com[1.2.3.4],
delay=2, status=sent (250 Ok: queued as DD8F02787)
```

The message was successfully delivered to the recipient joe@example.com via the mail.example.com SMTP relay. When accepting the message, the remote server said:

```
 250 Ok: queued as DD8F02787
```

So now we know the queue ID that our message got at the other end.
This information may be useful if we need to contact the postmaster at example.com regarding this message:

```
Jan  6 01:41:31 jeeves postfix/qmgr[12661]: CBA844305: removed
```

Delivery completed, queue file removed.

You are probably starting to get a grip on the general format of the logs emitted for a message, so the next example will only show log fragments.

Example: Connection Problems upon SMTP Delivery

The following example shows what happens when multiple hosts are set up in DNS to receive messages for a domain but some of the hosts are temporarily unreachable causing Postfix to try a few of them before the delivery can be made. We will only look at the logs of the delivery agent:

```
Jan  2 14:19:46 poseidon postfix/smtp[998]: connect to
mx4.hotmail.com[65.54.190.230]: Connection timed out (port 25)

Jan  2 14:20:16 poseidon postfix/smtp[998]: connect to
mx1.hotmail.com[64.4.50.50]: Connection timed out (port 25)

Jan  2 14:20:46 poseidon postfix/smtp[998]: connect to
mx3.hotmail.com[64.4.50.179]: Connection timed out (port 25)

Jan  2 14:20:47 poseidon postfix/smtp[998]: 940C132ECE:
to=<postmaster@hotmail.com>, relay=mx4.hotmail.com[65.54.167.230],
delay=92, status=sent (250  <20050102131914.B7C4B32ECF@example.com>

Queued mail for delivery)
```

Clearly, three of the receiving mail hosts for hotmail.com were unreachable when Postfix attempted the delivery. Notice how the connection attempts are evenly spread out at 30-second intervals. This is not a coincidence; the default value of the smtp_connect_timeout parameter, which controls how long Postfix will wait for a connection, is indeed 30 seconds. These three 30-second timeouts also explain why the delivery delay logged by the last message is 92 seconds. Also do notice that the acceptance message that Hotmail gives us does not contain any queue ID but instead the message ID.

Getting More Detailed Log Messages

In most cases, Postfix's default logging is enough to resolve a problem but sometimes more details are needed. For those rare cases, you can ask Postfix's daemon processes to log more detailed messages by making sure they are given at least one -v startup option. This is done by editing master.cf and adding -v to the end of the line for the daemon from which you want to get more detailed logging. For example, to get verbose logging from the SMTP server, smtpd, change the line:

```
smtp      inet  n       -       n       -       -       smtpd
```

to this:

```
smtp      inet  n       -       n       -       -       smtpd -v
```

Depending on your configuration, the first line may look slightly different, but the important part is what is in the last column, the name of the daemon. In the case of the SMTP server, busy servers may produce insane amounts of logging with this setting. If such is the case, the debug_peer_list parameter can come in handy.

This parameter accepts one or more hostnames or network addresses for which the level of logging will be increased. This makes sense only in contexts where there is a network peer, such as in the SMTP server and SMTP client.

If you are having problems sending messages to a particular remote server, say mail.example.com, you can set

```
debug_peer_list = mail.example.com
```

and watch the increased logging when Postfix connects to that particular host. When using debug_peer_list, there is no reason to touch master.cf.

Troubleshooting Lookup Tables with Postmap

The postmap command is not only useful for rebuilding indexed lookup tables. You can also use it to query lookup tables in order to check if the lookups work as you expect them to. This is especially useful for regular expression lookup tables and complex lookup tables' types like MySQL, LDAP, and PostgreSQL. Before taking new lookup tables into use in Postfix, you should debug them with postmap first. To perform lookups with postmap, use the -q option:

```
$ postmap -q postmaster@example.com mysql:/etc/postfix/mysql-aliases.cf
jack@example.com
```

You can also examine the exit status of the command to determine whether the lookup succeeded. As always, a zero exit status indicates success. The UNIX shell stores the exit status of the last process in the $? environment variable.

If a lookup does not work as you expect, you can (just as with the Postfix daemons) use one or more -v startup options to increase the verbosity of the messages.

Note that postmap performs 'raw' queries. For example, if you want to know whether the IP address 1.2.3.4 is matched by the following access map line:

```
1.2.3                           REJECT
```

You *cannot* test it with the following command:

```
$ postmap -q 1.2.3.4 hash:/etc/postfix/client_access
```

The postmap command does not know about Postfix's rules for how IP addresses are matched in access map context, and even if it did it has no way of knowing that 1.2.3.4 is an IP address.

Getting Help

The mailing list for Postfix is a very valuable resource when one is stuck with a Postfix problem. Links to the archives of the list as well as instructions for how to subscribe can found at `http://www.postfix.org/lists.html`.

Although the people on the list are very helpful, they do expect you to do your homework before requesting help. This means that you should search the list archives to see if your question has been asked before, and most importantly, you should read the documentation first.

When asking a question, do not forget to state the bigger goal you are trying to achieve. This is often forgotten, and the question is just too specific. Not only will an understanding of the bigger picture make it easier to help you, but it will also reveal if the solution method you have chosen is completely wrong. However, do not be too verbose in your description! After all, the people reading the Postfix-users list are humans too, and they do get bored with over-long postings.

Because they are humans, they are also not psychic. Therefore, be sure to provide complete configuration and any log messages that may be relevant to your question. Obtain your configuration by running `postconf -n`. That command will print the values of all parameters that your have set in your `main.cf`. Do not post the complete contents of your `main.cf`, or the output of `postconf` (without the `-n`). The contents of the `master.cf` are rarely needed.

Summary

The time has come to summarize what has been learned in this chapter:

- We began with a quick look at how the Postfix mail transfer agent works and then looked at how to install the software and prepare the basic configuration.
- We then examined various methods to stop spam and other unwanted messages.
- We introduced virtual alias domains to fully enable your mail server to host many domains.
- Finally, we took a look at a few structured techniques to help analyze and solve Postfix problems.

3

Incoming Mail with POP and IMAP

Postfix will receive e-mail and deliver it to the user's inbox, but additional software is required to read it with ease. There are two standards for retrieval of e-mail from a host. The first is called **Post Office Protocol (POP)**. POP3 is most commonly used. This is normally used to read e-mail from the server, store it in a client application, and remove the e-mail from the server. This is often used by **Internet Service Providers (ISPs)**. The e-mail is subsequently manipulated by the client application, for example, Outlook Express or Mozilla Thunderbird.

The second protocol is called **Internet Message Access Protocol (IMAP)**. The IMAP system is usually used when the e-mail is to stay on the server. IMAP allows users to create folders for e-mail and to move or copy e-mail between the folders. The client application accesses the e-mail on the server, but does not have to store it on the client machine. The e-mail server must be able to store all of the e-mail for all of its users, and the amount of data is expected to grow constantly—users rarely delete e-mail. IMAP is therefore more frequently used in large organizations with centralized IT facilities.

There are many POP3 and IMAP servers. Some perform only one of the tasks. The Courier-IMAP suite of software contains both a POP3 and IMAP servers, and is covered in detail in this chapter.

Courier-IMAP operates by accessing the maildir of the user. An overview of the operation is shown on the following page:

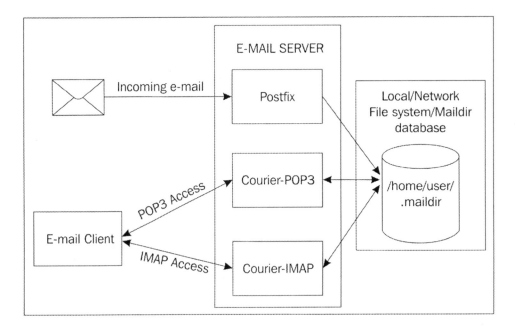

Downloading and Installing Courier-IMAP

Courier is a suite of programs, and includes a full-fledged MTA. This book assumes that the MTA used is **Postfix**. It is important that only the POP3 and IMAP components of Courier are installed and configured—an e-mail system would be very unstable if there were two MTAs operating at once.

> The term "Courier" is often used to refer to the complete suite of Courier software, including the MTA. **Courier-IMAP** is normally used to refer to the IMAP and POP3 portions of the server. Ensure that you only install Courier-IMAP.

There are a couple of ways to install Courier-IMAP. Courier-IMAP **Redhat Package Managers (RPMs)** for several different distributions of Linux are available. These will either be available from the manufacturer of the distribution, or may have been built by a third party, typically an enthusiast or developer of Courier. If a package of Courier-IMAP is not available in RPM, then it has to be built from source.

Installing Courier-IMAP from RPM

It is important to get an RPM that matches the distribution in use. An RPM meant for another distribution may not work correctly, and may also make existing software unstable.

To locate an RPM of Courier-IMAP, first check if one is provided by the Linux distributor. If so, then download and use it. If the vendor does not provide a package, then it is possible that a suitable package will be provided by another organization or individual. To check this, search the Web. There is a database of RPMs available at www.rpmfind.net, and searching for courier, coupled with the name of the distribution, will locate any suitable packages. It is best to use a package designed for a particular version of a distribution. For example, a package for Mandrake Linux 8.0 should not be used for Mandrake Linux 8.1. If you are not sure then it is best to install Courier-IMAP from source as described in the next section.

To install Courier-IMAP from RPM, firstly download the RPM, and change to the directory containing the file using the command prompt. As root, use the rpm command to install the RPM:

```
# rpm -ivh Courier-imap-mandrake-8.1.rpm
```

The RPM command may fail if all the prerequisite software is not present. In this case, the output will name the software required. The appropriate package can be downloaded and installed using the rpm command as above. Once all the prerequisite software has been installed, you can install Courier-IMAP using the rpm command shown above.

Due to the complexities of managing dependent packages, a graphical interface can be used during the installation process of Courier-IMAP. This may work for Courier-IMAP only if the RPM is provided by the distributor, but should be successful in installing prerequisite software.

If the rpm command was used to install Courier-IMAP, then it can be used to uninstall it. The command will be similar to the following:

```
# rpm -e Courier-IMAP
```

Installing Courier-IMAP from Source

Installing Courier-IMAP from source is not a difficult task on a modern Linux distribution. On older versions of Linux, and on other UNIX platforms such as AIX, Solaris, and HP/UX, problems may arise, particularly if the rest of the system software is not up to date.

Prerequisites

The following prerequisites are required to install Courier-IMAP:

- **A working C++ compiler**: We recommend the **GNU C++ Compiler**, which is part of virtually every Linux distribution and is available free for most platforms. If an RPM or other package of GCC is available (and it almost certainly will be) then it should be used in preference to building from source.

- **A** make **utility**: We recommend the GNU make utility, which will be available with most platforms, or can be downloaded from www.gnu.org/software/gcc/gcc.html.

- **The GNU linker**: This is available at www.gnu.org/software/binutils/.

- **GNU** libtool: This is available at www.gnu.org/software/libtool/.

- **Berkeley DB library or GDBM library**: These are libraries that allow programs to make databases in files. Again, these should be available in packaged form, but can be downloaded from www.sleepycat.com/ and http://www.gnu.org/software/gdbm/gdbm.html respectively. One or both of these will almost certainly be installed already.

- **The Courier-IMAP source code**

To install Courier-IMAP successfully, all the above prerequisites must be installed first.

Installing Versions below Courier-IMAP 4.0 from Source

In January 2005, Courier-IMAP 4.0 was introduced. Generally, when a major version of an open-source package is released, distributions tend to delay its implementation for a period of months or even years. However, the new package always offers major improvements and new features. We recommend that you install the latest version available, wherever possible. Often, only the latest version of a package is actively maintained, and bugs or security errors in a package may only be fixed in the latest version. For an application that listens for connections on an internet connection, security vulnerabilities can be very serious.

However, there are often good reasons for using an older version—documentation is abundant and help is often readily available. An older version often has a "tried and tested" reputation that is appealing.

If you wish to install a version of Courier-IMAP below 4.0, then the instructions are similar to the ones mentioned in the *Building Courier-IMAP* section, but there is no need to download and install the Courier Authentication Library. Please skip the following section and proceed to the *Building Courier-IMAP* section.

Building the Courier Authentication Library

There are two phases to installing Courier-IMAP. First, the **Courier Authentication Library**, called `Courier-authlib`, must be built. Once this is done, Courier-IMAP can be installed.

> Although instructions to install Courier-IMAP are given here, it is always a good idea to read the README, READ.ME, or INSTALL files that are supplied with the package. If problems are encountered while installing the software, then always check that the problem is not mentioned in any of the supplied documentation.

The `Courier-authlib` source can be downloaded from `www.courier-mta.org/authlib/` or SourceForge.net at `http://sourceforge.net/project/showfiles.php?group_id=5404`. As with many open-source packages, the Courier Authentication Library uses a configuration script to detect system capabilities, then uses the `make` command to build and install the software.

To build the Courier Authentication Library, enter the following commands. You should see responses similar to those below:

```
$ cd /tmp
$ tar xfj /path/to/courier-authlib-0.52.tar.bz2
$ cd  courier-authlib-0.52
$ ./configure
checking for a BSD-compatible install... /bin/install -c
checking whether build environment is sane... yes
checking for gawk... gawk
... (lots more output appears)
config.status: creating authlib.html
config.status: executing depfiles commands
config.status: creating README_authlib.html
config.status: executing depfiles commands
#
# make
make[1]: Entering directory `/tmp/courier-authlib-0.52-r1/
Making all in libltdl
make[2]: Entering directory `/tmp//courier-authlib-0.52/libltdl'
make  all-am
make[3]: Entering directory `/tmp/courier-authlib-0.52/libltdl'
...(lots more output)
cp imap/pop3d.cnf .
cp -f ./maildir/quotawarnmsg quotawarnmsg.example
make[2]: Leaving directory `/var/tmp/portage/courier-imap-
4.0.1/work/courier-imap-4.0.1'
make[1]: Leaving directory `/var/tmp/portage/courier-imap-
4.0.1/work/courier-imap-4.0.1'
#
# make install
Making install in numlib
make[1]: Entering directory `/var/tmp/portage/courier-imap-
```

```
4.0.1/work/courier-imap-4.0.1/numlib'
make[2]: Entering directory `/var/tmp/portage/courier-imap-
4.0.1/work/courier-imap-4.0.1/numlib'
...(lots more output)
  usr/sbin/imaplogin
  usr/sbin/pop3login
  usr/sbin/courier-imapd
  usr/sbin/courier-pop3d
  usr/lib/courier-imap/makedatprog
  usr/lib/courier-imap/couriertcpd
  usr/bin/maildirmake
#
```

After the commands have executed successfully, the Courier Authentication Library will be installed. Before it can be started, some configuration is required.

$ ./configure

If you are using RedHat Linux, or one of its derivatives, such as Fedora Core or Centos, then the **./configure** script detects this and suggests that you use an RPM:

```
$ ./configure

configure: WARNING: === I think you are trying to run this
configure script
configure: WARNING: === on Red Hat/Fedora. You're doing too much
    work!
configure: WARNING: === It's much faster to create installable
binary RPMs
configure: WARNING: === like this: http://www.courier-
mta.org/FAQ.html#rpm
configure: WARNING: === When you do this you may find that RPM
will tell you
configure: WARNING: === to install some other software first,
before trying to
configure: WARNING: === build this one, and even tell you the
name of RPMs you
configure: WARNING: === need to install from the distribution CD.
    That's much
configure: WARNING: === easier than trying to figure out the same
    from some
configure: WARNING: === cryptic error message.
configure: WARNING:
configure: WARNING: === Even if you don't intend to use
everything you need to
configure: WARNING: === have in order to build via RPM, you
should still do as
configure: WARNING: === you're told. All the extra stuff (LDAP,
SQL, etc...)
configure: WARNING: === goes into RPM sub-packages, which do not
need to be
configure: warning: === installed.
configure: WARNING: === But, if you insist, you can simply add '-
-  with-redhat'
```

```
configure: WARNING: === parameter to this configure script and
not see this
configure: WARNING: === error message. You should also do this
when upgrading
configure: WARNING: === and you didn't use RPM with the older
    version.
configure: error: ... in either case you better know what you're
    doing!
In this case, use the --with-redhat flag when running .configure:
$ ./configure --with-redhat
```

Configuring the Courier Authentication Library

Several decisions need to be made once the authentication library is installed.

The Courier Authentication Library provides the system administrator with flexibility in authenticating users. Authentication is when a user proves their identity, typically by providing a valid username and corresponding password. The following authentication methods are available:

Authentication Method	Description
authshadow	By default, most Linux distributions hold user passwords in the /etc/shadow system file. Using authshadow for authentication validates passwords against system accounts. This is suitable only when users have system accounts, i.e. they can log onto the machine using Telnet or ssh.
authpwd	On older systems, passwords were stored in the /etc/passwd file. The authpwd module allows users to be authenticated against their system password. Again, users must have system accounts.
authuserdb	Unlike authshadow, where each user needs a system account, authuserdb stores user details separately from the system accounts. This allows a **virtual mailbox** facility, where users can be defined without having real accounts on the machine. A number of scripts are used to administer the database, which is usually held in /etc/userdb. (Many distributions place it in /etc/courier/authlib/userdb.)
authmysql	This is similar to authuserdb, but uses a MySQL database instead of the files used in authuserdb. MySQL is a popular relational database provided by most Linux distributions, and offers both advantages and disadvantages over the other methods. Using a relational database such as MySQL adds

Authentication Method	Description
	complexity to an email server, but it is possible that the authentication will be quicker, and a relational database will allow the data to be shared with other applications, if required.
authpam	Authentication is provided by the **Programmable Access Method** (**PAM**) library. PAM is a commonly used library, and is provided by most Linux distributions. PAM is flexible, and can in turn authenticate users from a variety of sources, including the system password database (typically the /etc/passwd file).
authcustom	This allows the system administrators to develop their own, custom authentication method.

Choosing an authentication method can be a difficult decision. Here are some guidelines:

- If all users have system accounts, then authshadow, authpwd, or authpam can be used. If PAM is already installed and configured, then it should be used in preference.

- If a virtual e-mail system is required, then use either authdb, or authmysql. For small sites, there is little advantage in choosing authmysql over authdb.

In this book, only simple authentication with authshadow (or authpwd) is covered, although if PAM is installed and configured, then no additional configuration will be required. Authuserdb and authmysql require further configuration, which is described in the documentation for the authentication library.

The /usr/local/etc/courier/authlib directory contains the configuration files for the Courier Authentication Library. For security purposes, it's best to make the whole directory readable only by certain users. The default authdaemonrc file can be copied from the installation directory.

```
# mkdir -p /usr/local/etc/courier/authlib
# chown mail:mail /usr/local/etc/courier/authlib/
# chmod 755 /usr/local/etc/courier/authlib/
# cp /tmp/courier-authlib-0.52/authdaemonrc /usr/local/etc/courier/authlib
```

To complete the configuration, edit the /usr/local/etc/courier/authlib/ authdaemonrc file and alter the following entries:

```
authmodulelist="authshadow"
daemons=3
authdaemonvar=/var/lib/courier/authdaemon
DEBUG_LOGIN=0
DEFAULTOPTIONS=""
```

Enter the module(s) that you wish to use in the `authmodulelist` line.

The `daemons=` line lists how many processes should wait to authenticate users. Unless there will be a very high number of users, a value of 3 to 5 should suffice. The larger the number of daemons, the more memory will be used up by the authentication library. Moreover, there will be less available for other processes, which may affect overall system performance.

The `authdaemonvar` line lists where the Courier Authentication Library places its run-time files, in particular the socket used to connect to it. The directory listed here (in this example, it is `/var/lib/courier/authdaemon`) should exist and be only readable by the root user. Use the following commands as `root` to create the directory:

```
# mkdir -p /var/lib/courier/authdaemon
# chmod 750 /var/lib/courier/authdaemon
# chown mail:mail /var/lib/courier/authdaemon
```

For security purposes, it's best to make the `authdaemonrc` file readable only by certain users:

```
# chown mail:mail /usr/local/etc/courier/authlib/authdaemonrc
```

The authentication daemon needs to be started when the system boots. Typically, a script is placed in `/etc/init.d/` to enable easy starting and stopping of a daemon. A sample script is included with the source of the authentication library, in `./courier-authlib.sysvinit`. This file should be placed in `/etc/init.d`:

```
# cd /tmp/courier-authlib-0.52
# cp courier-authlib.sysvinit /etc/init.d/courier-auth
```

The service can in future be started and stopped with the commands:

```
# /etc/init.d/courier-auth start
# /etc/init.d/courier-auth stop
```

Initially, we should run the daemon directly from the command line. If there are any errors, they will be displayed.

```
# /usr/local/sbin/authdaemond start
/usr/local/sbin/authdaemond: line 16:
/usr/local/etc/authlib/authdaemonrc: No such file or directory
```

In the above example, the `/usr/local/etc/authlib/authdaemonrc` file was missing.

If the service is started correctly, then it can be stopped by passing it the `stop` parameter:

```
# /usr/local/sbin/authdaemond stop
```

Consult the documentation for the distribution to get the service to start automatically when Linux boots. On RedHat systems, the `service` command can be used to configure a service to start automatically:

```
# service courier-auth add default
```

For other distributions, the chkconfig command might be used:

```
# chkconfig -add imapd
```

Resolving Errors

Errors can be generated at each phase of the build. Errors while running the configure script will probably relate to a missing dependency. Check the README and INSTALL files supplied with the software and ensure that all dependencies are installed. If the problem is not obvious from the error message generated then an internet search for the exact error message may find a solution.

An error at build time is unusual, as most errors will be prevented by the configure script. Again, the error message should provide a good clue to the source of the error, and use of an internet search engine may pay off.

Run-time errors are generally due to erroneous configuration. There are few configuration options with the Courier Authentication Library, but errors do occur.

If an answer can't be found, there is a Courier mailing list, which can be approached for help. As always, first search list archives for your problem, and consult the FAQ. For Courier-IMAP, the mailing list is at http://lists.sourceforge.net/lists/listinfo/courier-imap/, searchable list archives are available at http://sourceforge.net/mailarchive/forum.php?forum_id=7307/, and the FAQ is available at http://www.courier-mta.org/FAQ.html.

Building Courier-IMAP

The Courier-IMAP source code is available in a tarball— a package of all the files, similar to a ZIP file. This should be downloaded from www.courier-mta.org/, or from sourceforge.net/projects/courier/, but be careful to download the source for Courier-IMAP and not for the Courier MTA.

> Although details are given here on how to install Courier-IMAP, it is always a good idea to read the README, READ.ME, or INSTALL files that are supplied with the package. If problems are encountered when installing the software, then always check that the problem is not mentioned in any of the supplied documentation.

To install Courier-IMAP, a few commands must be entered. As with much free software, a configuration script is run first. The configuration script checks the software installed on our machine and configures the software so that it will build correctly.

When Courier-IMAP is used as an IMAP server, it assumes that its clients are going to follow the IMAP standard exactly. Unfortunately, this is not the case and if

Courier-IMAP expected the clients to conform to the IMAP standard exactly then the clients would not function correctly. The Courier-IMAP developers recognize this, and have built the capability to work with non-standard clients, by passing the --enable-workarounds-for-imap-client-bugs flag to the configure script.

Courier-IMAP also includes a check functionality while building it. Unfortunately, using --enable-workarounds-for-imap-client-bugs prevents the check from working successfully. As the check functionality is useful, we will build the software twice. First without the --enable-workarounds-for-imap-client-bugs, then run check, and then build again with the flag, and install the software.

To build Courier-IMAP, enter the following commands as a non-root user. Choose a suitable directory to build the software. In this example, we choose /tmp, and the software unpacked itself into the courier-imap-3.0.8 directory. As noted above in the case of the Courier Authentication Library, the configure script will detect when a RedHat-derived Linux Distribution is being used, and the --with-redhat flag can be passed to configure.

```
$ cd /tmp
$ tar xfj /path/to/courier-imap-3.0.8.tar.bz2
$ cd /tmp/courier-imap-3.0.8
$ ./configure --with-redhat
checking for gcc... gcc
checking for C compiler default output file name... a.out
checking whether the C compiler works... yes
... (a lot more output follows)
config.status: creating config.h
config.status: executing depfiles commands
$ make check
Making check in numlib
make[1]: Entering directory `/tmp/courier-imap-3.0.8/numlib'
Compiling atotimet.c
... (a lot more output appears)
 rm -f '/tmp/courier-imap-3.0.8/=install-check/usr/lib/courier-
imap/etc/pop3d.cnf'
 rm -f '/tmp/courier-imap-3.0.8/=install-check/usr/lib/courier-
imap/etc/quotawarnmsg.example'
make[2]: Leaving directory `/tmp/courier-imap-3.0.8'
make[1]: Leaving directory `/tmp/courier-imap-3.0.8'
$ ./configure -enable-workarounds-for-imap-client-bugs
checking for gcc... gcc
checking for C compiler default output file name... a.out
checking whether the C compiler works... yes
checking whether we are cross compiling... no
... (a lot more output follows)
config.status: creating config.h
config.status: executing depfiles commands
$ make
make all-gmake-check FOO=BAR
make[1]: Entering directory `/tmp/courier-imap-3.0.8'
make[1]: Leaving directory `/tmp/courier-imap-3.0.8'

-----------------------------------------------------------
```

```
                              NOTE
All questions regarding ANY vpopmail-related problems,
such as compiling/building failures, or login errors
should be referred to the vpopmail mailing list.
Vpopmail questions sent to the sqwebmail or Courier
mailing lists will be IGNORED.
-------------------------------------------------------
(lots more output appears)
cp imap/pop3d-ssl.dist .
cp imap/imapd.cnf .
cp imap/pop3d.cnf .
make[1]: Leaving directory `/tmp/courier-imap-3.0.8'
$ su -c "make install"
Password: (enter password for root)
Making install in numlib
make[1]: Entering directory `/tmp/courier-imap-3.0.8/numlib'
make[2]: Entering directory `/tmp/courier-imap-3.0.8/numlib'
(lots more output appears)
 /bin/install -c 'makeuserdb' '/usr/lib/courier-
imap/share/makeuserdb'
 /bin/install -c 'pw2userdb' '/usr/lib/courier-
imap/share/pw2userdb'
make[2]: Leaving directory `/tmp/courier-imap-3.0.8'
make[1]: Leaving directory `/tmp/courier-imap-3.0.8'
$ su -c "make install-configure"
Password: (enter password for root)
make[1]: Entering directory `/tmp/courier-imap-3.0.8/numlib'
make[1]: Leaving directory `/tmp/courier-imap-3.0.8/numlib'
make[1]: Entering directory `/tmp/courier-imap-3.0.8/gdbmobj'
(lots more output appears)
authdaemonrc:
  authmodulelist: new
  authmodulelistorig: new
  daemons: new
  version: new
  authdaemonvar: new
make[1]: Leaving directory `/tmp/courier-imap-3.0.8'
$
```

If the output appears similar to above, then Courier-IMAP has been successfully installed and you may skip the next section on error handling.

Handling Errors

It is possible that the configure command will fail. Configuration attempts to detect existing software, and ensure that Courier-IMAP works with it, but it occasionally makes an error.

```
checking for getspent... yes
configure: error: /var/vpopmail/etc/lib_deps does not exist - upgrade
vpopmail to the current version or fix the permissions on this file
configure: error: /bin/sh './configure' failed for authlib
```

In this example, the `configure` command assumed that `vpopmail` was installed, and failed when it couldn't find parts of `vpopmail`. In reality, `vpopmail` was not installed, and could not be detected. We get the following from the `INSTALL` file:

```
...configure should automatically detect if you use vpopmail, and
compile and install the authvchkpw authentication module.
```

This suggests that the `authvchkpw` is used for `vpopmail`. Further up the `INSTALL` file we read:

```
    * authvchkpw - this module is compiled by default only if the
vpopmail account is defined.
```

Upon checking the `/etc/passwd` file, we find that there is an account for `vpopmail`, which explains the detection. The lack of `vpopmail` files explains the failure of the `configure` script. In the `INSTALL` file, the parameters to the configure script are described:

```
    Options to configure:
    ...
    * --without-module - explicitly specify that the authentication
module named "module" should not be installed. See below for more
details.
        Example: --without-authdaemon.
```

The solution, therefore, is to use the `--without-authvchkpw` option:

`$ ./configure –without-authvchkpw`

Most problems can be solved in a similar way. It is best not to be put off by terms and names that aren't understood—without understanding anything about `vpopmail`, just by searching for the term 'vpopmail' (which was mentioned in the original error message), it is possible to resolve the error by reading the documentation.

If you can't find an answer, there is a Courier mailing list that can be approached for help. Details are given in the *Resolving Errors* section.

Using POP3

As mentioned in the introduction, POP3 is typically used when e-mail is to be stored on a client computer. It is most often used when there is an intermittent connection to the e-mail server, for example, while using a dial-up line to access an e-mail account at an ISP. This approach has the advantage that the e-mail is always available to the client, who can work when not connected to the e-mail server. E-mails can be read, and replies created ready for when the user is next on line.

The main disadvantage of using POP3 is that e-mail is generally only available on the client PC. If the client PC fails, or is stolen, then the e-mail is lost, unless a backup has been made.

POP3 clients can be configured to keep e-mail on the POP3 server, for other clients to access, but IMAP is more often used in this situation.

Configuring Courier-IMAP for POP3

The configuration files are located in /usr/lib/courier-imap/etc/courier-imap/, if Courier-IMAP was built from source. If you are using a packaged distribution, they may be located in /etc/courier-imap. The pop3d file contains the settings for the POP3 server.

If you are using a packaged distribution of Courier-IMAP, then the configuration files can be found with this command:

```
# find / -name pop3d 2>/dev/null
/usr/lib/courier-imap/etc/pop3d
/usr/lib/courier-imap/bin/pop3d
```

Edit the file and locate and alter the following settings:

Setting	Description
PIDFILE	The pop3d daemon keeps track of the process ID that it uses. Specifies a valid path and a name, which suggests the use of the file. Typically, this might be /var/run/pop3d.pid.
MAXDAEMONS	This specifies the maximum number of pop3d process that can run at one time. This number limits the number of users that can connect at one time. A number higher than the expected number of users may be wasteful, but users attempting to connect are also included in this number. Set this to a number around the maximum number of users who may connect at one time, or a little higher.
MAXPERIP	This specifies the maximum number of connections from each IP address. A low number prevents malicious acts such as denial-of-service attacks, where an attempt is made to use up all the connections on the mail server.
AUTHMODULES	This specifies the authentication method to be used. If the Courier Authentication Library daemon is used, as with Courier-IMAP v4.0 and later, then set this to authdaemon.
POP3AUTH	If the Courier Authentication Library daemon is used, set this to blank, otherwise set it to indicate the type of login authentication performed. For versions prior to 4.0, this should be set to LOGIN.
PORT	This specifies the port that the daemon listens on. The standard port is 110, and a different one should only be chosen if all client software is configured to use the non-standard port.

Setting	Description
ADDRESS	This specifies the IP address to listen on. If the machine has multiple network interfaces, then Courier-IMAP can be configured to listen only on one of the addresses. A value of 0 indicates that all network interfaces should be used.
TCPDOPTS	These are options to be used. Typical ones used include -nodnslookup, which prevents the POP3 daemon from attempting to resolve the name of each connection, and -noidentlookup, which prevents it from attempting an ident query for the incoming connection. Specifying both of these settings can decrease the time taken to authenticate a user connection.
MAILDIRPATH	This is the path to a typical user's maildir. Specify the appropriate value for your system, for example, .maildir.

A sample pop3d configuration file is shown below.

```
PIDFILE=/var/run/pop3d.pid
MAXDAEMONS=40
MAXPERIP=4
AUTHMODULES="authdaemon"
POP3AUTH=""
PORT=110
ADDRESS=0
TCPDOPTS="-nodnslookup -noidentlookup"
MAILDIRPATH=.maildir
```

Once the POP3 server has been configured, it is time to test it. If you are using a distribution-supplied version of Courier-IMAP, then use the distributors' startup script called /etc/init.d/courier-imap. This will attempt to start imapd as well as pop3d, but as most of the configuration will have been done by the distributors, IMAP should start successfully.

> If you are using Courier-IMAP version 4.0 or later, then courier-authdaemon must be running before the POP3 or IMAP services. Ensure that you start them as described previously.

To start the POP3 service for testing, run the following command:

```
# /usr/lib/courier-imap/libexec/pop3d.rc start
```

Once the POP3 and IMAP services are configured correctly, they can be started automatically when the machine boots. This is explained in the *Testing the IMAP Service* section. The instructions can be followed, even if IMAP is not required.

Testing the POP3 Service

The easiest way to test a service like POP3 is by using the **Telnet** utility and connecting to the appropriate port. This avoids any problems there may be with network connectivity or client configuration. POP3 uses port 110, so connect Telnet to port 110 on the local machine:

```
$ telnet localhost 110
Trying 127.0.0.1...
Connected to localhost.
Escape character is '^]'.
+OK Hello there.
USER username
+OK Password required.
PASS password
+OK logged in.
STAT
+OK 82 1450826
LIST
+OK POP3 clients that break here, they violate STD53.
1 5027
2 5130
3 6331
4 3632
5 1367
... all emails are listed, with their sizes in bytes
82 6427
.
RETR 1
+OK 5027 octets follow.
Return-Path: <user@domain.com>
X-Original-To: user@localhost
Delivered-To: user@machine.domain.com
Received: from isp (isp [255.255.255.255])
... email is listed
.
QUIT
+OK Bye-bye.
Connection closed by foreign host.
```

The POP3 protocol is based on text commands, and so it is easy to emulate a client with Telnet. Initially, use the USER and PASS commands to authenticate a user. If the user is authenticated correctly, then the STAT command lists all e-mails and their combined size in bytes. LIST lists each e-mail and its size. The RETR command retrieves (or lists) an e-mail when the e-mail number is specified with the command. The DELE command (not shown in the example) will delete an e-mail from the server.

Now that POP3 is working, it is time to configure an e-mail client to collect e-mail.

Retrieving E-Mail via POP3 with Outlook Express

Outlook Express is a popular e-mail client, shipped with most versions of Windows. It includes POP ability. Follow the following steps to set up a Windows client:

These instructions are for Outlook Express 6, shipped with Windows XP. Other versions can be configured in a similar way.

1. Start Outlook Express by clicking on the icon on the desktop, or locate it in the Start menu hierarchy. Select the Tools | Accounts menu.

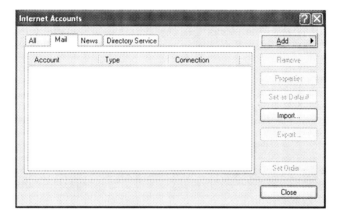

2. Click on the Add button, and select Mail from the menu. The Internet Connection Wizard is displayed.

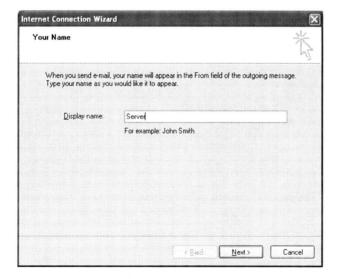

3. Enter a descriptive name for the server as the Display Name, and click Next.

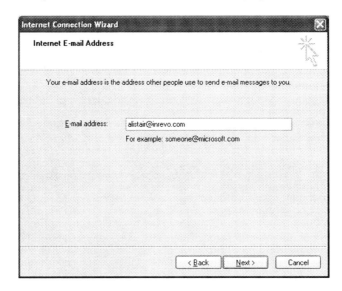

4. Enter your e-mail address and click Next.

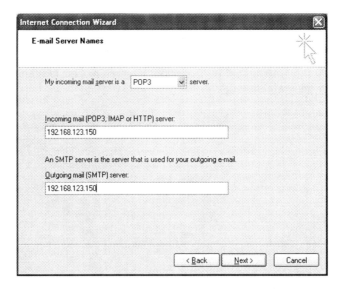

5. Enter the IP address of the e-mail server in both the Incoming mail and the Outgoing Mail fields. Ensure that POP3 is selected in the list of server types at the top of the screen. Click Next.

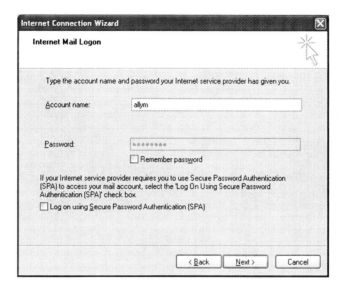

6. Enter the Account name. This is the system account on the e-mail server. If desired, leave the Remember Password box checked and enter a password, otherwise leave the password field empty. Click Next once more.

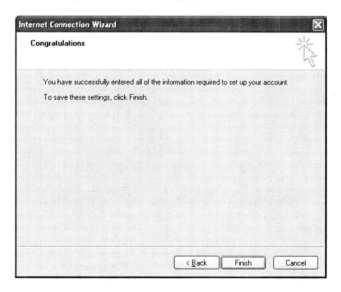

7. Click Finish to complete the wizard.

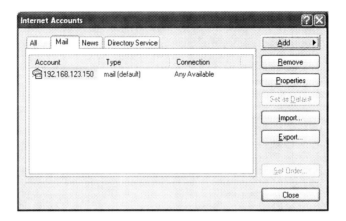

8. The account has been added to the Internet Accounts screen. Press Close. If some of the details need to be changed, select the account and press the Properties button.
    You can modify the account at a later time by returning to this screen and selecting the account in the list and pressing the Properties button.

9. To retrieve mail, select the Tools | Send and Receive | Send and Receive All menu. Even if you did not provide a password, you will be prompted for one.

10. Enter the password and click OK, and e-mail will be downloaded.

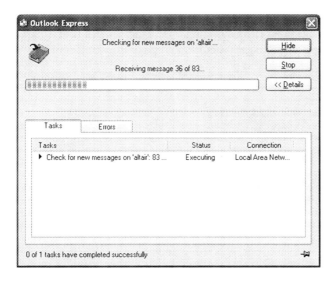

Now that POP3 has been successfully configured, it is time to move on to IMAP.

Using IMAP

IMAP stands for **Interactive Mail Access Protocol**. It is another method of communicating with an e-mail server. Generally, the mail is held on the server, and not on the client. This makes it ideal for organizations with a central administrative function, as it eases backups and also allows users to change the client computers they work at. As long as the e-mail client is installed, users can access their e-mail from any computer on the network, or even from home or another office.

In contrast to POP3, IMAP allows users to create folders on the server, so that related e-mails can be stored together.

Configuring Courier for IMAP

After Courier-IMAP has been installed, either from package or from source as described earlier, it needs to be configured before it can be used.

> If you have configured and tested POP3 as described earlier, then you should stop the Courier-IMAP daemons while you configure IMAP. If you are using a version of Courier-IMAP greater than 4.0, then you can leave the authentication daemon running.

The configuration files are located in `/usr/lib/courier-imap/etc/courier-imap/` if Courier-IMAP was built from source. In a packaged distribution, they may be located in `/etc/courier-imap`. The imapd file contains the settings for the IMAP server.

If you are using a packaged distribution of Courier-IMAP, then the configuration files can be found with this command:

```
# find / -name imapd 2>/dev/null
/usr/lib/courier-imap/etc/imapd
/usr/lib/courier-imap/bin/imapd
```

Once the file has been located, it can be modified as appropriate. Here are the main configuration directives:

Setting	Description
PIDFILE	The imapd daemon keeps track of the process ID that it uses. It specifies a valid path and a name, which suggests the use of the file. Typically, this might be /var/run/imapd.pid.
MAXDAEMONS	This specifies the maximum number of imapd process that can run at a time. This number limits the number of users that can connect at one time. A number higher than the expected number of users may be wasteful, but users *attempting* to connect are also included in this number. Set this to a number around the maximum number of users who may connect at one time, or a little higher.
AUTHMODULES	This specifies the authentication method to be used. If the Courier Authentication Library daemon is used, as with Courier-IMAP v4.0 and later, then set this to authdaemon.
POP3AUTH	If the Courier Authentication Library daemon is used, set this to blank, otherwise set it to indicate the type of login authentication performed. For versions prior to 4.0, this should be set to LOGIN.
PORT	This specifies the port that the daemon listens on. The standard port is 143, and a different one should only be chosen if all client software is configured to use the non-standard port.

Setting	Description
ADDRESS	This specifies the IP address to listen on. If the machine has multiple network interfaces, then Courier-IMAP can be configured to listen only on one of the addresses. A value of 0 indicates that all network interfaces should be used.
TCPDOPTS	These are options to be used. Typical ones used include -nodnslookup, which prevents the IMAP daemon from attempting to resolve the name of each connection, and -noidentlookup, which prevents it from attempting an ident query for the incoming connection. Specifying both of these settings can decrease the time taken to authenticate a user connection.
MAILDIRPATH	This is the path to a typical user's maildir. Specify the appropriate value for your system, for example, .maildir.
MAXPERIP	This specifies the maximum number of connections from each IP address. A low number prevents malicious acts such as **denial-of-service** attacks, where an attempt is made to use up all the connections on the mail server.
IMAP_CAPABILITY	This describes the IMAP capabilities that the server reports to clients. It should be left on the default setting.
IMAP_EMPTYTRASH	This specifies how long e-mail messages should be kept in certain folders. Messages older than the date specified are automatically deleted, when the user logs in or logs out. This can be used to automatically delete e-mail from the trash folder after a certain period. This works for all folders, so e-mail in the Sent items folder could be deleted after a longer period has expired.
	For example, IMAP_EMPTYTRASH=Trash:7,Sent:30 specifies that e-mails in the Trash folder are deleted after 7 days, and those in the Sent folder will be deleted after 30 days.
	If very large numbers of e-mails are present in the folders specified, then performance will suffer, as each file will be checked every time the user logs in or logs out of the IMAP server. In this case, it would be better to disable this setting and run a separate script once (or more often) a day to remove old files.

Setting	Description
IMAP_IDLETIMEOUT	This is the length of time (in seconds) that a client can be idle for (not make any request to the server), before the connection is closed. Values lower than the default of 60 may results in client connections being terminated prematurely, but a well-written client will reconnect without notifying the user. Higher values should be used if users report particular problems.
IMAP_TRASHFOLDERNAME	This specifies the folder to be used when e-mail is deleted.
SENDMAIL	This specifies the path to sendmail, for sending e-mail.

Here is a sample imapd configuration file:

```
ADDRESS=0
AUTHMODULES="authdaemon"
IMAP_CAPABILITY="IMAP4rev1 UIDPLUS CHILDREN NAMESPACE
THREAD=ORDEREDSUBJECT THREAD=REFERENCES SORT QUOTA IDLE"
IMAP_EMPTYTRASH=Trash:7
IMAP_IDLE_TIMEOUT=60
IMAP_TRASHFOLDERNAME=Trash
MAILDIRPATH=.maildir
MAXDAEMONS=40
MAXPERIP=4
PIDFILE=/var/run/imapd.pid
PORT=143
SENDMAIL=/usr/sbin/sendmail
TCPDOPTS="-nodnslookup -noidentlookup"
```

Testing the IMAP Service

To start the IMAP service for testing, run the following command:

```
# /usr/lib/courier-imap/libexec/imapd.rc start
```

The easiest way to test a service like IMAP is by using the Telnet utility and connecting to the appropriate port. This avoids any problems there may be with network connectivity or client configuration. IMAP uses port 143, so telnet to port 143 on the local machine:

```
$ telnet localhost 143
Connected to localhost.
Escape character is '^]'.
* OK [CAPABILITY IMAP4rev1 UIDPLUS CHILDREN NAMESPACE
THREAD=ORDEREDSUBJECT THREAD=REFERENCES SORT QUOTA IDLE ACL
ACL2=UNION STARTTLS] Courier-IMAP ready. Copyright 1998-2004
Double Precision, Inc.  See COPYING for distribution information.
```

```
1 capability
* CAPABILITY IMAP4rev1 UIDPLUS CHILDREN NAMESPACE
THREAD=ORDEREDSUBJECT THREAD=REFERENCES SORT QUOTA IDLE ACL
ACL2=UNION STARTTLS
1 OK CAPABILITY completed
2 login "username" "password"
2 OK LOGIN Ok.
3 namespace
* NAMESPACE (("INBOX." ".")) NIL (("#shared." ".")("shared."
"."))
3 OK NAMESPACE completed.
```

Each command is prefixed with an identifier—here we use unique numbers. The first command asks the IMAP server to list its capabilities. The second command is a user login, and includes the username and password. If this is successful, then the final namespace command shows that the server has accepted the login and the client can determine where in the folder hierarchy the user is placed.

This is enough to confirm that the user can log in and issue commands. The whole IMAP command set is quite large and complex, and does not lend itself to be used by Telnet.

Once the POP3 and IMAP services are configured correctly, they can be started automatically when the machine boots. If you have installed from a package, then the distributor will probably have created a suitable startup script in /etc/init.d. Depending on the distribution, this may start when the machine boots. For RedHat Linux, the command will be:

```
# service courier-imap add default
```

For other distributions, the chkconfig command might be used:

```
# chkconfig -add imapd
```

Now that IMAP is configured correctly, it is time to configure an e-mail client.

Retrieving Mail via IMAP with Mozilla Thunderbird

Mozilla Thunderbird is a popular open-source e-mail client and can be downloaded from http://www.mozilla.org/. It can be used with a variety of operating systems, including Windows and Linux.

Here are steps to configure it to connect to a Courier-IMAP server:

1. From the main Thunderbird screen, select Tools | Account Settings.

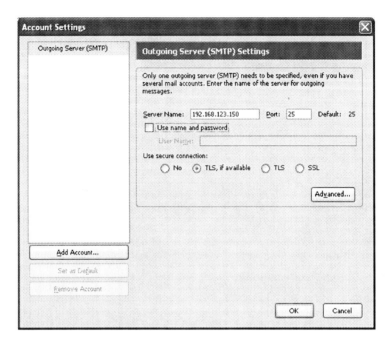

2. Click on the Add Account... button. On the next screen, choose Email Account and then click Next. The Identity screen opens. Enter your user name and e-mail address, then click Next.

3. On the Server Information screen, enter the name or the IP address of the servers for incoming and outgoing e-mail. Then click the Next button.

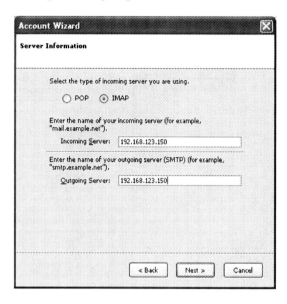

4. On the next screen, enter the Incoming User Name. This will normally be the Linux account name.

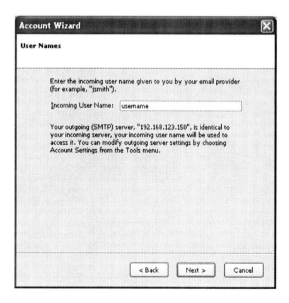

5. Finally, provide a useful tag for the e-mail account in the Account Name field, in case more than one account is defined in the future. Click Next.

6. On the next screen, the details are summarized. Click Finish to save the account details and to exit the Account Wizard.

7. Finally, the Account Settings screen is shown, listing the account you just defined. Click OK.

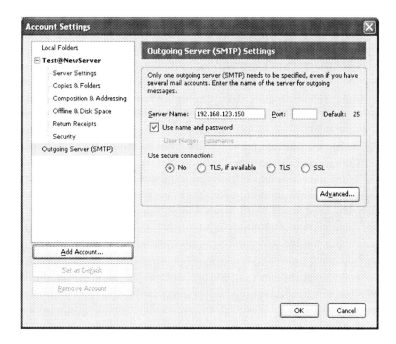

To retrieve messages, click on File | Get New Messages, and select the account you just created form the menu.

Thunderbird will prompt you for the password. Enter the correct password and press *Enter*. Thunderbird will then connect to Courier-IMAP and retrieve details of all the e-mail. If you click on an e-mail, Thunderbird will retrieve it using the IMAP protocol.

Summary

In this chapter, we covered the following:

- The POP3 and IMAP protocols were introduced.

- The best method of installing Courier-IMAP is to use a package provided with your Linux distribution, but it can be installed from source if desired.

- After installation, Courier-IMAP may require configuration. We saw how to configure and test both the POP3 and IMAP services.

- We included examples of how to configure popular e-mail clients to use POP3 and IMAP.

4
Providing Webmail Access

You've learned how to set up and configure an e-mail server in the previous chapters. Now that your e-mail server is ready to serve, how will your users access it? In this chapter, you will learn about the following:

- The benefits and disadvantages of a webmail access solution
- The SquirrelMail webmail package
- Setting up and configuring SquirrelMail
- What SquirrelMail plug-ins are and what they can do
- How to make SquirrelMail more secure

In the next section, we will introduce the SquirrelMail software package and examine the pros and cons of this and other webmail access solutions. After that, we will follow the installation and configuration of SquirrelMail step by step. Next, we will examine the installation of plug-ins, and include a reference of useful plug-ins. Finally, we will include some tips on how to secure SquirrelMail.

The Webmail Solution

A **webmail** solution is a program or a series of scripts that is run on a server, is accessible over the Web, and provides access to e-mail functions similar to a conventional mail client. You may already be familiar with various different forms of webmail: it is used by Yahoo! Mail, Microsoft Hotmail, and Google GMail as the primary interface to their e-mail solutions.

Though we will be examining SquirrelMail webmail solution specifically, the benefits and drawbacks of SquirrelMail apply to most webmail systems on the market. From this point of view, we will approach the issue from a general perspective, and then in detail for the SquirrelMail package.

The Benefits

This section will focus on the advantages offered by installing and maintaining a webmail solution. As with any list, it is not entirely comprehensive. Many benefits will be specific to a particular case; it is important to carefully examine and consider how the following qualities impact on your individual situation.

The main benefits we will explore in this section are as follows:

- Easy and quick access with little or no setup
- Easy remote access
- No need to maintain clients
- User interface to configure mail server options
- Possible security benefits

Easy and Quick Access

Traditional mail access solutions, although well suited to certain situations, can often be difficult to set up and maintain. Generally, this involves installing software on a client's local computer, and configuring it. This can be difficult, especially in cases where users need to set up the said software themselves. Configuration can often be even more problematic—some users may not computer savvy enough to follow even a very detailed set of instructions. These instructions also need to be provided and maintained for many different mail clients on many different platforms.

A webmail solution, however, does not have most of these problems. All of the user's settings can be configured on the server since the application itself resides on the server. This translates to almost zero set-up time for the user—once they have received their login credentials, they can visit the webmail site and instantly have access to all of their mail. The user is able to access the site instantly to send and receive e-mail.

Although webmail is a fairly new concept compared to more traditional mail access software, many internet users are familiar with it through popular web sites like Microsoft Hotmail and Yahoo! Mail, which offer free e-mail services. Your users' level of comfort with SquirrelMail depends on their level of familiarity with these web sites.

It is also worth mentioning that a webmail solution can offer what certain traditional mail clients offer as **groupware** features. These features let groups communicate and co-ordinate in ways that complement e-mail communication. Examples of groupware applications are private calendars, shared calendars, meeting scheduling, TODO lists, and similar tools.

These applications can also be pre-configured so that a user can instantly begin using them without having to configure them on their own. Several SquirrelMail plug-ins are available from the SquirrelMail web site that implement these features.

Easy Remote Access

Another problem with traditional mail access software is that it is not portable as it needs to be installed and configured on the client. Once it has been downloaded, installed, and configured as client for a particular computer, it is accessible only on that computer. If you ever use the Internet from a friend's place, travel, or want to access your work e-mail from home, you can't. E-mail will be accessible only from the computer where the software client has been installed.

In a webmail solution, however, e-mail can be accessed from any location with an Internet connection—assuming it is deemed safe to allow so. Employees can access their work e-mail from home; they can access e-mail from a public terminal such as those that can be increasingly found at many hotels and airports while traveling.

As the administrator, you can allow or deny users from checking their e-mail in these situations. By requiring the connection to be encrypted, you can also ensure that when a user is in a remote location, their communication with the server is secure.

No Need to Maintain Clients

Even if software mail clients have been installed and properly configured, they must be maintained. When a new version is released, all clients must be updated. This is not necessarily an easy task—upgrading a software client often unleashes a thunderstorm of unpredictable and difficult-to-solve problems.

One by one, each computer must be updated. This is a very large administrative burden. In fact, many expensive software packages are designed for the specific purpose of updating software on individual machines automatically. Despite this, often problems specific to each local machine arise and must be solved individually.

In contrast to this, a webmail solution is centrally maintained and administered. The webmail application resides on the server. The webmail package is the only component that needs to be upgraded—any exceptions or problems that arise can be dealt with before or during the upgrade. Although changes in settings are rare with SquirrelMail, it is possible to update a user's settings to make them compatible with the changes introduced in an updated version.

Additionally, while upgrading or changing a mail server platform, there is only one client to test—the webmail application. There is no need to test on all of the possible clients and software platforms. It may also be difficult to convey instructions or notifications to remote branch locations. With a webmail solution, this is not necessary.

User Interface to Configure Mail Server Options

Many traditional mail clients are just that, mail clients. Often there is no support for other essential tasks—such as changing the access password—that are performed on behalf of a mail user. Certain configuration options that reside on the server may require additional software applications or external solutions to provide for these needs. Examples of mail server options that may need to be configured include each user's password and junk mail filtering settings.

Often, in the interest of space and budget restrictions, the webmail application is integrated on the same physical machine as the main mail server. In this case, the webmail application can be easily extended to modify those options specific to the mail server that the user may need to modify. The application can take input from the user, apply it to the mail server on which it resides, and return the results to the user. This operation does not require any separate software—these features are included in plug-ins to the webmail application.

In the case of the SquirrelMail webmail application, many plug-ins have been developed that provide these features. For example, a user is able to change his or her password directly from the webmail interface. Also, there are plug-ins and systems that allow users to easily sign up without any direct human intervention. This may be useful if you are interested in providing a service where users can sign up without needing an administrative overhead.

Possible Security Benefits

This issue can be seen in two different ways—it is for this reason that the title is listed as *"Possible" Security Benefits*. Nonetheless, this is still an interesting point to examine.

In the software client access model, e-mail is traditionally downloaded onto the local user's computer. From a security perspective, this may be a bad thing. Users of the system may not be as conscientious or knowledgeable about computer security as a trained computer administrator might be. It is often much easier to gain unauthorized access to an end user's computer than a properly configured and secured server.

With e-mail being distributed in such a fashion, it is also very difficult to control. Even if an employee is terminated, he or she may still have access to all of the e-mail that resides on his or her local office computer. It may take a certain amount of time before important information may be secured. A disgruntled worker might easily connect an external storage source to their local office computer and download any data they desire.

It is also worth noting that in a webmail model, all e-mail is centrally stored. If an attacker were to gain access to the central e-mail server, he or she might access all the e-mail stored on that server. However, it is possible that an attacker will gain access to all the e-mail if the central mail server is compromised even if a webmail system is *not* used.

The Disadvantages

This section focuses on the disadvantages resulting from providing and supporting a webmail solution. The warning given in the previous section applies: This list is not entirely comprehensive. Each situation is unique, and may bring its unique disadvantages.

We will go over the following disadvantages of a webmail solution:

- Performance issues
- Not well suited to large e-mail volumes
- Not well suited to e-mail attachments
- Security issues

Performance

The traditional mail client is designed in the client-server model. One server performs the functions needed to negotiate mail with other mail servers, and deliver the mail to the proper destinations. The mail client, however, goes well above and beyond downloading mail from the mail server and offers many additional productivity-enhancing features. Examples of these features might be message sorting, searching, contact list management, attachment handling, and more recently, spam filtering and message encryption.

Each of these features may require a certain amount of processing power. This required level may be negligible on an individual level but may be problematic when applied on a larger scale.

When examining the performance issue, it is important to consider the number of potential users that will access the webmail application. A single server may be able to easily handle 300 total users, for example. If the total user base for a single server is increased to 10,000, server load may become an issue.

For example, searching through several years' worth of archived mail may take a few seconds on a client's computer. This load is equal on the server. When many clients request this operation at short intervals, it may be difficult for the server to accomplish, and may begin overloading the server's resources. This may result in pages being served at a slower rate, or, in extreme circumstances, the server failing to respond.

Optimally, load testing in the appropriate conditions should be performed if there is any concern that a server may not be able to handle a particular load of users.

Not Well Suited to Large E-Mail Volumes

This disadvantage is related to the previous one, but with a twist. Even with a relatively low number of users, a large volume of e-mails *may* be difficult to manage in a webmail application. This may be due to a couple of reasons:

First, a large e-mail folder may take a very long time to load from the web server. Since the entire application is web based, SquirrelMail must first access the mailbox, directly from the server. As opposed to storing messages locally, all e-mail message information must be retrieved from the server. This can cause long wait times, while the server software fetches e-mail information from the e-mail server.

Additionally, each action on the webmail application generally requires a user to wait for the next page to load. Managing a large volume of e-mail may take longer than with a traditional mail access client. Each operation—deleting a message, reading a message, moving a message, replying to a message—requires the user to wait while the next page loads. If a user receives a large volume of e-mail, the process of managing and sorting the incoming mail may take a long time.

Not Well Suited to E-Mail Attachments

By virtue of the fact that a webmail application resides on a remote server, any and all e-mail attachments must first be uploaded onto that server. For a couple of reasons, it may be difficult or impossible to accomplish this operation with too many attachments, or with attachments that are large.

Difficulties uploading large attachments may arise due to limited storage space on the webmail server. Large attachments may take a long time to upload over the HTTP protocol and even longer over HTTPS. Additionally, many file size limits may be imposed on uploaded files. PHP imposes a 2MB limit on uploaded files in its default configuration.

In this case, the nature of a webmail access solution—e-mail and the mail access software reside on the server—may offer an advantage. In a traditional mail client, e-mail is often downloaded before the user is aware of the contents or size of the particular e-mail message. As opposed to this, in the case of webmail, the user is able to view e-mail with large attachments without downloading the attachments, a particular benefit to those without high-speed internet connections.

Finally, downloading and uploading large e-mail attachments from the server may cause a performance issue with the user interface. Many users are frustrated by an attachment's upload time in the webmail application, especially since the message cannot be sent until the attachment is uploaded. In a traditional mail client, the attachment is attached instantly, while the message takes time to send.

Security Issues

The last issue we will examine is the potential for security shortcomings. One large feature of a webmail access solution also creates a potential problem. The benefit of remote access gives way to the potential insecurity of the local machines upon which the user accesses his or her mail.

A computer that is not directly under your control may be controlled by a third party intent on accessing your information. Normally, a computer does not record a user's individual keystrokes. A computer running malicious software, however, may monitor this and much more. A user must type in his or her password or login credentials to gain access to the system.

When these credentials are captured and stored on the computer with malicious software, they can be intercepted and used by third parties for unauthorized access.

Even if we take malicious intent out of the picture, there are still certain situations that may prove to pose security risks. For example, many modern web browsers offer the option of saving a password whenever it is entered. This password is stored on the local computer where the web site is visited. If a user logs in to the webmail application, and accidentally saves their password on the local computer, this password may be accessible to any user with access to that local computer.

Finally, users may inadvertently leave themselves logged in to the webmail application. Without logging out, any user with access to that specific computer within a short range of time could gain access to the user's mail account.

The SquirrelMail Webmail Package

SquirrelMail was chosen as the webmail package of choice for this book. The following screenshot shows the SquirrelMail login screen:

This choice is based on the combination of features it provides:

- It is a proven, stable, and mature webmail platform.
- It has been downloaded over two million times.
- It is standards-based and renders pages in pure HTML 4.0 without requiring the use of JavaScript.

SquirrelMail also includes the following features (and many more, via the flexible plug-in system). The screenshot that follows shows an inbox where you can see some of them.

- Strong MIME support
- Address book functionality
- A spell checker
- Support for sending and receiving HTML e-mail
- Template and theme support
- Virtual host support

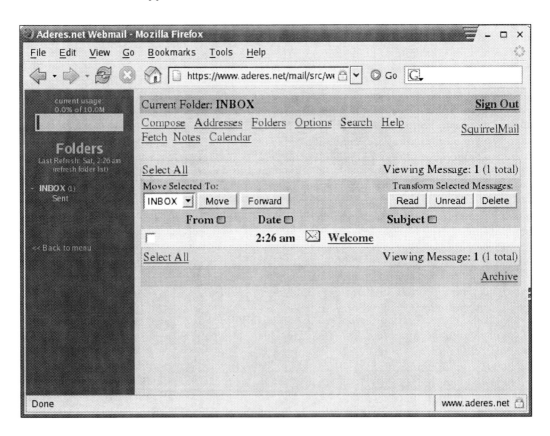

SquirrelMail Installation and Configuration

This section will examine the following:

- The Prerequisites to a SquirrelMail installation
  - Basic requirements
  - Configuration requirements
- Installing SquirrelMail
  - Binary or source installation
- Configuring SquirrelMail

Prerequisites to Installation

SquirrelMail requires both PHP and a web server that supports PHP scripts to be installed before proceeding. In our case, we will be using the Apache web server, although others will work as well.

First, we will go over the basic requirements, and what to do if you do not meet them. Next, we will go over some more advanced requirements that may impact on certain features within SquirrelMail.

Basic Requirements

At the time of writing, the most current stable version of SquirrelMail available is 1.4.4. The following instructions apply to this version. There are two basic requirements to SquirrelMail installation.

Apache

Any modern version of Apache that supports PHP will do the trick. To query for an Apache installation, on an RPM package management-based system, issue the following command at the prompt.

```
$ rpm -q apache
apache-1.3.20-16
```

If, as in the example above, a version of Apache is returned, then the Apache web server is installed on your system. Similar commands are available for other systems using other package management systems.

If you do not have an Apache installation present, it is best to first look to your distribution for a copy of Apache—such as on your operating system installation CDs. Alternatively, you may visit the home for the Apache foundation at http://www.apache.org.

PHP

The PHP programming language is required in order to install SquirrelMail. PHP version 4.0.6 or greater is required. To query for a PHP installation on an RPM-based system, issue the following command:

```
$ rpm -q php
php-4.0.6-7
```

If version 4.0.6 or higher of PHP is present, then you are good to go. Otherwise, you will need to install or upgrade your current installation. As with Apache, it is often best to look to your distribution for a copy to install—more than likely, a copy was included on the installation CD-ROMs that came with your operating system. Alternatively, you may also visit http://www.php.net.

Once you have verified that these packages are installed on your system, you may choose to read the following section, where we will discuss some configuration options that may impact on your SquirrelMail installation.

Configuration Requirements

You may wish go over php.ini, the PHP configuration file. On most Linux systems, this file may be found in /etc/php.ini. If you want users to be able to upload attachments, make sure that the option file_uploads is set to On:

```
; Whether to allow HTTP file uploads.
file_uploads = On
```

The next option within the php.ini file you may want to change is upload_max_filesize. This setting applies to uploaded attachments and determines the maximum file size of an uploaded file. It may be helpful to change this to something reasonable, like 10M.

```
; Maximum allowed size for uploaded files.
upload_max_filesize = 10M
```

SquirrelMail Installation

SquirrelMail may be installed either though **binaries** or **source code**. While no source code compilation takes place in either method, upgrades are facilitated in the binary installation method through the local package management system.

Many of the various Linux and UNIX distributions include the SquirrelMail package. Install the appropriate package from your distribution to use the binary method. On many Linux distributions, this may be an RPM file that begins with squirrelmail....

However, an updated version of SquirrelMail may not be included or available for your specific distribution.

Source Installation

If you do not install SquirrelMail through your distribution, you will need to obtain the appropriate tarball. To do so, visit the SquirrelMail web site at `http://www.squirrelmail.org`, and click download. At the time of writing, this link is: `http://www.squirrelmail.org/download.php`.

There are two versions available for download, a **stable version**, and a **development version**. Unless you have specific reasons for choosing otherwise, it is generally best to choose the stable version. Download and save this file to an intermediate location.

```
$ wget
http://voxel.dl.sourceforge.net/sourceforge/squirrelmail/squirrelmail-
1.4.4.tar.gz
```

Next, unpack the tarball (`.tar.gz`) file. You may use the following command.

```
$ tar zxf squirrelmail-1.4.4.tar.gz
```

Move the folder just created to your web root folder. In this case, we will assume that /var/www/html is your web root. We will also rename the clumsy `squirrelmail-1.4.3a` folder to a more simple `mail` folder. You will need to have superuser `root` privileges in order to do this on most systems.

```
# mv squirrelmail-1.4.4 /var/www/html/mail
# cd /var/www/html/mail
```

It is also useful and secure to create a `data` directory for SquirrelMail that is outside the main web root. We do this so that this folder will be inaccessible from the Web.

```
# mv /var/www/html/mail/data /var/www/sqmdata
```

It is important to make this newly created folder writable by the web server. To be able to do this, you must know the user and group that your web server runs under. This may be nobody and nobody, apache and apache, or something else. You will want to verify this; it will be listed in your `httpd.conf` file.

```
# chown -R nobody /var/www/sqmdata
# chgrp -R nobody /var/www/sqmdata
```

Finally, we will create a directory in which to store attachments. This directory is special in that, although the web server should have write access to write the attachments, it should not have read access. We create this directory and assign the correct permissions with the following commands.

```
# mkdir /var/www/sqmdata/attachments
# chgrp -R nobody /var/www/sqmdata/attachments
# chmod 730 /var/www/sqmdata/attachments
```

SquirrelMail has now been properly installed. All of the folders have been correctly set up with correct permissions that will secure intermediate files from prying eyes.

> If a user aborts a message that contains an uploaded attachment, the attachment file on the web server will not be removed. It is good practice to create a cron job on the server that erases excess files from the attachment directory. For example:
>
> ```
> rm `find /var/www/sqmdata/attachments -atime +2 | grep -v "\."|
> grep -v _
> ```

Configuring SquirrelMail

SquirrelMail is configured through the config.php file. To aid the configuration, a conf.pl perl script has also been provided. These files are located within the config/ directory in the base installation directory.

```
# cd /var/www/html/mail/config
# ./conf.pl
```

Once you have run this command, you should run into the following menu.

```
SquirrelMail Configuration : Read: config_default.php (1.4.0)
---------------------------------------------------------------
Main Menu --
1.  Organization Preferences
2.  Server Settings
3.  Folder Defaults
4.  General Options
5.  Themes
6.  Address Books (LDAP)
7.  Message of the Day (MOTD)
8.  Plugins
9.  Database

D.  Set pre-defined settings for specific IMAP servers

C.  Turn color on
S   Save data
Q   Quit


Command >>
```

To select an item in the menu, enter the appropriate letter or number, followed by the *Enter* key. To load a default configuration for your IMAP server, enter the D option.

```
Please select your IMAP server:
    cyrus        = Cyrus IMAP server
    uw           = University of Washington's IMAP server
    exchange     = Microsoft Exchange IMAP server
```

```
    courier      = Courier IMAP server
    macosx       = Mac OS X Mailserver
    quit         = Do not change anything


Command >> courier
```

You will be presented with the following options. Type courier, in this case, and press *Enter* twice. You are now at the main menu. We will be moving through the various subsections of the menu, and configuring the appropriate options.

Type 1 and then press *Enter*.

```
SquirrelMail Configuration : Read: config_default.php (1.4.0)
---------------------------------------------------------------

Organization Preferences
1.   Organization Name      : SquirrelMail
2.   Organization Logo      : ../images/sm_logo.png
3.   Org. Logo Width/Height : (308/111)
4.   Organization Title     : SquirrelMail $version
5.   Signout Page           :
6.   Default Language       : en_US
7.   Top Frame              : _top
8.   Provider link          : http://www.squirrelmail.org/
9.   Provider name          : SquirrelMail
```

In this section, you may wish to edit the Organization Name, Organization Logo, and Organization Title fields. Once you have modified these to your satisfaction, enter R to return to the main menu.

After this, type 2 followed by the *Enter* key. You will see options similar to the ones you've already seen.

```
Server Settings

General
-------
1.   Domain                 : example.com
2.   Invert Time            : false
3.   Sendmail or SMTP       : SMTP


A.   Update IMAP Settings   : localhost:143 (courier)
B.   Update SMTP Settings   : localhost:25
```

It is important that you update the Domain field to the proper value.

In our case, the Update IMAP Settings and Update SMTP Settings values should be correct. If you would like to use an IMAP or SMTP server that is located on a different machine, you may wish to update these values.

Press R followed by the *Enter* key to return to the main menu.

Next, type 4 followed by the *Enter* key.

```
General Options

 1.  Default Charset             : iso-8859-1
 2.  Data Directory              : ../data/
 3.  Attachment Directory        : $data_dir
 4.  Directory Hash Level        : 0
 5.  Default Left Size           : 150
 6.  Usernames in Lowercase      : false
 7.  Allow use of priority       : true
 8.  Hide SM attributions        : false
 9.  Allow use of receipts       : true
10.  Allow editing of identity   : true/true
11.  Allow server thread sort    : false
12.  Allow server-side sorting   : false
13.  Allow server charset search : true
14.  Enable UID support          : true
15.  PHP session name            : SQMSESSID
```

You will need to modify two options in this section.

Modify 2. Data Directory to be /var/www/sqmdata.

Modify 3. Attachment Directory to be /var/www/sqmdata/attachments.

```
General Options

 1.  Default Charset        : iso-8859-1
 2.  Data Directory         : /var/www/sqmdata/
 3.  Attachment Directory   : /var/www/sqmdata/attachments/
```

Type in R followed by the *Enter* key to return to the main menu. Enter S followed by the *Enter* key twice to save the settings to the configuration file. Finally, enter Q followed by the *Enter* key to exit the configuration application.

We have finished configuring the SquirrelMail settings needed for basic operation. You may return to this script at any time to update any settings you have set. There are many other options to set, including those regarding **Themes** and **Plugins**.

SquirrelMail Plug-Ins

Plug-ins are pieces of software that extend or add functionality to a software package. SquirrelMail was designed from the ground up to be very extensible, and includes a powerful plug-in system. Currently, there are 193 different plug-ins available on the SquirrelMail web site. They may be obtained at `http://www.squirrelmail.org/plugins.php`.

The functionality they provide includes administration tools, visual additions, user interface tweaks, security enhancements, and even weather forecasts. In the following section, we will first go over how to install and configure a plug-in. After that, we'll go over some useful plug-ins, what they do, how to install them, and more.

Installing Plug-Ins

These SquirrelMail additions were designed to be simple to set up and configure. In fact, the majority of them follow exactly the same installation procedure. A few, however, require custom setup instructions. For all plug-ins, the installation process is as follows.

1. Download and unpack the plug-in.
2. Perform custom installation if needed.
3. Enable the plug-in in `conf.pl`.

Example Plug-In Installation

In this next section, we will go over the installation of the **Compatibility plug-in**. This plug-in is required in order to install plug-ins created for older versions of SquirrelMail. No matter how bare-bones your installation, the `Compatibility` plug-in will most likely be part of your setup.

Download and Unpack the Plug-In

All available plug-ins for SquirrelMail are listed on the SquirrelMail web site at `http://www.squirrelmail.org/plugins.php`.

Certain plug-ins may require a specific version of SquirrelMail—verify that you have this version installed. Once you have located a plug-in, download it to the `plugins/` directory within the SquirrelMail root folder.

You may locate the `Compatibility` plug-in by clicking the Miscellaneous category. Click on Details, and then Download under the Version 1.3 heading.

> **Plugins - Compatibility**
> Category: Miscellaneous
>
> Provdies a standard API for plugin authors who need certain functionalities that may not be available in older versions of SquirrelMail. Also makes it easier to upgrade plugins for SM 1.4 compatibility. SquirrelMail administrators only need to download this plugin if any of the plugins they have require it. This plugin has no functionality in and of itself.
>
> **Version 1.3**
> by Paul Lesneiwski on Apr 23, 2004
> [download]   **Requires: (none)**
> *Description:*
>
> - Added compatibility_check_plugin_setup() that helps verify that a plugin has been installed and set up correctly
> - Added new $compatibility_sm_path variable for easier plugin coding...
> - Updated for compatibility (!) with new version reporting API

Download the tarball to your SquirrelMail plug-in directory.

```
# cd /var/www/mail/plugins
# wget http://squirrelmail.org/plugins/compatibility-1.3.tar.gz
```

Once you have downloaded the plug-in to the plugins directory, unpack it using the following command:

```
# tar zxvf compatibility-1.3.tar.gz
```

> If a plug-in of the same name has already been installed, its files may be overwritten. Verify that you either do not have a plug-in of the same name, or save the files before you unpack the tarball.

Perform Custom Installation if Needed

The Compatibility plug-in does not require any additional configuration. However, certain other plug-ins may require custom installation. Once you have unpacked the plug-in package, the installation instructions will be listed in the INSTALL file within the newly created plugin directory. It is advisable to check the installation instructions before enabling the plug-in in the configuration manager, as some plug-ins may require custom configuration.

Enable the Plug-In in conf.pl

Within the main menu of the configuration editor, option number 8 is used to configure and enable plug-ins. Start up conf.pl and select option 8.

```
# cd /var/www/mail/plugins
# cd ../config
# ./conf.pl
```

```
SquirrelMail Configuration : Read: config_default.php (1.4.0)
------------------------------------------------------------
Main Menu --
[...]
7.  Message of the Day (MOTD)
8.  Plugins
9.  Database
[...]

Command >>
```

The first time you select this option you should get a display similar to the following:

```
SquirrelMail Configuration : Read: config.php (1.4.0)
----------------------------------------------------
Plugins
  Installed Plugins

  Available Plugins:
    1.  info
    2.  translate
    3.  squirrelspell
    4.  spamcop
    5.  filters
    6.  calendar
    7.  abook_take
    8.  fortune
    9.  administrator
    10. newmail
    11. bug_report
    12. sent_subfolders
    13. mail_fetch
    14. listcommands
    15. message_details
    16. delete_move_next
    17. compatibility

R    Return to Main Menu
C.   Turn color on
S    Save data
Q    Quit

Command >>
```

All the plug-ins that have been installed and enabled are listed under the Installed Plugins list. All the plug-ins that have been installed but not enabled are listed under the Available Plugins list.

Once you have unpacked a plug-in within the plugins/ directory, it will show up under Available Plugins. As you can see above, there are a number of installed plug-ins, but none enabled. Since a malfunctioning or wrongly configured plug-in can cause

SquirrelMail to stop functioning properly, it is advisable to enable plug-ins one by one, and verify that SquirrelMail works after each one. To enable the Compatibility plug-in, enter 17, and press the *Enter* key. The same process will disable a plug-in once it is enabled. Save and quit with S then *Enter* twice and Q then *Enter*. The Compatibility plug-in is now installed.

Useful Plug-Ins

We'll now see some useful SquirrelMail plug-ins that you may consider installing.

The information has been compiled to provide a helpful reference while deciding whether to install a plug-in. Each plug-in contains four specific categories:

- **Category**: The category in which the plug-in is listed on the SquirrelMail site
- **Authors**: Authors who wrote the plug-in, in chronological order
- **Description**: A short description of the plug-in's functionality
- **Requirement**: A list of prerequisites for the plug-in's successful installation

Compatibility Plug-In (v1.3)

Category:	Miscellaneous
Authors:	Paul Lesneiwski
Description:	Provides a standard plug-in API for functions that may not be available in older versions of SquirrelMail, and makes it easy to upgrade plug-ins for SquirrelMail 1.4 compatibility. Required by certain plug-ins.
Requires:	Nothing

Secure login (v1.2)

Category:	Logging in
Authors:	Graham Norbury, Paul Lesneiwski
Description:	Prevents plain text passwords and e-mail contents being transmitted over the unencrypted internet by requiring an HTTPS connection during log-in and while using SquirrelMail.
Requires:	SquirrelMail >= 1.2.8, the Compatibility Plug-in, SSL-capable web server

HTTP Auth (v1.1)

Category:	Logging in
Authors:	Frederic Connes
Description:	This plug-in will use the username and password provided by HTTP authentication to automatically bypass the login screen.
Requires:	SquirrelMail >= 1.4.0

Password Forget (v2.1)

Category:	Logging in
Authors:	Paul Lesneiwski
Description:	Changes the name of the username and password input box on the login form to make it difficult for modern browsers to remember these values.
Requires:	SquirrelMail >= 1.0.1, the Compatibility Plug-in

HTML Mail (v2.0)

Category:	Compose
Authors:	Paul Lesneiwski
Description:	Allows users to compose e-mail with HTML style additions.
Requires:	SquirrelMail >= 1.4.0, the Compatibility Plug-in

Quick Save (v2.0)

Category:	Compose
Authors:	Ray Black III, Paul Lesneiwski
Description:	JavaScript plug-in that allows recovery of a message that is being composed if it is abandoned or lost.
Requires:	SquirrelMail >= 1.0.0, the Compatibility Plug-in, JavaScript-capable browser

G/PGP Encryption Plug-In (v2.0)

Category:	Compose
Authors:	Brian G. Peterson
Description:	A general-purpose encryption, decryption, and digital signature plug-in for SquirrelMail that implements the OpenPGP standard using GPG.
Requires:	SquirrelMail >= 1.4.2 recommended, GnuPG

Quota Usage (v1.3)

Category:	Compose
Authors:	Bill Shupp, Paul Lesneiwski
Description:	This plug-in displays the current e-mail quota usage just above the folder list.
Requires:	IMAP Server with QUOTA Extension capability

Sent Confirmation (v1.6)

Category:	Miscellaneous
Authors:	Paul Lesneiwski
Description:	Displays a confirmation message after a message is successfully sent, as well as other features.
Requires:	SquirrelMail >= 1.2.0, the Compatibility Plug-in

Timeout User (v1.6)

Category:	Miscellaneous
Authors:	Ray Black III, Paul Lesneiwski
Description:	Automatically logs a user out if they are idle for a specified amount of time.
Requires:	The Compatibility Plug-in

E-Mail Footer (v0.4)

Category:	Miscellaneous
Authors:	Ray Black III, Paul Lesneiwski
Description:	Tacks a footer on to all sent messages.
Requires:	SquirrelMail >= 1.4.2

Change Password (v2.7-1.4.x)

Category:	Change Password
Authors:	Tyler Akins, Seth E. Randall
Description:	Allows a user to change their password using PAM or Courier authentication modules.
Requires:	SquirrelMail >= 1.4.0

Address Book Import-Export (v0.8)

Category:	Address Book
Authors:	Lewis Bergman, Dustin Anders, Christian Sauer
Description:	Imports addresses from a CSV-formatted address book.
Requires:	SquirrelMail >= 1.4.0

Plugin Updates (v0.7)

Category:	Administrator's Relief
Authors:	Jimmy Conner
Description:	Checks for updates to your currently running plug-ins.
Requires:	SquirrelMail >= 1.4.2

Many other plug-ins exist that handle vacation messages, calendars, shared calendars, notes, TODO lists, exchange server integration, bookmarks, the weather, and much more. Check the Plugins section in the SquirrelMail web site for all of the available plug-ins.

Securing SquirrelMail

The SquirrelMail package, in and of itself, is fairly secure. It is well written, and does not require JavaScript to function. However, there are a few precautions that may be taken to allow SquirrelMail to run as a secure mail handling solution:

- **Require an SSL connection**: By requiring an SSL connection, you may be certain that all communications will be handled over an encryption medium. This may be accomplished through the installation of the **Secure Login plug-in**. Obviously a web server configured for secure SSL access will also be required; certificates will most likely need to be generated or acquired.

- **Time-out inactive users**: Users may leave themselves logged in and neglect to log out once they are finished. To fight this, inactive users should be logged out after a certain amount of time. The **Timeout User plug-in** accomplishes this.

- **Fight 'Remembered Passwords'**: Many modern-day browsers will offer to remember a user's password. Although a convenience, this may be a large security vulnerability, especially if the user is located at a public terminal. To fight this, install the **Password Forget plug-in**. This plug-in will always change the names of the username and password input fields, to make it more difficult for a browser to suggest them to future users.

- **Do not install security-compromising plug-ins**: Plug-ins such as **Quick Save**, **HTML Mail**, and **View As HTML** may compromise security.

Summary

Now that you've finished this chapter, you should have a working SquirrelMail installation, as well as a greater understanding of the benefits and disadvantages to a webmail solution. You should be familiar with:

- The features of the SquirrelMail package

- The benefits of SquirrelMail and a webmail solution such as a speedy setup, easy remote access, the advantage of not needing to maintain local clients, and the ability for users to configure mail server options directly, as well as possible security benefits

- The disadvantages of SquirrelMail such as the performance issues when dealing with large e-mail or attachment volumes, as well as the security drawbacks of allowing remote access

- The basic prerequisites to a SquirrelMail installation—Apache and PHP—and the configuration of PHP for optimal SquirrelMail use

- How to install SquirrelMail either through a binary installation, or by source, as well as the benefits of each option.

- How to configure SquirrelMail to work with Courier, to set your organization's settings, and to work with a more secure data directory.

- What SquirrelMail plug-ins are, and how to retrieve and install them.

- The step by step installation of the `Compatibility` plug-in.

- Several useful plug-ins and some helpful information about each one of them.

- Tactics to secure SquirrelMail.

5
Securing Your Installation

Of all the bad things that can happen to your SMTP server, the worst is probably having it abused as an open relay—a server that relays mail for third parties without your permission. This will consume a lot of bandwidth, eat up server resources, and cost you a lot of money. Worse than that, your server will end up on a blacklist, and any server consulting this list will refuse to accept mail from your server until you have proven it to be relay-safe. If you need your mail server for business, you will have a big problem.

This chapter will tell you how to protect Postfix from relay abuse. You will learn the difference between statically and dynamically assigned IP addresses when it comes to relay protection. Then you will be shown how to configure relay permissions for both types of IP addresses.

Postfix provides means to protect users from unwanted content such as spam and other harmful content. Finally, as an introduction to its vast functionality, you will learn how to configure Postfix to defeat or at least slow down **Dictionary Attacks**. The chapter will end with a demonstration of how Postfix can give a hard time to those who are trying to give Postfix a hard time.

Setting Up a Permanent Authorized Relay for an IP Address or Range of IP Addresses

Back in the good old days of Internet no one had to protect their mail servers from relay abuse. Actually, not many people had a mail server and permitting others to relay was considered a service for the ones that didn't have one.

This changed with the advent of people who soon became known as spammers. They would abuse open relays to send out advertisements to large numbers of remote recipients leaving the owner of the mail server to pay for the traffic.

This is when postmasters started to handle relay permissions restrictively. They used to separate the wheat from the chaff by permitting relaying only for trusted IP addresses. A trusted IP address in this context was an IP address that could be associated statically (refer the *Static IP Ranges* section) with a host that belonged to a known user, or a range of IP addresses known to belong to a trusted network. It worked well as most computers would have static IP addresses (the IP address wouldn't change over time).

However a new approach had to be found when users became mobile or would use dial-up providers to access the Internet and wanted to use a mail server in a totally different location. Access providers would give these users dynamic IP addresses i.e. their IP address would change every time they dialed in.

Suddenly the criteria to tell the good user from the bad user were gone. Postmasters would either have to loosen their relay permissions to permit a whole network of potentially untrusted IPs to use the relay, or would have to find another way to handle relaying for dynamic IP addresses. Over time several approaches to handle relaying for dynamic IP addresses emerged:

- SMTP-after-POP
- Virtual Private Networks
- SMTP Authentication

All of the three approaches differ in their requirements and how they work. The following sections will give you a closer insight.

SMTP-After-POP

Usually a mail client sends mail first (SMTP) and then checks the server (POP) to see if there is any new mail— the SMTP part happens before the POP part.

This makes it impossible for the SMTP server to find out if the sender should be permitted to relay, because the dynamic IP is in no relation with any other criteria that would make the sender's host a trusted host.

Not so with SMTP-after-POP, which reverses the procedure—the POP part takes place before the SMTP part. Accessing one's mail on a POP server requires sending a username and a password to get access to the messages.

This makes it possible for an SMTP server to identify a trusted IP address, because the moment a POP users authenticates as valid user, the POP server can write the user's IP address to a file the SMTP server can read from—any IP address in there belongs to a valid user and the SMTP server may let its client relay mail.

The disadvantages of SMTP-after-POP are that you need a POP server even if you only want to allow relaying of messages. A POP server will complicate the setup on a server if you don't need it. It might also bind updates of your SMTP server to your POP server to keep compatibility.

Virtual Private Networks

Virtual Private Networks (VPNs) assign the client another private IP address if the authentication to the VPN succeeds. The SMTP server knowing and trusting the range of private IP addresses will permit relaying for a mail client coming from the VPN.

Again, just as with SMTP-after-POP, running a VPN just for the sake of relaying mails is way beyond reasonable efforts. It only pays off if you provide additional resources and services in the VPN.

SMTP Authentication

SMTP Authentication, also known as **SMTP AUTH**, uses a different method to identify valid relay users. It requires mail clients to send a username and a password to the SMTP server during the SMTP dialogue and if the authentication succeeds they may relay.

It is less complex than running a full-blown POP server and it solves the problem where it arises—in the SMTP server. You will learn what it takes to offer SMTP AUTH after you've configured your server to handle static IP addresses.

Static IP Ranges

By default Postfix will only allow hosts from its own network(s) to relay messages. Trustworthy networks are those you configured for your network interfaces. Run `ifconfig -a` to get a list of what has been configured on your system.

If you want to change the default, you can either use some generic values using the `mynetworks_style` parameter or provide explicit ranges of IP addresses noted as values for the `mynetworks` parameter in `main.cf`.

Generic Relay Rules

To configure generic relay rules you need to add one of the following values to the `mynetworks_style` parameter in `main.cf`.

- `host`: If you configure `mynetworks_style = host`, Postfix will permit only the IP addresses of the host it runs on to send messages to remote destinations.

- `class`: If you configure `mynetworks_style = class`, Postfix will allow every host in the network class (Network class A/B/C) it serves to relay.

- `subnet`: If you configure `mynetworks_style = subnet`, the only hosts allowed to relay messages are those from the subnet(s) Postfix is part of.

> This option will be deprecated in Postfix 2.2 to simplify the upcoming implementation of IPv6 functionality.

Explicit Relay Rules

Explicit relay rules allow for finer-grained relay permissions. Simply add a list of remote and local hosts and/or networks to the `mynetworks` parameter in `main.cf`. If you want to permit localhost, all hosts in your LAN (in the following example the IP addresses `10.0.0.0` to `10.0.0.254`), and your static IP from home (here `192.0.34.166`) you note them as a list in CIDR notation as shown in this example:

```
mynetworks = 127.0.0.0/8, 10.0.0.0/24, 192.0.34.166/32
```

Once you reload Postfix the new settings will take effect.

Dynamic IP Ranges

In the previous section you saw how to permit relaying for static IP addresses. This section will show how you can configure Postfix to permit relaying for dynamic IP addresses.

As mentioned in this chapter's introduction there are several ways to achieve this. The only method described in the following sections is SMTP Authentication. It provides a simple and stable mechanism, but the setup isn't trivial. The reason for this is that SMTP AUTH isn't processed by Postfix on its own. Another software module, Cyrus SASL, is required to offer and process SMTP AUTH to mail clients. You will need to configure Cyrus SASL, Postfix, and how they interoperate.

If you have never dealt with Cyrus SASL before, you should read the introduction to Cyrus SASL carefully. Most of the problems that people have with SMTP AUTH are not Postfix-related but stem from Cyrus SASL configuration problems.

Cyrus SASL

Cyrus SASL (`http://asg.web.cmu.edu/cyrus/`) is Carnegie Mellon University's implementation of a SASL. **SASL**, a **Simple Authentication and Security Layer**, is an authentication framework described in RFC 2222 (`http://www.rfc-editor.org/rfc/rfc2222.txt`).

SASL was written to provide an application-independent authentication framework for any application that needs to use or offer authentication services.

Cyrus SASL isn't the only SASL available today, but was the first to emerge and is used in various applications such as Postfix, Sendmail, Mutt, and OpenLDAP to name a few. In order to use Cyrus SASL you need to understand its architecture, how the various layers are made to work together, and how the layers' functionalities are configured.

SASL Layers

SASL consists of three layers: **authentication interface**, **mechanism**, and **method**. Each of these takes care of a distinct job when an authentication request is being processed.

An authentication process usually goes through the following steps:

1. A client connects to a server.
2. The server announces its capabilities.
3. The client recognizes the option to authenticate among the listed capabilities. It also recognizes a list of mechanisms it can choose to process authentication.
4. The client chooses one of the mechanisms and calculates a string. What goes into the string depends on the mechanism.
5. The client sends the "AUTH mechanism string" to the server.
6. The server receives the authentication request and hands it over to SASL.
7. SASL recognizes the mechanism and does some calculation on its own. What it calculates exactly depends on the mechanism.
8. SASL uses a method to contact an authentication back end in order to verify the information given by the client. What it exactly looks for depends on the mechanism used.
9. If it can verify the information it will tell the server and the server may permit the client to, say, relay a message. If it can't verify the information it will tell the server as well and the server may reject the client's wish to relay a message. In both cases the server will tell the client whether authentication was successful or if it failed.

Let's take a closer look at the three SASL layers in the following sections.

Authentication Interface

In steps 1 to 5 and step 9, you could see client and server exchange data to process authentication. This part of communication takes place in the authentication interface.

Though SASL defines *what* data must be exchanged it does not specify how it must be communicated between client and server. It leaves this to their specific communication protocol, which is why SASL can be used by various services, such as SMTP, IMAP, or LDAP.

> SASL is younger than the SMTP protocol (see: RFC 821). It was added later in RFC 2554 (`http://www.rfc-editor.org/rfc/rfc2554.txt`), which describes the **SMTP Service Extension for Authentication**.

An SMTP conversation where the server offers SMTP authentication among its other capabilities looks like this:

```
$ telnet mail.example.com 25
220 mail.example.com ESMTP Postfix
EHLO client.example.com
250-mail.example.com
250-PIPELINING
250-SIZE 10240000
250-VRFY
250-ETRN
250-AUTH PLAIN LOGIN CRAM-MD5 DIGEST-MD5 1)
250-AUTH=PLAIN LOGIN CRAM-MD5 DIGEST-MD5 2)
250 8BITMIME
QUIT
```

- 250-AUTH PLAIN LOGIN CRAM-MD5 DIGEST-MD5 1): This line tells the client that the server offers SMTP AUTH. It consists of two logical parts. The first part, 250-AUTH, announces SMTP AUTH capability and the rest of the line is a list of available mechanisms from which the client may choose the one it prefers.

- 250-AUTH=PLAIN LOGIN CRAM-MD5 DIGEST-MD5 2): This line repeats the line above, but differs in the way it announces SMTP authentication. Instead of whitespace after the 250-AUTH it adds an equal sign like this 250-AUTH=. This is for broken clients that do not follow the final specification of SASL.

Mechanism

Mechanisms (as described in steps 4 to 7) represent the second layer of SASL. They determine the verification strategy used during authentication. There are several mechanisms known to SASL. They differ in how they transmit data and their level of security during transmission. The most commonly used mechanisms can be grouped into **plaintext** and **shared-secret** mechanisms.

One mechanism you should never have Postfix offer to clients is the **anonymous** mechanism. We will have a look at this first.

- anonymous: The anonymous mechanism requires a client to send any string it likes to. It was designed to allow anonymous access to, say, global IMAP folders, but not for SMTP. An SMTP server offering ANONYMOUS in the AUTH line will be abused over time. You should never offer this in an SMTP server!

- plaintext: Cyrus SASL knows the **PLAIN** and **LOGIN** plaintext mechanisms. LOGIN is pretty much the same as PLAIN, but is used for mail clients that don't follow the final SASL RFC by the books, such as Outlook and Outlook Express. Both mechanisms require the client to calculate a base64-encoded string of the username and password and transmit it to the server for authentication. The great thing about plaintext mechanisms is that they are supported by nearly every mail client in use today. The bad news is plaintext mechanisms are not secure if used without **Transport Layer Security (TLS)**. This is because a base64-encoded string is merely encoded, but not encrypted—it can easily be decoded. It is safe though to use plaintext mechanisms to transmit one during a Transport Layer encrypted session. The TLS layer will protect the base64-encoded string from eavesdroppers.

- `shared-secret`: The shared-secret mechanisms available in Cyrus SASL are **CRAM-MD5** and **DIGEST-MD5**. Shared-secret based authentication has a totally different strategy to verify a client. It is based upon the assumption that client and server both share a secret. A client choosing a shared-secret mechanism will only tell the server the name of the specific shared-secret mechanism. The server will then generate a challenge, based upon their secret and send it to the client. The client then generates a response, proving that it knows the secret. During the whole authentication process neither a username nor a password is sent over the wire. That's why shared-secret mechanisms are a lot more secure than the ones mentioned before. However, the most popular mail clients Outlook and Outlook Express do not support shared-secret mechanisms.

> On a heterogeneous network you will probably end up offering plaintext and shared-secret mechanisms side by side.

This said on mechanisms there's only one layer left—the method layer. This is where lookups to data stores that hold credentials are configured and processed. The next section will tell you more about methods.

Method

The last layer SASL refers to is the method layer. Methods are represented by libraries in the Cyrus SASL install directory. They serve to access data stores, which Cyrus SASL not only refers to as methods but also as authentication back ends. Out of the number of methods SASL has the most commonly used are:

- `rimap`: The `rimap` method stands for **remote IMAP** and enables SASL to log in to an IMAP server. It uses the username and password given by the client. A successful IMAP login is a successful SASL authentication.

- `ldap`: The `ldap` method queries an LDAP server to verify a username and password. If the query succeeds the authentication succeeds.

- `kerberos`: The `kerberos` method checks a Kerberos ticket.

- `Getpwent/shadow`: The `getpwent` and `shadow` methods access your system's local user databases to verify an authentication request.

- `pam`: The `pam` method accesses any PAM module you configure in your PAM settings to verify an authentication request.

- sasldb: The sasldb method reads and even writes to Cyrus SASL's own database called sasldb2. Usually this database is used in conjunction with Cyrus IMAP, but you can use it without the IMAP server.

- sql: This method uses SQL queries to access various SQL servers. Currently these are MySQL, PostgreSQL, and SQLite.

Now that you know about the three layers of the SASL architecture, it's time to take a look at the SASL service that handles all the requests between them. It is called the **Password Verification Service** and will be described in the following section.

Password Verification Service

A password verification service handles an incoming authentication request from a server, does mechanism-specific calculations, calls a method to query an authentication back end, and finally returns the result to the server that sent the authentication request.

> In the case of Postfix the server that hands over the authentication request is the smtpd daemon. In the *Postfix SMTP AUTH Configuration* section you will learn how you can configure the smtpd daemon to choose the right password verification service.

Cyrus SASL version 2.1.20, the latest version at the moment, provides us with three different password verification services:

- saslauthd

- auxprop

- authdaemond

Mechanisms that your mail clients may use successfully and the methods that Cyrus SASL can access during authentication depend on the password verification service you tell Postfix to use.

- saslauthd: saslauthd is a standalone daemon. It can be run as root, which gives it the privilege to access sources accessible to root only. However saslauthd is limited in the range of mechanisms it supports; it can only handle plaintext mechanisms.

- auxprop: auxprop is the short name for **auxiliary property plugins,** a term used in the Project Cyrus mail server architecture. auxprop represents a library that is used by the server offering authentication. It accesses sources with the privileges of the server that uses it. Other than saslauthd, auxprop can handle every mechanism available within the Cyrus SASL authentication framework.

- authdaemond: authdaemond is a password verification service written especially to use Courier's authdaemond as password verifier. This way you can access any authentication back end that Courier can deal with. This auxprop plug-in can only deal with plaintext mechanisms.

The following table gives you an overview of the mechanisms the password verification services (methods) can handle:

Method/mechanisms	PLAIN	LOGIN	CRAM-MD5	DIGEST-MD5
saslauthd	yes	yes	no	no
auxprop	yes	yes	yes	yes
Authdaemond	yes	yes	no	no

Only the auxprop password verification service is able to handle the more secure mechanisms; saslauthd and authdaemond can only process plaintext mechanisms. All this said about the Cyrus SASL theory, it's about time we started to roll our own Cyrus SASL configuration. This is exactly what we do in the next sections.

Cyrus SASL Installation

Chances are you already have Cyrus SASL on your system. However various Linux distributions have begun to install Cyrus SASL in locations other than the default path /usr/lib/sasl2. To check if Cyrus SASL is on your server, either run your package manager and query for cyrus-sasl or run find. A query to the RedHat package manager (on Fedora Core 2) would return something like this if SASL is installed:

```
$ rpm -qa | grep sasl
cyrus-sasl-2.1.18-2.2
cyrus-sasl-devel-2.1.18-2.2
cyrus-sasl-plain-2.1.18-2.2
cyrus-sasl-md5-2.1.18-2.2
```

A find looking for libsasl*.* looks like this:

```
$ find /usr -name 'libsasl*.*'
/usr/lib/libsasl.so.7.1.11
/usr/lib/libsasl2.so
/usr/lib/libsasl.la
/usr/lib/libsasl2.so.2.0.18
/usr/lib/libsasl.a
/usr/lib/libsasl2.a
/usr/lib/libsasl2.la
/usr/lib/sasl2/libsasldb.so.2.0.18
/usr/lib/sasl2/libsasldb.so.2
/usr/lib/sasl2/libsasldb.so
/usr/lib/sasl2/libsasldb.la
/usr/lib/libsasl.so.7
/usr/lib/libsasl.so
/usr/lib/libsasl2.so.2
```

This proves that you have SASL installed on your system. To verify the location of the SASL libraries simply do an `ls` like this:

```
$ ls -l /usr/lib/sasl2
total 928
-rwxr-xr-x  1 root root       838 Oct  8 01:39 libanonymous.la
lrwxrwxrwx  1 root root        22 Oct 10 04:45 libanonymous.so ->
libanonymous.so.2.0.18
lrwxrwxrwx  1 root root        22 Oct 10 04:45 libanonymous.so.2 ->
libanonymous.so.2.0.18
-rwxr-xr-x  1 root root     12592 Oct  8 01:40 libanonymous.so.2.0.18
-rwxr-xr-x  1 root root       826 Oct  8 01:39 libcrammd5.la
lrwxrwxrwx  1 root root        20 Oct 10 04:45 libcrammd5.so ->
libcrammd5.so.2.0.18
lrwxrwxrwx  1 root root        20 Oct 10 04:45 libcrammd5.so.2 ->
libcrammd5.so.2.0.18
-rwxr-xr-x  1 root root     15116 Oct  8 01:40 libcrammd5.so.2.0.18
-rwxr-xr-x  1 root root       847 Oct  8 01:39 libdigestmd5.la
lrwxrwxrwx  1 root root        22 Oct 10 04:45 libdigestmd5.so ->
libdigestmd5.so.2.0.18
lrwxrwxrwx  1 root root        22 Oct 10 04:45 libdigestmd5.so.2 ->
libdigestmd5.so.2.0.18
-rwxr-xr-x  1 root root     41328 Oct  8 01:40 libdigestmd5.so.2.0.18
-rwxr-xr-x  1 root root       814 Oct  8 01:39 liblogin.la
lrwxrwxrwx  1 root root        18 Oct 10 04:45 liblogin.so ->
liblogin.so.2.0.18
lrwxrwxrwx  1 root root        18 Oct 10 04:45 liblogin.so.2 ->
liblogin.so.2.0.18
-rwxr-xr-x  1 root root     13036 Oct  8 01:40 liblogin.so.2.0.18
-rwxr-xr-x  1 root root       814 Oct  8 01:39 libplain.la
lrwxrwxrwx  1 root root        18 Oct 10 04:45 libplain.so ->
libplain.so.2.0.18
lrwxrwxrwx  1 root root        18 Oct 10 04:45 libplain.so.2 ->
libplain.so.2.0.18

-rwxr-xr-x  1 root root     13036 Oct  8 01:40 libplain.so.2.0.18
lrwxrwxrwx  1 root root        18 Oct 10 04:45 libplain.so.2 ->
libplain.so.2.0.18-rwxr-xr-x  1 root root  13036 Oct  8 01:40
libplain.so.2.0.18
-rwxr-xr-x  1 root root       894 Oct  8 01:39 libsasldb.la
lrwxrwxrwx  1 root root        19 Oct 10 04:45 libsasldb.so ->
libsasldb.so.2.0.18
lrwxrwxrwx  1 root root        19 Oct 10 04:45 libsasldb.so.2 ->
libsasldb.so.2.0.18
-rwxr-xr-x  1 root root    798308 Oct  8 01:40 libsasldb.so.2.0.18
-rw-r--r--  1 root root        83 Sep  6 02:21 sample.conf
-rw-r--r--  1 root root        25 Apr 15  2004 Sendmail.conf
-rw-r--r--  1 root root        88 Jul  2 20:48 smtpd.conf
```

As mentioned above, your distribution might put them somewhere else. In this case consult your distribution's documentation to find out where they should be.

If you don't have Cyrus SASL installed, you will have to either use your package manager to get it or install it manually.

One place to get it would be http://asg.web.cmu.edu/cyrus/download/. After you have downloaded and unpacked the source files, change into the source directory and run configure. A typical configuration of the sources goes like this:

```
$ ./configure \
    --with-plugindir=/usr/lib/sasl2 \
    --disable-java \
    --disable-krb4 \
    --with-dblib=berkeley \
    --with-saslauthd=/var/state/saslauthd \
    --without-pwcheck \
    --with-devrandom=/dev/urandom \
    --enable-cram \
    --enable-digest \
    --enable-plain \
    --enable-login \
    --disable-otp \
    --enable-sql \

    --with-ldap=/usr \
    --with-mysql=/usr \
    --with-pgsql=/usr/lib/pgsql
```

This will configure Cyrus SASL to give you plaintext and shared-secret mechanisms and will build saslauthd and give you the SQL method including support for MySQL and PostgreSQL.

After the configure script has finished, run make, become root, and then run make install. Cyrus SASL will install itself to /usr/local/lib/sasl2, but it will expect to find the libraries in /usr/lib/sasl2. You need to create a symbolic link like this:

```
# ln -s /usr/local/lib/sasl2 /usr/lib/sasl2
```

Finally you need to check if SASL log messages will be caught and written to a log file by syslogd. Cyrus SASL logs to the syslog auth facility. Check your syslogd configuration, usually /etc/syslog.conf, to see if it contains a line that catches auth messages.

If you can't find an entry add the following, save the file and restart syslogd:

```
auth.*                          /var/log/auth
```

Once you've got all this done, you are ready to configure SASL.

Cyrus SASL Configuration

It is absolutely necessary that you always configure and test Cyrus SASL before you turn to Postfix and work on Postfix-specific SMTP AUTH settings.

The reason to follow this procedure is quite simple: An authentication framework that cannot authenticate will be of no assistance to any other application using it. Chances are you will end up debugging Postfix for hours while the problem is Cyrus SASL-related.

To understand how and where you must configure SASL, recall that it's an authentication framework. It was designed to offer its service to many applications. These applications might have totally different requirements regarding the password verification service to be used, the mechanisms to be offered, and finally the method to use to access an authentication back end.

You might ask yourself: How can SASL tell which settings to use for which application? The answer to this is that it uses application-specific configuration files and it's part of each application's job to tell SASL which configuration to use.

The application handling SMTP AUTH concerning Postfix is the `smtpd` daemon. When it contacts SASL it not only sends authentication data, but also its application name, `smtpd`.

> The application name `smtpd` is a default value that is sent to Cyrus SASL from Postfix. You can change it using the `smtpd_sasl_application_name`, but usually this is not required. You need it only if you run different Postfix daemons that need different Cyrus SASL configurations.

When Cyrus SASL receives the application name it will append a `.conf` and start to look for a configuration file containing configuration settings.

By default the location for `smtpd.conf` is `/usr/lib/sasl2/smtpd.conf`, but for various reasons some Linux distributions have started to put it to other locations. On Debian Linux you will have to create the configuration at `/etc/postfix/sasl/smtpd.conf`. Mandrake Linux expects the file to be located at `/var/lib/sasl2/smtpd.conf`. All others are known to expect it at `/usr/lib/sasl2/smtpd.conf`.

Check your system and find out if `smtpd.conf` has already been created. If not a simple touch command will create it:

```
# touch /usr/lib/sasl2/smtpd.conf
```

All of the configuration that follows now will center on `smtpd.conf`. Here's a quick rundown of what we will put in there:

1. The name of the password verification service we want to use
2. The log level at which SASL should send log messages to the auth log
3. A list of mechanisms Postfix should advertise when offering SMTP AUTH to clients
4. Configuration settings specific to the password verification service chosen

Finally we will configure how the password verification service should access the authentication back end. How this needs to be done depends on the password verification service we choose and will be explained when we get there.

Selecting a Password Verification Service

The first configuration step will be to choose the password verification service SASL should use during authentication. The parameter that tells SASL which password verification service should handle authentication is pwcheck_method. The values you may provide are:

- saslauthd
- auxprop
- authdaemond

Depending on the password verification service you've chosen, you will have to add the correct value. The names should speak for themselves and tell you which password verification service will be called. A configuration that would use saslauthd would add the following line to smtpd.conf:

```
pwcheck_method: saslauthd
```

Choosing a Log Level

Cyrus SASL does not handle logging consistently. What Cyrus SASL will log depends on the password verification service and the method that is being used. The parameter to define a log level is log_level. A reasonable setting during setup would be log level 3:

```
log_level: 3
```

Here is a list of all the log levels Cyrus SASL knows:

log_level Value	Description
0	No logging
1	Log unusual errors; this is the default
2	Log all authentication failures
3	Log non-fatal warnings
4	More verbose than 3
5	More verbose than 4
6	Log traces of internal protocols
7	Log traces of internal protocols, including passwords

Choosing Valid Mechanisms

Your next step will be to choose the mechanisms that Postfix may offer when it advertises SMTP authentication to clients. The parameter in Cyrus SASL to configure a list of valid mechanisms is mech_list. The names of the mechanisms are exactly like the ones we used when we introduced them in the *Mechanism* section.

It is important to set the `mech_list` parameter and list only the mechanisms your password verification service can handle. If you don't do it Postfix will offer all mechanisms SASL provides and authentication will fail if your mail client chooses a mechanism that the SASL password verification service cannot handle.

> Recall that the password verification services `saslauthd` and `authdaemond` can only handle the two plaintext mechanisms PLAIN and LOGIN. Consequently a `mech_list` for those password verification services must only hold the values PLAIN and LOGIN. Any mail client capable of stronger mechanisms will always prefer the stronger over the weaker ones. It will do its calculation and send the result to the server. The server will fail to authenticate because neither `saslauthd` nor `authdaemond` is capable of handling non-plaintext mechanisms.

The following example would define valid mechanisms for `saslauthd` in `smtpd.conf`:

```
mech_list: PLAIN LOGIN
```

A list of valid mechanisms for any of the `auxprop` password verification services could go further and list the following mechanisms:

```
mech_list: PLAIN LOGIN CRAM-MD5 DIGEST-MD5
```

> The order of mechanisms in this list has no influence on the mechanism the client will choose. Which mechanism is selected depends on the client; it will usually choose the one that provides the strongest cryptography.

In the sections that follow, we will take a look at how you configure the password verification service to choose an authentication back end and how to provide additional information to pick the relevant data. This is, as mentioned before, handled differently by the three password verification services. We will have a look at each password verification service separately.

saslauthd

Before you can use `saslauthd`, you need to check whether it is able to establish a socket in a directory that `saslauthd` refers to as **state dir**. Check this carefully because there are two common problems related to the socket:

- **The directory does not exist**: In this case `saslauthd` will quit running and you will find a log message indicating the missing directory.

- **The directory is not accessible to applications other than** `saslauthd`: In this case you will find log messages in the mail log indicating that `smtpd` was unable to connect to the socket.

To get around these problems first you need to find out where saslauthd would like to establish the socket. Just fire it up as root as in the example below and look out for the line that has run_path in it:

```
# saslauthd -a shadow -d
saslauthd[32560] :main          : num_procs  : 5
saslauthd[32560] :main          : mech_option: NULL
saslauthd[32560] :main          : run_path   :
/var/state/saslauthd
saslauthd[32560] :main          : auth_mech  : shadow
saslauthd[32560] :main          : could not chdir to:
/var/state/saslauthd
saslauthd[32560] :main          : chdir: No such file or
directory
saslauthd[32560] :main          : Check to make sure the
directory exists and is
saslauthd[32560] :main          : writeable by the user this
process runs as.
```

As you can see in the example above, saslauthd would want to access /var/state/saslauthd as state dir. Since it cannot access the directory it quits immediately. Now there are two ways to deal with this. It depends whether you acquired saslauthd from a package or installed it from the source.

In the first case it is quite likely that the package maintainer built saslauthd with the default settings; choose a different location as state dir and configured the init-script to override the default path by giving the -m /path/to/state_dir option.

On RedHat systems, for example, you would typically find command-line options passed to saslauthd in /etc/sysconfig/saslauthd. The following listing gives you an overview of the settings for Fedora Core 2:

```
# Directory in which to place saslauthd's listening socket, pid file, and so
# on.  This directory must already exist.
SOCKETDIR=/var/run/saslauthd

# Mechanism to use when checking passwords.  Run "saslauthd -v" to get a list
# of which mechanism your installation was compiled to use.
MECH=shadow

# Additional flags to pass to saslauthd on the command line.  See saslauthd(8)
# for the list of accepted flags.
FLAGS=
```

Speaking for most Linux distributions typical locations for the state dir would be either /var/state/saslauthd or /var/run/saslauthd.

In the second case, that is if you built saslauthd manually, you should create a directory that matches the value of the --with-saslauthd parameter you used when you executed the configure script.

In the SASL configuration example above the value for --with-saslauthd was /var/state/saslauthd. Create this directory and make it accessible to user root and group postfix like this:

```
# mkdir /var/state/saslauthd
# chmod 750 /var/state/saslauthd
# chgrp postfix /var/state/saslauthd
```

Once you have verified saslauthd can create a socket and pid file in your state dir, you can start configuring saslauthd to access the authentication back end of your choice.

> The following examples presume that you don't have to provide an extra run path to saslauthd. If you need to do so, just add it to the examples given.

Using an IMAP Server as Authentication Back End

Specify the -a option together with the value rimap to have Cyrus SASL log in to an IMAP server with the credentials given by the mail client. Additionally you must use the -o option to tell saslauthd which IMAP server it should turn to like this:

```
# saslauthd -a rimap -o mail.example.com
```

Upon successful login into an IMAP server, saslauthd will report an authentication success to Postfix and Postfix may permit the mail client to hand over the credentials to the relay.

Using an LDAP Server as Authentication Back End

Verifying credentials with an LDAP server is a little more complex than asking an IMAP server. It requires by far more configuration and that's why you don't give all the options to saslauthd on the command line but put them into a configuration file. By default saslauthd expects the LDAP configuration to be located at /usr/local/etc/saslauthd.conf. If you choose a different location, you need to tell it on the command line:

```
# saslauthd -a ldap -o /etc/cyrussasl/saslauthd.conf
```

In the example above, the value ldap tells saslauthd to turn to an LDAP server and the -o option provides the path to the configuration file. Your configuration file might hold the following parameters:

```
ldap_servers: ldap://127.0.0.1/ ldap://172.16.10.7/
ldap_bind_dn: cn=saslauthd,dc=example,dc=com
ldap_bind_pw: Oy6kOqyR
ldap_timeout: 10
ldap_time_limit: 10
ldap_scope: sub
```

```
ldap_search_base: dc=people,dc=example,dc=com
ldap_auth_method: bind
ldap_filter: (|(&(cn=%u)(&(uid=%u@%r)(smtpAuth=Y)))
ldap_debug: 0
ldap_verbose: off
ldap_ssl: no
ldap_start_tls: no
ldap_referrals: yes
```

As you might have expected, you will have to accommodate the settings to suit your LDAP tree and other settings specific to your LDAP server. For a complete list of all LDAP-related parameters—there are many more than listed here—take a look at the LDAP_SASLAUTHD readme that comes with the Cyrus SASL sources and is located in the saslauthd subdirectory.

Using the Local User Accounts

This is the configuration that most people use saslauthd for. You can either configure saslauthd to read from the local password file or configure it to read the local shadow password file on systems that support shadow passwords.

To have it read from /etc/passwd, use the -a getpwent option like this:

```
# saslauthd -a getpwent
```

If you want saslauthd to read from /etc/shadow instead run it as root like this:

```
# saslauthd -a shadow
```

Using PAM

It is also possible to use **PAM (Pluggable Authentication Modules)** as authentication back end, which in turn has to be configured to access other authentication back ends. Start by running saslauthd like this:

```
# saslauthd -a pam
```

Then create a /etc/pam.d/smtp file or a section in /etc/pam.conf and add PAM-specific settings to it. If you installed Cyrus SASL from a package chances are you already have such a file. For example, it looks like the following lines on RedHat:

```
#%PAM-1.0
auth        required        pam_stack.so service=system-auth
account     required        pam_stack.so service=system-auth
```

> The name of the configuration file must be smtp. This has been defined in RFC 2554, which says that the service name for SASL over SMTP is smtp. Postfix smtpd daemon passes the value smtp as service name to Cyrus SASL. saslauthd in turn passes it to PAM, which then looks in the smtp file for authentication instructions.

auxprop

Auxiliary Property Plug-ins or **auxprop** are configured differently from what you've learned about saslauthd. Instead of passing command-line options, you simply add auxprop-specific settings to your smtpd.conf. Any auxprop configuration that you setup in your smtpd.conf should begin with these three lines:

```
log_level: 3
pwcheck_method: auxprop
mech_list: PLAIN LOGIN CRAM-MD5 DIGEST-MD5
```

To tell Cyrus SASL which plug-in you want to use, you need to add an additional parameter to the configuration. The parameter is called auxprop_plugin and we will examine its use in the following sections.

Configuring the sasldb Plug-In

The auxprop plug-in sasldb is the default plug-in that Cyrus SASL will use even if you don't set the auxprop_plugin parameter.

> This tends to irritate people, who try to set up a different plug-in and have something wrong in their configuration. Cyrus SASL will fail with the wrong configuration and will fall back to the default sasldb plug-in. When you get an error message that says Cyrus SASL can't locate sasldb you know you probably have a typo in your configuration if you didn't go for sasldb in the first place.

To use sasldb, first of all you need to create a sasldb database. Use the following command as root to create a sasldb2 file and add a user.

sasldbpasswd2 -c -u example.com username

This command will create a sasldb2 file and will add a user username with the realm of example.com. It is important that you pay special attention to the realm you add, because it will be part of the username the mail client will have to send later.

> The realm is part of the concept of a **KERBEROS** infrastructure. By adding a realm you can define a context—for example, a domain or host—in which the user may do something. If you don't add a realm, sasldbpasswd2 will add the hostname of your server by default.

Now that you have created the database and added a user you need to change access permissions on sasldb to have Postfix access the database as well. Simply give access to the group postfix to sasldb2 like this:

chgrp postfix /etc/sasldb2

> Don't get irritated because the sasldb is called sasldb2. The format of sasldb changed when Cyrus SASL major version 2.x came out. For reasons of compatibility the new sasldb file is called sasldb2.

Once you've created the database you need to tell Cyrus SASL to use it. Add the auxprop_plugin parameter to smtpd.conf like this:

```
auxprop_plugin: sasldb
```

That's all you need to do and you should be ready to start testing (see the *Testing Cyrus SASL Authentication* section). If for any reason you need to put sasldb in a location that differs from the default you can use the following, additional parameter:

```
sasldb_path: /path/to/sasldb2
```

Configuring the sql Plug-In

The **sql auxprop plug-in** is a generic plug-in that gives you access to MySQL, PostGreSQL, and SQLite. As an example we will show you how to configure the sql plug-in to access a MySQL database. Configuring access to the other two databases is pretty much the same with one exception that we will note.

First of all you need to create a database. This, of course, is specific to the database you use. Connect to MySQL and create a database if you don't have one already:

```
mysql> CREATE DATABASE `mail`;
```

Then add a table that holds everything you need to SASL-authenticate users. It will look similar to this:

```
CREATE TABLE `users` (
  `id` int(11) unsigned NOT NULL auto_increment,
  `username` varchar(255) NOT NULL default '0',
  `userrealm` varchar(255) NOT NULL default 'example.com',
  `userpassword` varchar(255) NOT NULL default 'GjpCok82',
  `auth` tinyint(1) default '1',
  PRIMARY KEY (`id`),
  UNIQUE KEY `id` (`id`)
) TYPE=MyISAM COMMENT='Users';
```

The table has fields for a username, the userrealm, the userpassword, and an additional field, auth, which we will use later to determine if a user may relay or not. This way we can use the table for other authentication purposes as well—for example, for granting access to specific folders over httpd in conjunction with the mysql module for Apache.

> Don't forget to set a default value for the userpassword, like GjpCok82 in the example above, or all that would be required to get relay permissions would be sending a username.

Once you've created the table, add a user like this for testing purposes:

```
INSERT INTO `users` VALUES (1,'test','example.com','testpass',0);
```

Then add a user for postfix to access the database to MySQLs user database like this:

```
mysql> CONNECT mysql;
mysql> INSERT INTO user VALUES
('localhost','postfix','','Y','Y','Y','Y','Y','Y','Y','Y','Y','Y','Y','Y
','Y','Y');
mysql> UPDATE mysql.user SET password=PASSWORD("Pgdk1Cf4") WHERE
user='postfix' AND host='localhost';
mysql> GRANT SELECT, UPDATE ON mail.users TO 'postfix'@'localhost';
mysql> FLUSH PRIVILEGES;
```

Once you're done setting up MySQL you need to add sql auxprop-specific parameters to your smtpd.conf. These are the parameters available:

- sql_engine: Specifies the database type. You can pick mysql, pgsql, or sqlite. We will use mysql in our example. If you go for a different database you will need to change this is value.

- sql_hostnames: Specifies the database server name. You can specify one or more FQDNs or IP addresses separated by commas. If you pick localhost, the SQL engine tries to communicate over a socket.

- sql_database: Tells Cyrus SASL the name of the database to connect to.

- sql_user: The value you set here must match the name of the user that connects to the database.

- sql_passwd: The value you set here must match the password of the user that connects to the database. It must be a plaintext password.

- sql_select: The sql_select parameter defines the SELECT statement to authenticate a user.

- sql_insert: The sql_insert parameter defines an INSERT statement that would allow Cyrus SASL to create users in the SQL database. You would use the saslpasswd2 program to do so.

- sql_update: The sql_update parameter defines the UPDATE statement that would allow Cyrus SASL to modify existing entries in your database. If you choose to configure this you will have to use it in combination with the sql_insert parameter.

- sql_usessl: You can set either yes, 1, on, or true to enable SSL to access the MySQL over an encrypted connection. By default this option is off.

A straightforward configuration bringing all parameters together would look like this:

```
# Global parameters
log_level: 3
pwcheck_method: auxprop
mech_list: PLAIN LOGIN CRAM-MD5 DIGEST-MD5
# auxiliary Plugin parameters
auxprop_plugin: sql
sql_engine: mysql
sql_hostnames: localhost
sql_database: mail
sql_user: postfix
sql_passwd: Pgdk1Cf4
```

```
sql_select: SELECT %p FROM users WHERE username = '%u' AND userrealm
= '%r' AND auth = '1'
sql_usessl: no
```

As you can see, macros have been used in the `sql_select` statement. Their meaning is:

- **%u:** This macro is a placeholder for the username that is to be queried for during authentication.

- **%p:** This macro is a placeholder for the password.

- **%r:** The r stands for realm and whatever was given as realm by the client will be inserted at `%r`.

- **%v:** This macro is only used in combination with the `sql_update` or `sql_insert` statement. It represents the submitted value that should replace an existing value.

> Take special notice of the notations. Macros must be quoted using single quotation marks (`'`).

That's it. If you followed the instructions up to here you are ready to start testing.

authdaemond

authdaemond was created especially to work together with Courier IMAP. If you configure Cyrus SASL to use `authdaemond`, it will connect to Courier authlib's authdaemond socket asking Courier authlib to verify the credentials of the mail client sent in. On the one hand Cyrus SASL benefits from the various back ends Courier authlib can turn to for user verification, but on the other hand Cyrus SASL's `authdaemond` password verification service is limited to plaintext mechanisms, which doesn't give you the mileage you get when you use auxprop plug-ins.

Setting up the **Authdaemond Password Verification Service** is pretty straightforward. We will take a look at it in the following sections.

Setting the authdaemond Password Verification Service

Your first step is to configure Postfix to use the `authdaemond` password verification service. Just as with `saslauthd` or auxprop, you add the `pwcheck_method` parameter to your `smtpd.conf` and choose it to be `authdaemond`:

```
log_level: 3
pwcheck_method: authdaemond
mech_list: PLAIN LOGIN
```

Due to the limitations of `authdaemond` you must also limit the list of mechanisms to PLAIN and LOGIN—the only plaintext mechanisms available.

Configuring the authdaemond Socket Path

Then you need to tell Cyrus SASL where it can find the socket that has been created by Courier authlib's `authdaemond`.

Use the `authdaemond_path` parameter to provide the full path including the socket name:

```
authdaemond-path:     /var/spool/authdaemon/socket
```

Finally check the permissions of the `authdaemond` directory and verify that at least the user `postfix` may access the directory. All this done you are ready to start testing.

Testing Cyrus SASL Authentication

There are no testing utilities, but you can use the sample applications `sample-server` and `sample-client` to test authentication without any other application (e.g. Postfix) interfering with the test. You can find them either in the `sample` subdirectory of the Cyrus SASL sources or in the `devel-packages` of your distribution. We will use them to test the Cyrus SASL configuration we've created in `smtpd.conf`. However, the programs don't expect to find their configuration in `smtpd.conf`, but in `sample.conf`. We will simply create a symbolic link from sample.conf to smtpd.conf to meet the requirements:

```
# ln -s /usr/lib/sasl2/smtpd.conf /usr/lib/sasl2/sample.conf
```

Next we need to start the server application to have it listen for incoming connections. If you can't find it on your computer, check if you have installed the cyrus-sasl-devel package from your distribution as the two utilities are usually bundled with the development libraries. If you installed Cyrus SASL from source, take a look at the sample subdirectory—you should find them there. Start the server like this:

```
# server -s rcmd -p 8000
trying 10, 1, 6
socket: Address family not supported by protocol
trying 2, 1, 6
```

The server will listen on port 8000 for incoming connections. Next open a new terminal and start the client using the same port and the mechanism PLAIN and point to `localhost` where your server utility should be listening. A successful authentication looks like this:

```
# client -s rcmd -p 8000 -m PLAIN 127.0.0.1
receiving capability list... recv: {11}
PLAIN LOGIN
PLAIN LOGIN
please enter an authentication id: test
please enter an authorization id: test
Password:
send: {5}
PLAIN
send: {1}
Y
send: {18}
test[0]test[0]testpass
successful authentication
closing connection
```

You should be able to see some logging in the auth log. If you are going to use saslauthd, start it on a separate terminal in debug mode and you will be able to follow the authentication like this:

```
# saslauthd -m /var/run/saslauthd -a shadow -d
saslauthd[4547] :main : num_procs : 5
saslauthd[4547] :main : mech_option: NULL
saslauthd[4547] :main : run_path : /var/run/saslauthd
saslauthd[4547] :main : auth_mech : shadow
saslauthd[4547] :ipc_init : using accept lock file:
/var/run/saslauthd/mux.accept
saslauthd[4547] :detach_tty : master pid is: 0
saslauthd[4547] :ipc_init : listening on socket:
/var/run/saslauthd/mux
saslauthd[4547] :main : using process model
saslauthd[4548] :get_accept_lock : acquired accept lock
saslauthd[4547] :have_baby : forked child: 4548
saslauthd[4547] :have_baby : forked child: 4549
saslauthd[4547] :have_baby : forked child: 4550
saslauthd[4547] :have_baby : forked child: 4551
saslauthd[4548] :rel_accept_lock : released accept lock
saslauthd[4548] :do_auth : auth success: [user=test]
[service=rcmd] [realm=] [mech=shadow]
saslauthd[4548] :do_request : response: OK
saslauthd[4548] :get_accept_lock : acquired accept lock
```

Only if you were able to authenticate successfully, proceed to configure SMTP AUTH in Postfix. If your authentication fails, follow the log and iterate through the instructions on how to set up and configure SASL from above.

Postfix SMTP AUTH Configuration

Configuring SMTP AUTH in Postfix is pretty straightforward now that you have managed to set up and configure Cyrus SASL. The first thing you need to do is to check if Postfix was built to support SMTP authentication. Point the ldd utility to the Postfix smtpd daemon and check if it has been linked to libsasl:

```
# ldd /usr/libexec/postfix/smtpd | grep libsasl
        libsasl2.so.2 => /usr/lib/libsasl2.so.2 (0x00d7f000)
```

If you don't get any output you will probably have to rebuild Postfix. Read the SASL_README from the Postfix README_FILES directory to get detailed information on what you must include in the CCARGS and AUXLIBS statements.

Preparing the Configuration

Once you've verified that Postfix supports SMTP AUTH you need to verify that the smtpd daemon does not run chrooted while you configure SMTP AUTH. Many people spend hours with a chrooted Postfix that cannot access the saslauthd socket before they realize that the reason is the chroot jail. A Postfix smtpd daemon that does not run chrooted has an n in the chroot column in /etc/postfix/master.cf:

```
# ================================================================
# service type  private unpriv  chroot  wakeup  maxproc command +
args
#                (yes)   (yes)   (yes)   (never) (100)
# ================================================================
smtp        inet n       -       n       -       -        smtpd
```

Reload Postfix if it was running chrooted after you changed the chroot settings for smtpd and turn to main.cf.

Enabling SMTP AUTH

The first thing you will do is enable SMTP AUTH by adding the smtpd_sasl_auth_enable parameter and setting it to yes:

```
smtpd_sasl_auth_enable = yes
```

This will make Postfix offer SMTP AUTH to clients that use ESMTP, but you still need to configure a few settings before you can start testing.

Setting the Security Policy

Next you will have to decide which mechanisms Postfix should offer using the smtpd_sasl_security_options parameter. This parameter takes a list of one or more of the following values:

- noanonymous: You should always set this value or Postfix will offer anonymous authentication to mail clients. This almost makes you an open relay and should not be used for SMTP servers.

- noplaintext: The noplaintext value will prevent Postfix from offering the plaintext mechanisms PLAIN and LOGIN. Usually you don't want that because the most widespread clients support only LOGIN. If you set this option, the clients will not be able to authenticate.

- noactive: This setting excludes SASL mechanisms that are susceptible to active (non-dictionary) attacks.

- nodictionary: This keyword excludes all mechanisms that can be broken by means of a dictionary attack.

- mutual_auth: This form of authentication requires the server to authenticate itself to the client as well as the other way around. If you set it only servers and clients capable of doing this form or authentication will be able to authenticate. This option is hardly ever used.

A common setting for the smtpd_sasl_security_options parameter adds the following line to main.cf:

```
smtpd_sasl_security_options = noanonymous
```

This prevents anonymous authentication and permits all others.

Including Broken Clients

Next you have to decide if Postfix should offer SMTP AUTH to broken clients. Broken clients, in the context of SMTP AUTH, are clients that will not recognize a server's SMTP AUTH capability if authentication has been offered the way RFC 2222 requires. Instead they adhere to a draft of the RFC that had an additional = in the line that shows SMTP AUTH capability during SMTP communication. Among the clients that are broken are Microsoft Outlook Express and Microsoft Outlook. To get around this problem just add the broken_sasl_auth_clients parameter to main.cf like this:

```
broken_sasl_auth_clients = yes
```

Postfix will print out an additional AUTH line when it lists its capabilities to the mail client. This line will have the extra = in it and the broken clients will take notice of the SMTP AUTH capability.

Finally, if you want to limit the users that may relay to a group with the same realm, add the smtpd_sasl_local_domain parameter and provide the realm as value like this:

```
smtpd_sasl_local_domain = example.com
```

Postfix will append the value to all usernames that get sent by mail clients successfully limiting relaying to those users whose username contains the smtpd_sasl_local_domain value in their username.

Once you're done with all the configuration steps from above reload Postfix to let the settings become active and start testing.

Testing SMTP AUTH

When you test SMTP authentication, don't use a regular mail client as the mail client may introduce some problems itself. Instead use the Telnet client program and connect to Postfix in an SMTP communication. You will need to send the username and password of your test user in a base64-encoded form so the first step will be to create such a string. Use the following command to create a base64-encoded string for the user test using the password testpass:

```
$ perl -MMIME::Base64 -e 'print encode_base64("test\0test\0testpass");'
dGVzdAB0ZXN0AHRlc3RwYXNz
```

> Note the \0 that separates the username from the password as well as that the username will have to be repeated twice. This is because SASL expects two, possibly different usernames (userid, authid) to support additional functionality that isn't used for SMTP authentication.

> Also keep in mind that if your username contains the @ character you will need to escape it with a prepended \ or Perl will interpret the @ and will come up with a non-functional base64-encoded string.

Once you have the base64-encoded string at hand, use the Telnet program to connect to port 25 on your server like this:

```
$ telnet mail.example.com 25
220 mail.example.com ESMTP Postfix
EHLO client.example.com
250-mail.example.com
250-PIPELINING
250-SIZE 10240000
250-VRFY
250-ETRN
250-STARTTLS
250-AUTH LOGIN PLAIN DIGEST-MD5 CRAM-MD5
250-AUTH=LOGIN PLAIN DIGEST-MD5 CRAM-MD5
250-XVERP
250 8BITMIME
AUTH PLAIN dGVzdAB0ZXN0AHR1c3RwYXNz
235 Authentication successful
QUIT
221 Bye
```

You can see that in the above example the authentication was successful. First the mail client sent an EHLO during the introduction and Postfix responded with a list of capabilities. If you set the broken_sasl_auth_clients parameter to yes as we did in our example, you will also have noted the additional AUTH line containing the =.

Authentication took place when the client sent the AUTH string along with the mechanism it wanted to use and, in the case of the plain mechanism, appended the base64-encoded string. If your authentication did not succeed, but you were able to authenticate during the SASL testing, take a look at the parameters in main.cf and double-check the chroot status of smtpd in master.cf.

Enabling Relaying for Authenticated Clients

If authentication has been successful then all that is left to be done is tell Postfix to let those who have authenticated relay messages. This is done by adding the permit_sasl_authenticated option to your list of restrictions in smtpd_recipient_restrictions like this:

```
smtpd_recipient_restrictions =
    ...
    permit_sasl_authenticated
```

```
permit_mynetworks
reject_unauth_destination
...
```

Reload Postfix and start testing with a real mail client. Make sure its IP address is not part of mynetworks as Postfix might be allowed to relay for that reason and not because SMTP AUTH worked out. You might want to limit relaying to the server only during the test. Change the mynetwork_classes = host setting so that clients from other machines automatically will not be part of the Postfix network.

If you still experience problems with SMTP AUTH take a look at saslfinger (http://postfix.state-of-mind.de/patrick.koetter/saslfinger/). It's a script that gathers all kinds of useful information about SMTP AUTH configuration and gives you output that you can append to your mail when you ask on the Postfix mailing list.

Securing Plaintext Mechanisms

We already noted that SMTP AUTH using plaintext mechanisms isn't really safe because the string that is sent during authentication is merely encoded and not encrypted. This is where **Transport Layer Security (TLS)** comes in handy because it can shield the transmission of the encoded string from curious eyes.

In the following example it is presumed that you already have a private key and a valid certificate that was signed by a certification authority. If you don't have one take a look at cacert.org, where you can get your certificate request signed for free.

Enabling Transport Layer Security

To enable TLS you must add the smtpd_use_tls parameter to main.cf and set it to yes:

```
smtpd_use_tls = yes
```

Then you will need to tell smtpd where it can find the key and the certificate by adding the smtpd_tls_key_file and smtpd_tls_cert_file parameters:

```
smtpd_tls_key_file = /etc/postfix/certs/mail.example.com.key
smtpd_tls_cert_file = /etc/postfix/certs/mail.example.com.crt
```

A mail server that sends a certificate to prove its identity must also keep a copy of the certification authority's public certificate on hand. Presuming that you've already added it to your server's local CA root store, you use the following parameter:

```
smtpd_tls_CAfile = /usr/share/ssl/certs/ca-bundle.crt
```

If the CA certificates aren't all in one file, but in separate files in the same directory, use the following parameter instead:

```
smtpd_tls_CApath = /usr/share/ssl/certs/
```

Once you have all this configured, you're done with the basic TLS configuration and you can take care of securing plaintext authentication.

Configuring Security Policy

There are several ways you can secure plaintext authentication using TLS. The most radical approach is to use `smtpd_tls_auth_only` parameter and set it to yes. If you use it, SMTP AUTH will be announced only once the mail client and mail server have established an encrypted communication layer.

However, this punishes all the other mail clients that are capable of using other safer mechanisms such as shared-secret mechanisms. If you want to handle this a little more selectively you should go for the following approach that disables plaintext authentication over an unencrypted wire, but permits it as soon as an encrypted communication has been established.

First of all you need to reconfigure your `smtpd_sasl_security_options` parameter to exclude plaintext mechanisms from being offered to mail clients:

```
smtpd_sasl_security_options = noanonymous, noplaintext
```

Then you set the additional `smtpd_sasl_tls_security_options` parameter that controls the same settings, but applies to TLS sessions only:

```
smtpd_sasl_tls_security_options = noanonymous
```

As you can see the `smtpd_sasl_tls_security_options` parameter will not exclude plaintext mechanisms. This way clients that can use other non-plaintext mechanisms don't have to go for TLS and those that can only do plaintext mechanisms can do it safely once they have established an encrypted session.

Once you've reloaded Postfix you are ready to test.

> Don't forget to add the certificate of the certification authority that signed your server's certificate request to your mail client's CA root store or it will at the very minimum complain that it cannot verify the server's identity when it presents its server certificate.

Dictionary Attacks

Dictionary attacks are attacks where clients try to send mail to countless potential recipients, whose e-mail addresses are derived from words or names in a dictionary:

```
anton@example.com
bertha@example.com
...
zebediah@example.com
```

If your server doesn't have a list of valid recipient addresses, then it must accept these mails regardless whether the recipient actually exists. Then, this onslaught of e-mails needs to be processed as usual (virus check, spam check, local delivery) until, at some stage, the system realizes that the recipient does not even exist!

Then a non-delivery report will be generated and sent back to the sender.

So, for every non-existing recipient, one mail is being accepted and processed and additionally another e-mail (the bounce) is generated, and is subject to delivery attempts.

As you can see this course of action wastes precious resources on your servers. Because the server is busy trying to deliver mail it should never have accepted in the first place, legitimate mail is falling behind in the flood of spam.

Recipient Maps

Postfix is able to verify recipient addresses before it accepts a message. It can run checks

- For local domains (listed in `mydestination`)
- For relay domains (listed in `relay_domains`)

Checking Local Domain Recipients

The `local_recipient_maps` parameter controls which recipients Postfix will hold to be valid local recipients. It defaults to the following:

```
local_recipient_maps = proxy:unix:passwd.byname $alias_maps
```

With this setting Postfix will check the local `/etc/passwd` file for recipient names as well as any map that has been assigned to the `alias_maps` parameter in `main.cf`. To expand this list, simply add the path to the map that holds additional local recipients.

Checking Relay Domain Recipients

The `relay_recipient_maps` parameter controls which recipients are valid for relay domains. It is empty by default, and in order to have Postfix get more control, you need to build a map where Postfix can look up valid recipients.

Let's say your server relays mail to and from `example.com` then you would create the following configuration:

```
relay_domains = example.com
relay_recipient_maps = hash:/etc/postfix/relay_recipients
```

The `relay_domain` parameter would tell Postfix to relay mail for recipients in the `example.com` domain and the `relay_recipient_maps` parameter would point to a map that holds valid recipients. In the map you would create a list like this:

```
adam@example.com     OK
eve@example.com      OK
```

Then run the `postmap` command to create an indexed map like this:

```
# postmap /etc/postfix/relay_recipients
# postfix reload
postfix/postfix-script: refreshing the Postfix mail system
```

This will allow only adam@example.com and eve@example.com as recipients for the domain example.com. Mail to snake@example.com would be rejected with a User unknown in relay recipient table error message.

Rate-Limiting Connections

Rejecting mail for non-existing recipients helps a lot, but when your server is subject to a dictionary attack, then it will still accept all the client's connections and produce an appropriate error message (or accept the mail, should a valid recipient address have been hit by chance).

Postfix's anvil server maintains short-term statistics to defend your system against clients that hammer your server with either of the following cases within a configurable period of time:

- Too many simultaneous sessions
- Too many successive requests

Since the hardware and the software you use limit the number of mails your server is able to process per given time unit, it makes sense not to accept (much) more mail than your server can handle.

```
anvil_rate_time_unit = 60s
```

The above line specifies the time interval used for all the following limits:

- smtpd_client_connection_rate_limit = 40: This specifies the number of connections a client can make during the period specified by anvil_rate_time_unit. In this case, it's 40 connections per 60s

- smtpd_client_connection_count_limit = 16: This gives the maximum number of simultaneous connections any client is allowed to make to this service per anvil_rate_time_unit.

- smtpd_client_message_rate_limit = 100: This is an important limit, since a client could reuse an established connection and send many mails using just this single connection.

- smtpd_client_recipient_rate_limit = 32: This gives the maximum number of recipient addresses that any client is allowed to send to this service per anvil_rate_time_unit regardless of whether or not Postfix actually accepts those recipients.

- smtpd_client_event_limit_exceptions = $mynetworks: This can be used to exempt certain networks or machines from the rate limiting. You may want to exempt your mailing list server from the rate limiting, since it will undoubtedly send lots of mails to many recipients during a short period.

anvil will emit detailed logging about the maximum connection rate (here: 5/60s) and which client reached that maximum (212.227.51.110) and when (Dec 28 13:19:23)

```
Dec 28 13:25:03 mail postfix/anvil[4176]: statistics: max connection
rate 5/60s for (smtp:212.227.51.110) at Dec 28 13:19:23
```

This second log entry shows which client established the most concurrent connections and when:

```
Dec 28 13:25:03 mail postfix/anvil[4176]: statistics: max connection
count 5 for (smtp:62.219.130.25) at Dec 28 13:20:19
```

If any limit is being exceeded, anvil will log this as well:

```
Dec 28 11:33:24 mail postfix/smtpd[19507]: warning: Connection rate
limit exceeded: 54 from pD9E83AD0.dip.t-dialin.net[217.232.58.208]
for service smtp

Dec 28 12:14:17 mail postfix/smtpd[24642]: warning: Connection
concurrency limit exceeded: 17 from hqm-
smrly01.meti.go.jp[219.101.211.110] for service smtp
```

Any client that exceeds these limits will be given a temporary error code, thus signaling it to retry at a later time. Legitimate clients will honor that and retry. Open proxies and trojaned machines will most likely not retry.

Summary

The topic of Chapter 5 was how you could secure your installation and we went straight into business with Cyrus SASL. As you've seen throughout the chapter SASL is quite a complex piece of software, but the benefit you gain—once you've got it up and running— pays off. Once you have it up and running you can:

- Permit relaying based upon successfully authenticated clients
- Prevent abuse of envelope sender addresses by matching them with SASL login names

Then, at the end of the chapter we went for another protection method and had a look at the anvil daemon, and you learned to:

- Limit clients that connect to often within a given timeframe
- Limit clients that open too many connections at the same time

The measures shown in this chapter will make your life as a postmaster a lot easier.

6

Getting Started with Procmail

In this section we will see how a mail filtering system can be set up on the server to handle the repetitive sorting and storing tasks that you would rather not spend your time on every day. Procmail is designed to handle a wide variety of processing and filtering tasks on mail being received by users within the system. Filtering only applies to users who have an account on the system—not to virtual users—and may be applied system wide to all users or individual users may add their own filters. By the end of the chapter you will understand the basics of the filtering process—how to set up the system to perform filtering, and how to perform a number of very simple but extremely useful filtering operations on your own mail. All of which will help you keep on top of all the mail you are already or will soon be receiving.

How can a Filtering System Help Me?

By now you should have an e-mail system up and running, and sending and receiving e-mails. You have probably registered with a number of useful mail groups with messages arriving at varying intervals. You should also be receiving messages informing you of the status of the system. All this extra low priority information can easily distract and get in the way of the important e-mails that you need to read ahead of others.

How you organize your mail is up to your own personal taste; if you are very organized you may have already set up some folders in your e-mail client and move messages into appropriate locations when you have read them. Nevertheless, one thing you have probably realized is that it would be very useful to be able to have some messages stored automatically by the system in a different location than your important e-mail.

What you will need to think about while setting up an automatic process is how you identify what the mail item is about. The most important indicators are to whom it was sent, the title or subject line, and also the sender details. If you take a few minutes now to make a few notes on how you already handle your mail, the types of messages that arrive—for instance, mails from mail groups and messages generated by the system, discussed overleaf—and what you do with them, you will have a clearer idea of what automatic processes you may want to set up.

- **Membership of mail groups**: Mail arriving from a mail group is normally easy to identify from the sender information or possibly, from the subject line. A number of groups send messages every few minutes while others may only send a couple of messages a month. Typically different mail group items are identified by different pieces of information. For example, some groups send messages with the From address being that of the real sender while others add a fake or system-generated From address. Some groups may, say, automatically add a prefix to the Subject field.

- **Automated system messages**: Your server generates a number of messages each day. Although normally they are sent only to the system administrator or root user, one of the first things to do is to make sure that you receive a copy of the mail so that you are kept informed of the system status and events. This you would do by editing the default destinations in the /etc/mail/aliases or /etc/aliases file depending on how your system is set up. These system-generated messages are nearly always identifiable as originating from a small number of specific system user IDs. These are typically root and cron.

After completing the work in this chapter you should have the tools and knowledge to start to examining mail in more detail and set up some basic filtering operations.

Potential Uses for Mail Filtering

E-mail was one of the first communication services to be implemented when computers were first starting to be connected together. It predates the Internet as we see it today. In its earliest implementations it utilized a set of computer-to-computer dial up connections and a simple map of the network to route items to be between computers and users. This very simple but powerful ability to send messages between computers was very quickly utilized for more than sending simple text messages between people or for system applications to send messages to human operators. It very quickly became possible to create applications that could read an e-mail and perform actions on the message contents or the subject line.

The basic mail system you have already set up has some inbuilt abilities of its own to process incoming mail according to a user setup. The default operation would be for messages to go to your Inbox; other options are to automatically forward all your mail to another user if, for example, you had multiple mail accounts on different systems and wanted all your mail to end up in one particular mail account. You could have mail sent to a particular file, or have mail passed to a program or application to allow it to do its own work.

The downside of this setup is that all your mail has to follow one particular route, so over time a number of options have been created to intelligently filter mail. One of the most powerful and popular of these is Procmail.

Filtering and Sorting Mail

This may be viewed from the perspectives of two differing groups—**System Users** and **System Administrators**. Procmail provides powerful capabilities to both of these roles.

For system administrators, Procmail offers a range of facilities for applying rules and operations to all the mail being received by users of the system. Such actions may include making a copy of all mail for historical purposes or in businesses where the content of e-mail messages may be used in some form of legal or business situation.

Elsewhere in this book we will be discussing ways of identifying e-mail-borne viruses or something that is becoming the bane of all businesses these days, **spam**; Procmail can take the information provided by these processes and perform actions based upon the information added by these processes such as storing all mail items containing a virus in a secure mail folder that is checked by system administrators.

For a system user the most common operation to perform on incoming mail is to sort it into some organized layout so that you can easily find the items you are looking for, based on the topic area that you are interested in. A typical organizational layout could be a hierarchical one similar to the following.

```
/mailgroups/Procmail
/mailgroups/postfix
/mailgroups/linux
/system/cron
/system/warnings
/system/status
/inbox
```

If you plan on keeping mail in store for long periods of time for historical reference, it may be worth adding an extra layer or two to separate the mail into years and months. This makes it easier in the future to archive or purge older e-mail and it also means that searching and sorting can be quicker.

Forwarding Mail

Sometimes you may get lots of e-mail that is easily identified as needing to be sent to another user at another e-mail address. In this case rather than storing the file on the system, you may set up a rule that will forward the e-mail to one or more other e-mail addresses. Of course you need to be careful to make sure that the forwarding does not end up coming back to you and creating a never-ending loop.

Forwarding of mail in this way has a big advantage over the manual forwarding of mail from within your mail client software, quite apart from not needing any manual intervention. Mail forwarded by Procmail is transparent, in that to the recipient it appears as if the mail has arrived directly from the original sender, whereas if it was forwarded using a mail client it would appear as though it had been sent by the person or account doing the forwarding.

Where all mail items for a single address need forwarding to a single other address a more efficient way to achieve this is using the aliasing mechanism of the Postfix mailing system. Procmail should only be used where an intelligent filtering of the mail is required dependant upon factors that can only be determined at the time of receipt of the message.

Processing the Mail in an Application

Some mail items could be suitable for passing through to an application where the application program does some work on the e-mail. Perhaps it could read the contents and then store the information in a bug-tracking database or update the company history log for a client activity. These are more advanced topics that are briefly covered in the following chapter.

Acknowledgements and Out of Office/Vacation Replies

If you wanted to send an automatic reply to certain messages, a filter or rule could be set up to send such a message. When you are away from the office for a prolonged period of time on holiday, vacation, or perhaps illness it is possible to set up a reply service to inform the sender that it will be some time before you are able to respond to their mail and perhaps give them alternative contact details or ask them to contact another person.

It is important that you organize such a feature carefully. You shouldn't send such a reply to a mailing group or keep sending repeated replies to people who already know that you are away but need to send you information for your return. This requires that a log of the addresses that the message is sent to is kept to avoid repeat messages being sent. We will investigate the setting up of such a service in the next chapter.

File Locking and Integrity

An important concept to keep in mind during all your work with Procmail is that it is always possible for multiple mail messages to be arriving at the same time, all vying to be processed. It is quite possible therefore that two or more messages are going to be stored in the same location at the same time—a recipe for disaster exists. Assume the simple example of two items arriving at the same time. The first mail opens the storage location and starts to write the contents of the message, and then the second process does the same. A variety of possible results could occur from this ranging from one message being lost totally through to both messages being stored intertwined and totally illegible.

To make sure that this doesn't happen, a strict locking protocol needs to be observed to ensure that only one process can write at a time and all other applications need to wait their turn patiently. Procmail itself has the ability to enforce a locking protocol appropriate to the type of process being applied and will, by default, lock the physical file in which a mail is being stored in.

In some cases the mail is being processed by an application and Procmail can be instructed by the use of flags within the rule to use an appropriate locking mechanism. This is covered more completely in Chapter 7.

Introduction to Procmail

The following introduction from the Procmail Source Distribution http://www. procmail.org/ describes the intended uses for Procmail:

> "… can be used to create mail-servers, mailing lists, sort your incoming mail into separate folders/files (real convenient when subscribing to one or more mailing lists or for prioritising your mail), preprocess your mail, start any programs upon mail arrival (e.g. to generate different chimes on your workstation for different types of mail) or selectively forward certain incoming mail automatically to someone."

Who Wrote It and When

Version 1.0 was released in late 1990's and has evolved to represent one of the best and most common mail filtering solutions for UNIX-based mail systems. Procmail was originally designed and developed by Stephen R. van den Berg (srb@cuci.nl). In the fall of 1998, recognizing that he didn't have the time to maintain Procmail on his own, Stephen created a mailing list for discussion of future development and deputized Philip Guenther (guenther@sendmail.com) as a maintainer.

What Procmail Is Not Suitable For

There are some very specific mail filtering and processing requirements for which Procmail may be considered to be suitable and in most cases, it is flexible and capable enough to perform the task at least at a rudimentary level. Such tasks could be filtering of spam-related e-mails or filtering out viruses or running a mailing list operation. For each of these there are a number of solutions available that go beyond the capabilities of using just Procmail filters. We will be looking at SpamAssassin for performing spam filtering and a virus filtering solution later in Chapter 8.

We have already mentioned that Procmail is suitable only for users having accounts on the system that Procmail runs on. Nevertheless, it is worth reinforcing that Procmail is unable to process mail that is being delivered to a virtual user and such mails will end up on another system. If it is necessary to process mail for such a user it is possible to create a 'real' user account on the system and then use Procmail to perform the final forwarding as part of its filtering processes. This is not an ideal use as the Postfix system is much more efficient if it is allowed to do this work rather than using Procmail.

Versions Used

Procmail has been stable since Version 3.22 was released in September 2001 so most recent installations will have this latest version installed.

Downloading and Installation

As the software is now reasonably mature, there are very few binary downloads available on the Internet other than the specific solutions for your own server version. Indeed the Procmail software may already be installed on your system, or may be available for installation on the disks supplied with the system. To check if the software is already installed on your system you could try using the following commands:

```
which procmail
```
or
```
find / -name procmail -print
```

For completeness, we will go through the basic steps of a simple installation procedure for the latest version of the software available.

Web Site Location

Procmail may be obtained from a number of sources but the official distribution is maintained and available from www.procmail.org. There you will find links to a number of mirror services from which you can download the source files. The version used in this book can be downloaded from http://www.procmail.org/procmail-3.22.tar.gz.

It can be downloaded by use of the wget command as follows:

```
wget http://www.procmail.org/procmail-3.22.tar.gz
```

Installing and Configuring Procmail

For Fedora users the simple way to install Procmail if it isn't already installed is to use the yum command as follows:

```
yum install procmail
```

This will ensure that the binary of Procmail is correctly installed on your system and you can then decide how you want it to integrate into your Postfix system.

Installation Options/Considerations

For most people following the implementation, throughout this book you will be the system administrator of the machine or machines you are managing and will probably be applying the installation to process all mail for all users on the system. If you are not an administrator, or you wish only a limited number of people on the system to take advantage of the features of Procmail then you can install Procmail for individual users.

Individual Installation

If you are installing Procmail for your own use or for only a few people on your server, the most common method is to call the Procmail program directly from the .forward file in your home directory on the server (this file needs to be world-readable). You will also need to install a .procmailrc file in the home directory—this is the file that holds the rules that Procmail will use to filter your e-mail.

System-Wide Installation

If you are a system administrator, you can decide to install Procmail globally. This has the advantage that users do not need to have a .forward file anymore. Simply having a .procmailrc file in each user's HOME directory will suffice. The operation is transparent in this case—if no .procmailrc file is present in the HOME directory, the mail will be delivered as usual.

A global .procmailrc file can be created that takes effect before the user's own file. In this case you need to be careful to ensure that the configuration has the following instruction included so that messages are stored with the end user's privileges rather than the root user's privileges.

```
DROPPRIVS=yes
```

This also helps protect against weaknesses in your system security. This file is normally stored in the /etc directory as /etc/procmail where it is intended to provide a default set of personal rules for all users as they are added to the system. It will be worth configuring a .procmail file in the skeleton account that is used by the add user capabilities of your system. Consult your Linux documentation for information on how this can be set up.

Integration with Postfix Mail Service for System-Wide Delivery

To integrate Procmail into the Postfix system is now a simple step but, as with any other configuration change, care must be taken. Postfix runs all external commands such as Procmail with the User ID of nobody. So it would be unable to deliver mail to the user root. To ensure that important system messages are still received you should make sure that an alias is configured so that all mail intended for the root user is forwarded to a real user who will read the mailbox. (It is worthwhile doing this for any other system account that may receive mail.)

Create an Alias for System Accounts

To create an alias for the root user you must edit the appropriate alias file, normally found in /etc/aliases or /etc/mail/aliases.

If you are unable to find the file use the following command:

```
postconf alias_maps
```

The entry in the alias file should be as follows with just a single tab character between the colon (:) and the start of the e-mail address and no trailing spaces:

```
root:    user@domain.com
```

After creating the text entry you should run the `newaliases` command to convert the text file into a database file ready for Postfix to read.

Add Procmail to the Postfix Configuration

For system-wide delivery of mail by Procmail it is necessary to modify the Postfix `main.cf` file to specify the application that will be responsible for the actual delivery.

Edit the `/etc/postfix/main.cf` file and add the following line:

```
mailbox_command = /path/to/procmail
```

When the change has been made you need to instruct Postfix that the file has changed using the following command:

```
postfix reload
```

Postfix-Provided Environment Variables

We will later on find out how to use information outside Procmail. Postfix exports information regarding the mail package by use of a number of environmental variables. The variables are modified to avoid any shell expansion issues by replacing all characters that may have special meaning to the shell, including whitespace, with the underscore character. The following is a list of variables that are exported and the meaning of each.

Variable	Meaning
DOMAIN	The text to the right-hand side of the @ in the recipient address
EXTENSION	Optional address-extension part
HOME	The recipient's home directory
LOCAL	The text to the left-hand side of the @ in the recipient address, for example, $USER+$EXTENSION
LOGNAME	The recipient username
RECIPIENT	The entire recipient address, $LOCAL@$DOMAIN
SENDER	The complete sender address
SHELL	The recipient's login shell
USER	The recipient username

Basic Operations

When a mail item arrives and is passed to the Procmail program, the sequence of operations follows a set format. It starts by loading the various configuration files to obtain the rules that have been set up for that particular user. The message is then tested by each of these rules in turn and when a suitable match is made the rule is applied. Some rules terminate when they have completed while others return control so that the message can be assessed against remaining rules for potential processing.

Configuration File

System-wide configuration is normally made in /etc/Procmail, while personal configuration files are normally stored in the user's home directory and called .procmail. Individual rules can be stored in separate files or grouped together into a number of files and then included as part of the mail filtering process by the main .procmail file. Typically these files would be stored in the Procmail subdirectory of your home directory.

File Format

Entries in the configuration file are made in a simple text format according to a basic layout. Comments are allowed and are formed by the text following a # character; empty lines are simply ignored. Rules themselves do not have to be laid out in any particular format, though for ease of maintenance and readability it is well worth writing the rules in a consistent and simple format.

Configuration File Dissection

The Procmail configuration file contents can be classified into three main sections:

- **Variables**: Information necessary for Procmail to do its work may be assigned to variables within the configuration file in a manner similar to how they are used in shell programming. Some of the variables are obtained from the shell environment that Procmail is running in, others are created by Procmail itself for the use within the scripts, while other variables can be assigned within the script itself. A further use for variables is to set flags as to how Procmail itself should operate.

  A few useful variables can be set in most scripts:

```
PATH=/usr/bin: /usr/local/bin:.
MAILDIR=$HOME/Mail                        # Make sure it exists
DEFAULT=$MAILDIR/mbox
LOGFILE=$MAILDIR/from
LOG="
"
VERBOSE=yes
```

The VERBOSE variable is used to affect the level of logging that is performed, while the NEWLINE embedded in the LOG variable is deliberate and intended to make log files easier to read.

Chapter 7 also includes a short script that displays all the variables assigned within Procmail.

- **Comments**: A # character and all the following characters up to a NEWLINE are ignored. This does not apply to condition lines, which cannot be commented. Blank lines are ignored and may be used in conjunction with comments to document your configuration and to aid readability. What makes obvious sense today as you are writing your rules, may well defy explanation in six months time without checking the manual.
- **Rules or recipes**: "Recipe" is a common name for rules we create. A line starting with a colon (:) marks the beginning of a recipe. A recipe has the following format:

```
:0 [flags] [ : [locallockfile] ]
<zero or more conditions (one per line)>
<exactly one action line>
```

The :0 is a hangover from earlier versions of Procmail. The number following the : was originally intended to indicate the number of actions contained within the rule, this is now calculated automatically by the Procmail parser; however, the :0 is required for compatibility purposes.

Analyzing a Simple Rule

Let us assume that we are receiving large amounts of mail from a particular mail group that we subscribed to. The mail is interesting, but isn't important and we would prefer to read it at our leisure. The subject is mythical monsters and all e-mail arriving from this mailing list has a To address of mythical@monsters.com. We have decided that we will create a special folder just for these items of mail, and copy all the mail into this folder. This is a simple rule that you will be able to easily copy and modify to process your own mail in the future.

The Rule Structure

The following is an example copy of a very simple .procmail file taken from a user's home directory and is intended to explain some of the basic features of a Procmail configuration. The rule itself is designed to store all mail sent to a certain e-mail address, mythical@monsters.com, in a special folder called monsters. Most mail will be sent to multiple people including yourself and the To address can hold a useful indication of the mail contents. For example mail may be sent to a distribution list at info@yourcompany.com and you need to prioritize this e-mail.

Take a few moments to read the contents of the file and then we will break each section down in turn and analyze what its function is.

```
#
#    Here we assign variables
#
PATH=/usr/bin: /usr/local/bin:.
MAILDIR=$HOME/Mail                    # Make sure it exists
DEFAULT=$MAILDIR/mbox
LOGFILE=$MAILDIR/from
LOG="
"
VERBOSE=yes


#
#    This is the only rule within the file
#
:0:                                   # Anything to mythical@monsters.com
* ^TO_ mythical@monsters.com
monsters                              # will go to $MAILDIR/monsters
```

Variable Analysis

If we examine this file in detail we can start with the definition statements where the variables are assigned with specific values. These values will override any values that Procmail has already assigned. By doing this manual assignment we can ensure that paths are optimized for the script operation and that we are certain of what values are being used rather than assuming the values that Procmail may assign.

```
PATH=/usr/bin: /usr/local/bin:.
MAILDIR=$HOME/Mail                    # Make sure it exists
DEFAULT=$MAILDIR/mbox
LOGFILE=$MAILDIR/from
LOG="
"
VERBOSE=yes
```

These set up instructions to Procmail to define some basic parameters:

- The PATH instruction specifies where Procmail can find any programs it may need to execute as part of the processing.

- MAILDIR specifies the directory that all the mail items will be stored in.

- DEFAULT defines where mail will be stored if a specific location is not defined for the individual rule.

- LOGFILE is the file where all tracking information will be stored so that we can see what it is happening.

Rule Analysis

Next we have the recipe instructions beginning with :0. The second : instructs Procmail to create a lock file to ensure only one mail message is written to the file at a time in order to avoid corruption of the message store.

The single line rule may be broken down as follows:

- *: All rule lines begin with a *. This is the way Procmail knows that they are rules. There may be one or more rules per recipe.
- ^TO_: This is a special Procmail built-in macro that searches most headers that can carry your address in them, such as To:, Apparently-To:, Cc:, Resent-To:, and so on and will match if it finds the address mythical@monsters.com.

The final line is the action line and by default specifies a mail folder in the directory specified by the MAILDIR variable.

Creating and Testing a Rule

Procmail allows you to organize your rules and recipes into multiple files and then process each file in turn. This makes it much easier to manage the rules and also to switch rules on and off as the needs change. For this first test case we will create a special rule-set for testing and organize all our rules in a subdirectory of our home directory. Typically, the subdirectory is called Procmail but you are free to use your own name.

We will start off by looking at a simple personal rule and testing it for a single user. Later on in the chapter when we have covered all of the basics and you are comfortable with the process of creating and setting up rules we will show how to start applying rules to all system users.

'hello world' Example

Almost all books on programming start off with a very simple 'hello world' example to show the basics of the programming language. In this case we will create a simple personal rule that processes all e-mails received by a user and checks to see if the subject contains the words 'hello world'. If the mail subject contains these particular words then the mail message will be stored in a special folder. If it does not contain these magic words the mail will be stored in the user's normal inbox.

Create rc.testing

When you are working in a production environment, it is important to make sure that the rules being written and tested do not interfere with your normal day-to-day mail activities. One way of controlling this is to create a special file specifically for testing new rules and only include it in the Procmail processing when you are actually doing the testing work. When you are happy with the rule operation you can then move it to a specific file of its own, or add it to other similar or related rules. In this example we will create a new file for testing rules called rc.testing.

In the $HOME/Procmail directory use your favorite editor to create the file rc.testing and enter the following lines:

```
# LOGFILE should be specified early in the file so
# everything after it is logged
LOGFILE=$PMDIR/pmlog

# To insert a blank line between each message's log entry,
# Use the following LOG entry
LOG="
"
# Set to yes when debugging; VERBOSE default is no
VERBOSE=yes

#
#   Simple test recipes
#
:0:
* ^Subject:.*hello world
TEST-Helloworld
```

By now you are hopefully beginning to recognize the structure of the rules. This one is broken down as follows:

The first few lines set up variables that are applicable to our testing environment. As they are assigned within the testing script, they will only apply while the script is being included in the processing. As soon as we exclude the test script, the testing settings will, of course, not be applied.

Match all lines that begin (^) with the string Subject: and contain a string ending in hello world. We have deliberately not used a string such as test as a small number of systems can strip out messages that appear to be test messages. Remember that default operation of Procmail is to be case independent so we don't need to test for all variations such as Hello World.

The last line directs Procmail to store the output in the TEST-Helloworld file.

Perform Static Testing of the Script

Running the following command from the Procmail directory will generate the debugging output:

```
formail -s procmail -m rc.testing < testmail.txt
```

After running the command you can look at the log file for error messages. If everything worked fine, you would see the following output in the log:

```
procmail: [16640] Wed Feb 2 20:56:52 2005
procmail: Match on "^Subject:.*hello world"
procmail: Locking "TEST-Helloworld.lock"
procmail: Assigning "LASTFOLDER=TEST-Helloworld"
procmail: Opening "TEST-Helloworld"
procmail: Acquiring kernel-lock
procmail: Unlocking "TEST-Helloworld.lock"
From foo@bar Wed Feb 2 20:56:52 2005
 Subject: HEllo World Again
 Folder: TEST-Helloworld                                          88
```

If the Subject line had not contained the relevant matching phrase you might have seen the following output in the log:

```
procmail: [17012] Wed Feb 2 21:01:11 2005
procmail: No match on "^Subject:.*hello world"
From test@adepteo.net Wed Feb 2 21:01:11 2005
 Subject: lo World Again
 Folder: **Bounced**                                      0
```

Configure Procmail to Process rc.testing

You will need to edit your .procmail configuration file. There may well be some entries in there already, so it is worth making a backup of the file before you make any changes. Ensure that the following lines are included in the file:

```
# Directory for storing procmail configuration and log files
PMDIR=$HOME/Procmail

# Load specific rule sets
INCLUDERC=$PMDIR/rc.testing
```

Some lines are deliberately commented out using ##. These may be required if we need to do some more detailed debugging later.

Testing the Setup

Send yourself two messages. One should include the string hello world in the subject line and one should not include this particular sting

When you check your mail you should find that the message with the key word in the subject has been stored in the TEST-HelloWorld mail folder while the other message was left in the normal mail inbox.

Configuration Debugging

If this has all worked correctly, congratulations—you are well on the way to organizing your mail. If it didn't quite work as expected there are a number of simple things we can do to find out what the problem is.

Check for Typos in the Scripts

As with any programming process, if at first it doesn't work—check the code to make sure that there are no obvious typos introduced during the editing phase.

Look at the Log File for Error Messages

If that doesn't highlight anything you can look at the log file created by Procmail. In this case the log file is called pmlog in the ~/Procmail directory.

To look at just the last few lines use the following command:

```
tail ~/Procmail/pmlog
```

In the following example there is a missing :0 so that the rule lines are being skipped:

```
* ^Subject:.*hello world
TEST-HelloWorld
```

This would give the following errors:

```
procmail: [23821] Wed Feb  2 22:32:55 2005
procmail: Skipped "* ^Subject:.*hello world"
procmail: Skipped "TEST"
procmail: Skipped "-HelloWorld"
```

Here there is no storage instruction to follow the rule :0:

```
* ^Subject:.*hello world
```

This would give the following errors:

```
procmail: [23985] Wed Feb 2 22:35:06 2005
procmail: No match on "^Subject:.*hello world"
procmail: Incomplete recipe
```

Check File and Directory Permissions

Use the ls command to check the permissions on the ~/.procmailrc and ~/Procmail/* files and the ~/ home directory. The rules files should be writable by users other than the owner and should have permissions similar to the following:

```
rw-r--r-
```

and the home directory should have permissions such as the following where the ? may be either r or –:

```
drwx?-x?-x
```

Turn on Full Logging

When you are creating more complex rules, or if you still have a problem, then you need to enable the **Full Logging** capability of Procmail. To do this you need to remove the comment ## from the lines in the ~/.procmailrc file so that they are enabled as follows:

```
# Directory for storing procmail configuration and log files
PMDIR=$HOME/Procmail

# LOGFILE should be specified early in the file so
# everything after it is logged
LOGFILE=$PMDIR/pmlog

# To insert a blank line between each message's log entry,
# uncomment next two lines (this is helpful for debugging)
LOG="
"

# Set to yes when debugging; VERBOSE default is no
VERBOSE=yes
```

```
# Load specific rule sets
INCLUDERC=$PMDIR/rc.testing
```

Now resend the two sample messages and check the log file for the output information. The log file should indicate some areas of problems for you to investigate.

Taking Steps to Avoid Disasters

The following recipe inserted early on in the .procmailrc file will ensure that the last 32 messages received are each stored in the backup directory ensuring that valuable mail is not lost in cases where a recipe contains a fault or has an unexpected side effect.

```
# Create a backup cache of 100 most recent messages in case of mistakes.
# For this to work, you must first create the directory
# ${MAILDIR}/backup.
:0 c
backup

  :0 ic
  | cd backup && rm -f dummy `ls -t msg.* | sed -e 1,32d`
```

For now we will assume that this works, and in the next chapter we will analyze the recipe in detail to see exactly how it works and what it does.

Understanding E-mail Structure

In order to make full use of the capabilities of Procmail it is worth spending some time to understand the basic structure of a typical e-mail message. Over time, the structure has grown in complexity, but it can still be broken down into two discrete blocks.

Message Body

The message body is separated from the headers by a single blank line (all the headers must be on consecutive lines as any headers following a blank line will be assumed to be part of the message body).

The message body itself may be either a simple text message composed normally of simple ASCII characters or it may be a complex combination of parts encoded using something known as **MIME**. This has allowed e-mail to be able to transfer all forms of data ranging from simple text, HTML, or other formatted pages and to include information such as attachments or embedded objects such as images. Discussion of MIME encoding is beyond the scope of this book, and is not necessary for most processes that you are likely to come across in mail filtering.

If you decide to try to process data held in the message body, it is important to remember that what you see as the output of the mail program may be very different from the actual data transmitted in the raw mail message.

E-Mail Headers

The headers are the instructions that an e-mail contains that permit the various mailing components to send and process messages. The typical format of a mail header is a simple two-part construction composed of a keyword terminated by a : and followed by the information assigned to the keyword. The headers provide a lot of information about how the e-mail was created, what form of mail program created the message, from whom it came, to whom it should go, and how it reached your mailbox.

The following mail headers relate to an e-mail received from one of a number of mailing lists at freelancers.net. The most useful identifying feature of the e-mail is the subject line as most of the other mail groups use the same values for the other headers discussed:

Return-Path: <do-not-reply@freelancers.net>

Received: from fnmail.co.uk (ev1s-207-44-214-84.ev1servers.net [207.44.214.84] (may be forged))

> by delta.adepteo.net (8.12.5/8.12.5) with SMTP id iA3LGkGD002068

> for <projects@adepteo.net>; Wed, 3 Nov 2004 21:16:46 GMT

Received: (qmail 4477 invoked by uid 0); 3 Nov 2004 18:30:47 -0000

Date: 3 Nov 2004 18:30:47 -0000

Message-ID: <20041103183047.4476.qmail@fnmail.co.uk>

To: projects@adepteo.net

Subject: FN-PROJECTS Freelance Web Designers

From: Do Not Reply <do-not-reply@freelancers.net>

X-Mailer: http://www.phpclasses.org/mimemessage $Revision: 1.29 $

MIME-Version: 1.0

Content-Type: text/plain

X-Spam-Checker-Version: SpamAssassin 3.0.0 (2004-09-13) on delta.adepteo.net

X-Spam-Level:

X-Spam-Status: No, score=-2.3 required=5.0 tests=AWL,BAYES_00,COMBINED_FROM
autolearn=no version=3.0.0

Header Structure

The above example contains a large number of headers inserted by a number of processes that the mail has been through on its journey from sender to recipient. There is however a small number of key headers that are very useful for processing e-mail and are used in a significant number of recipes.

Official Definitions for Headers

All headers that do not begin with x- are assigned specific functions by the relevant standards authority. More information about them may be found in the **RFC (Request for Comment) Document 822** at `http://www.ietf.org/rfc/rfc0822.txt`.

Headers beginning with x- are user defined and are applicable to a specific application only. However, some applications may use the same header tag as other applications, but for different reasons and with a different format for the information provided.

Example Rule Sets

In order to help you understand the way Procmail rules work, we will go through the design and setup of several simple but very useful rule sets. This should help to get you into the swing of designing your own rule sets as you find more specific needs to filter your incoming mail items.

All these examples are based on the mail messages received from the Freelancers mailing list from which the previous example headers were taken. They all achieve the same result and once again prove that there is no one correct solution to a programming problem.

From Header

This header explains who the originator of the e-mail was. There are a variety of formats that may be used and are formed of various combinations of human-readable and computer-readable items of information. When you have looked at a few e-mails, you will begin to see the various patterns that can be used by differing mail systems and software. The actual formatting of this header is not necessarily important as you are looking to generate rules to match specific e-mails.

From: Do Not Reply <do-not-reply@freelancers.net>

Return-Path Header

This field is added by the final transport system that delivers the message to its recipient. The field is intended to contain definitive information about the address and route back to the message's originator.

Return-Path: <do-not-reply@freelancers.net>

Filtering by Return-Path

The majority of mailing lists use the Return-Path header:

```
:0:
* ^Return-Path: <do-not-reply@freelancers.net>
freelancers
```

This is a useful way of easily filtering mailing list items. Here, the ∧ character performs a special function that instructs Procmail to start the match process at the beginning of a new line. This means that lines that contain the phrase embedded in the middle of the line are not matched. The default operation for Procmail is to return a match if the string is found anywhere within the header or anywhere within the mail body depending on where the script has been set to search.

To and Cc Headers

Messages are normally sent to one or more people who are listed in the To: or Cc: headers of the e-mail. Like the From: header, these addresses may be formatted in several ways. These headers are visible to all mail recipients and allow you to see all the public recipients listed.

To: projects@adepteo.net

There is a third recipient header that is not quite as common as the To: and Cc: but is used quite a lot in bulk mailings. This is the Bcc: (Blind Carbon Copy). Unfortunately, as the name implies, this is a blind header and so the information is not included in the actual header information and hence not available for processing.

Filtering by To or Cc

Procmail has a number of special built-in macros that can be used to identify mail items. The special rule ∧TO_ is intended to search all the destination headers available. The rule must be written as exactly 4 characters with no spaces and with both T and O in capitals. The phrase being matched must follow immediately after the _ again without a space.

```
:0:
* ∧TO_ do-not-reply@freelancers.net
freelancers
```

Subject Header

The subject line is usually included in the e-mail headers unless the sender has decided not to include a subject line at all.

Subject: FN-PROJECTS Freelance Web Designers

In this example all the mail items sent to this particular list start with the phrase "FN-PROJECTS" and so are sometimes suitable for filtering.

Filtering by Subject

When mailing lists add a prefix to subject lines, this prefix may be suitable for filtering:

```
:0:
* ∧Subject: FN-PROJECTS
freelancers
```

System-Wide Rules

Now that we have covered all the basics of setting up rules, analyzing e-mails, and generally seeing how all of the processing operations interact we will look through a couple of examples for system-wide filtering, testing, and operations.

System Rule: Remove Executables

In Chapter 9 we will see how to integrate a complete virus checking system into the Postfix mail architecture. This will perform accurate virus signature recognition and add suitable flags to the mail headers to indicate if a virus is present in the mail. However, if it is not possible to set up such a system, this rule will provide an alternative but more brutal approach to block all e-mails with executable attachments.

If you place the following in /etc/procmailrc it will affect all mail traveling through the system that contains certain types of documents as attachments.

```
# Note: The whitespace in the [ ] below comprises a space and a tab character
:0
*  < 256000
*  ! ^Content-Type: text/plain
{
    :0B
    * ^(Content-(Type|Disposition):.*|[   ]*(file)?)name=("[^"]*|[^
]*)\.(bat|cmd|com|exe|js|pif|scr)
    /dev/null
}
```

The rule starts with the customary :0 instruction.

The conditions are applied as follows:

Firstly, ensure that we are only going to filter messages less than 256KB in size. This is primarily for efficiency and most spam is smaller than this size. You could obviously increase it if you are getting viruses that are bigger, but there could be a higher load on your system.

The next line says that we also only look at those messages that are MIME types (i.e. not plain text), as attachments, by definition, cannot be included in a plain text message.

We have a subfilter between the curly braces. The :0B says we are processing the body of the message, rather than the headers. We have to do this because attachments come in the body, not the headers. We then look for lines that have the signature of being a MIME heading for an executable file. You can amend the filename extensions if you wish; these are simply ones that are commonly used to transmit viruses.

The action in this case is to send this message to /dev/null if it matches. Note that this means no message bounce or error message to the sender; the message is simply dropped, never to be seen again. You may of course store the messages in a secure location and nominate someone to monitor the account for valid messages that do not contain viruses. For a more elegant solution to this problem, remember to check Chapter 9.

System Rule: Large E-Mails

With the ever-increasing use of high speed, always-on-Internet connections, people are starting to send larger and larger e-mail messages. Once upon a time it was considered rude to have more than four lines in your signature file, nowadays people happily include images and wallpapers, and send both HTML and text versions of the e-mail all without realizing the size of message they are sending.

Storing such large messages in your inbox adds considerably to the processing overhead to search through your mail messages. One simple solution is to move all messages over a certain size into an oversize folder. This can be achieved very simply by using the following rule that looks for messages over 100,000 bytes in size and stores them in the `largemail` folder.

```
:0:
* >100000
largemail
```

The downside of this rule is that your users need to remember to check on a regular basis both their Inbox and the `largemail` folder. A more elegant solution will allow you to copy the first few lines of the message together with the headers and subject line and store that in the Inbox and inform you that the complete version needs to be checked for. Such a solution can be seen in the examples at the end of the next chapter.

Summary

In this chapter we have discovered some of the basics of Procmail. By now you should be familiar with the various files that Procmail uses to load scripts, the core principles of filtering, and the options available. In this chapter we have analyzed e-mails, set up individual and system wide filters, and looked at some of the simple testing, logging, and debugging options we have to help us manage a company's mail more effectively.

We have just scratched the surface of what is possible, but hopefully this little blemish has already provided you with a whole load of ideas about how you could go about processing and filtering your daily overload of e-mail. It may well have given you ideas for more advanced filters and the next chapter will provide more advice and explanations of how to go about setting these up.

7

Advanced Procmail

Now that you have got the basics of Procmail under your belt, we can move on and start putting together a more complete mail-handling system. We will be using a number of more advanced Procmail capabilities in this chapter. By the end of this chapter you should have a useful tool chest of routines for putting together your own set of Procmail recipes and getting your mail under control

Delivering and Non-Delivering Recipes

So far we have covered only those recipes that either do a final delivery of the mail to a program or a file, or forwarded a message to another mail user. There is another option available, and to quote from the Procmail documentation:

> "...There are two kinds of recipes: delivering and non-delivering recipes. If a delivering recipe is found to match, Procmail considers the mail (you guessed it) delivered and will cease processing the .procmail file after having successfully executed the action line of the recipe. If a non-delivering recipe is found to match, processing of the .procmail file will continue after the action line of this recipe has been executed."

Non-Delivering Example

We introduced an example in the previous chapter that was intended to make backups of mail items in case a recipe that is being tested deletes all mail. This is a very useful non-delivering recipe example and may be found in the Procmail manual page procmailex.

If you are fairly new to Procmail and plan to experiment a little bit, it often helps to have a safety net of some sort. Inserting the following two recipes above all other recipes will make sure that the last 32 messages of all arriving mail will always be preserved. In order that this works as intended, you have to create a directory named backup in $MAILDIR prior to inserting these two recipes:

```
:0 c
backup
:0 ic
cd backup && rm -f dummy `ls -t msg.* | sed -e 1,32d`
```

The second recipe uses several features of Procmail that we will be exploring in more detail in later sections of this chapter.

If we work step by step through this recipe we will end up with a useful archive utility that records the last 32 mail items to be received and allows us to manually recover mail if we ever create a recipe that ends up destroying mail rather than storing it.

The first recipe performs a simple backup operation by delivering a copy or clone of the mail into the backup directory:

```
:0 c
backup
```

Before adding the second recipe, create the above recipe in your `.procmailrc` file and send a couple of mail messages to yourself. You will see that each mail item is stored in the backup directory (provided of course, that it exists and has the correct permissions).

The second recipe is just as simple but uses some more complex features of Linux system commands to delete all but the most recent 32 mail items in the backup directory.

```
:0 ic
| cd backup && rm -f dummy `ls -t msg.* | sed -e 1,32d`
```

This recipe works as follows. Firstly the rule flags state that:

Flag	Meaning
i	Ignore the return code of the subsequent pipeline command
c	Clone or copy the incoming data so that the original data is not affected

The | instructs Procmail to pass the data matched to the following pipeline command, which performs the following actions:

Command	Action
cd backup	Changes to the backup directory
ls -t msg.*	Obtains a list of files beginning with msg and sorts them in to time order
sed -e 1,32d	Deletes all but the last 32 lines—that is, most recent mail items
rm -f dummy...	The parameter dummy is to stop error messages in case there are no files to be deleted, and then the rm command continues to remove the files listed by the sed filter.

These two recipes are examples of unconditional recipes that are actioned for every single mail item to arrive. That they are unconditional can be inferred from the fact that there are no 'conditions lines', i.e. lines that begin with a *. As both the recipes include a c flag in the recipe, they are also defined as non-delivering recipes.

Ordering of Procmail Recipes

When you have collected a number of Procmail recipes, you will find that the order in which the recipes are processed can be important. By setting the order of processing correctly you can improve performance and reduce the time taken to process incoming mail. You can also make sure that more critical rules are applied to important messages earlier than more general rules that are intended to act on bulk messages. A typical scenario could be to apply rules in the following order:

- Process daemon or server messages first.
- Mailing lists should be handled as early as possible, but after the server messages, because you want your services handled first.
- Apply kill file to block any known spammers.
- Next come vacation replies. Do not send vacation replies before you have handled mailing lists to prevent annoying vacation replies to mailing lists.
- Save private messages.
- Check for **Unsolicited Bulk E-Mail** (**UBE**)—Spam. This avoids the high overhead of processing spam checks on known valid e-mail.

Formail

Formail is an external utility program (from Procmail) that is nearly always available on systems where Procmail is installed. Its function is to process mail messages and extract information from within the headers of the messages. It acts as a filter that can be used to force mail into a format suitable for storing in a Linux mail system. It can also perform a number of other useful functions such as 'From' escaping, generating auto-replying headers, simple header extracting, or splitting up a mailbox/digest/articles file.

The input data mail/mailbox/article contents needs to be provided using the standard input. So formail is ideally suited for use in pipeline command chains. Output data is provided on the standard output.

We are not going to go into the subtleties of formail in this document but as it is a useful tool, we will make reference to some of its functionality in some of our examples. More information can be obtained from the system manual pages.

Advanced Recipe Analysis

Here we have a much more complicated recipe that implements a form of vacation service to inform senders that you are away and unable to reply to e-mails. At first thought this could be a simple non-delivering recipe to send a message back to all messages received; however, this is not ideal as some people may end up receiving multiple delivery confirmation messages and you may also end up sending messages back to system utilities that have no way of understanding your well-meant reply.

The example is based upon the "vacation example" from the Procmail `procmailex` manual page.

The `vacation.cache` file is maintained by `formail`. It maintains a vacation database by extracting the name of the sender and inserting it in the `vacation.cache` file. This ensures that it always contains the most recent names. The size of the file is limited to a maximum of approximately 8192 bytes. If the name of the sender is new, an auto reply will be sent.

```
SHELL=/bin/sh # for other shells, this might need adjustment

:0 Whc: vacation.lock
# Perform a quick check to see if the mail was addressed to us
$TO_:.*\<$\LOGNAME\>

# Filter out the mail senders we don't want to send replies to - Ever
* !^FROM_DAEMON

# Make sure that we do not create an endless loop that keeps
# replying to the reply by checking to see if we have already
processed
# this message and inserted a loop detection header
* !^X-Loop: your@own.mail.address
| formail -rD 8192 vacation.cache


:0 ehc
# We are pretty certain it's OK to send a reply to the sender of this
message
| (
    formail -rA"Precedence: junk" \
    -A"X-Loop: your@own.mail.address" ; \
    echo "Hi, Your message was delivered to my mailbox,"; \
    echo "but I won't be back until Monday."; \
    echo "-- "; cat $HOME/.signature \
) | $SENDMAIL -oi -t
```

We will come back to this recipe at the end of this section and work through creating a slightly updated version using some of the things we have learned about Procmail. For now the example will help as a reference to understand some of the concepts we explore in the following breakdown of a general recipe structure.

Comments

Documentation, or adding comments to your rules and recipes, is always an important task. What may seem obvious to you now may no doubt seem incomprehensible and cryptic in six months time when you are struggling under pressure to sort out a problem. All comments begin with a # character and continue to the end of the line. In most cases, it is useful to place comments at the beginning of a line or with one or two tabs after a single line that you wish to document.

```
# Here is a full line comment
MAILDIR=${HOME}/index        #Make sure this directory exists. You
should also                          #create the directory
${MAILDIR}/backup at this
                        #time.
```

There is, however, one section of the rule file where comments *must* be included on their own lines and that is in the *Conditions* section.

Variable Assignments

In order to keep track of settings, results from tests, default values, and so on, we can store this information in variables. The assignment operation is simple and follows the same format as other Linux scripting languages. The basic format is `VARIABLENAME=VALUE`.

There must be no spaces within the variable name, and if there are spaces within the value being assigned, the whole of the variable should be stored between double quotes.

The correct way to access a variable is by enclosing the `VARIABLENAME` within braces, `{}`, and prefixing it all with a $ (dollar) sign. It is quite acceptable to use variables within other assignments. Some examples are as follows:

```
MAILDIR=${HOME}/index      # Set the value of the MAILDIR
LOGFILE=${MAILDIR}/log     # Store logfiles in the MAILDIR
```

Notice in the example above that `${HOME}` takes the value of the shell environment setting as it was set when the process was started.

Careful use of variables and their naming can make a script much easier to read and also to maintain.

Substitutions

Sometimes it will be necessary or useful to be able to replace a literal element with a variable that can only be calculated or evaluated at run time. Procmail allows the author to replace most literal elements with variable substitutions or command substitutions in most places. The simplest form of using a variable is by use of the `$varname` format common to a number of scripting languages:

Variable/Command	Substitution
$VAR	Wherever $VAR occurs in the recipe replace it with the value held by this variable.
${VAR}iable *	When you need to concatenate a variable with literal text use the {} to enforce the fact the name is ${VAR} rather than $VARiable.
$\VAR	The \ is a special instruction to Procmail to perform the variable substitution after the variable's contents have been backslash escaped. The output value will then be suitable for literal matching in condition lines.

> * If it is necessary to combine variables with fixed text or values, the {} elements allow absolute definition of the variable name to be established. Notice that this will not happen in condition lines unless you include the $ modifier.

Default Values

If you wish to be able to assign a default value to a variable to be used in cases where the variable has not been set or could not be calculated for some reason, it is possible to use the – or : – separator.

Separator	Action
${VAR:-value}	VAR is assumed to be set if it has a non-null value.
${VAR-value}	VAR is assumed to be set if it has any value assigned.

Command Output

It is possible to assign the output of a command to a variable by use of the ` (back tick) operator (the back tick (`) is ASCII value 96 and not a normal apostrophe (') having ASCII value 39):

```
`cmd1 | cmd2`
```

The above example will assign the output from the pipeline between the two back ticks to the variable or inline in the code as applicable.

Pseudo-Variables

There are a number of special variables or pseudo-variables assigned directly by Procmail; changing some of these values can actually change the way Procmail operates.

Mailbox Variables

Name	Action
MAILDIR	The default value for MAILDIR is taken from the value of the $HOME environment variable. It is also the value used for the current working directory for Procmail during execution. Unless the output file names include a path component, they will be created in this default directory.
MSGPREFIX	This option is used when you want files to be written sequentially to a directory. The MSGPREFIX appends a prefix to the name of the file created using this option. The default prefix is msg., so the file will be named msg.xyz.
DEFAULT	This is the location of the default mail storage area on your system. Normally you should not modify this variable.
ORGMAIL	This is used as a disaster recovery location for cases where DEFAULT is unavailable for any reason. This should definitely not be modified.

Program Variables

Procmail has reasonable defaults written in at compile time. Mostly these shouldn't need to be changed.

Name	Action
SHELL	This is a standard environment variable that specifies the shell environment within which Procmail needs to invoke sub-processes. The value assigned to it should be Bourne shell-compatible such as /bin/sh.
SHELLFLAGS	This specifies any optional flags that should be passed to the SHELL when starting it up
SENDMAIL	This instructs Procmail where to find the sendmail program used for sending mail on to other users (Usually not to be fiddled with).
SENDMAILFLAGS	Like SHELLFLAGS this specifies any flags or command-line arguments that should be passed to the SENDMAIL program when it is executed.

System Interaction Variables

Name	Action
UMASK	This gives the file permissions mode used when creating any files. See man umask for details.
SHELLMETAS	The shell pipeline is compared with the contents of SHELLMETAS before execution. If any characters from SHELLMETAS are found in

Name	Action
	the pipeline command, the command is considered too complicated for Procmail to manage itself and a sub-shell process is spawned. If you know that the a particular pipeline will always be simple enough for Procmail to manage itself but contains characters held in SHELLMETAS, you can temporarily assign an empty string to SHELLMETAS while processing the pipeline and then restore SHELLMETAS. This will avoid the overhead of spawning a sub-shell.

TRAP	Here you can assign a code segment to be executed at the end of execution of Procmail. An example use for it could be to delete temporary files created during execution of the recipes.
	
	`TEMPORARY=$HOME/tmp/pmail.$$`
	`TRAP="/bin/rm -f $TEMPORARY"`

EXITCODE	This is the value that is given back to the process that started Procmail when Procmail exits. Typically the value of 0 is returned for success and non-zero values indicate some form of failure. By modifying the EXITCODE value, you can return specific information about the processing performed. The exit code of a program started by Procmail is stored in $?

Logging Variables

Name	Action
LOGFILE	This specifies the location to which Procmail should write all its logging and debugging information. If this value is empty then output is sent to the **standard error output,** which means that it will be lost unless the program is running interactively or stderr is redirected somewhere.

LOG	If you wish to write something directly to the log file yourself, you can assign a value to the LOG variable, and it will be appended to LOGFILE. If you want to format the output and include a blank line after your log message remember to include a blank line in the message that you output.
	
	`LOG="Isn't working with procmail great - you can`
	`achieve so much`
	`"`

VERBOSE	This allows the output to be the basic 'default' or provide detailed information. Setting VERBOSE=1 will include detailed logging information that will aid in debugging your recipes. To reduce the amount of output information, remember to set VERBOSE=0 after the recipe has been run.

Name	Action
LOGABSTRACT	If LOGABSTRACT is set to all then all the deliveries will have information regarding the sender, subject, and size of the mail delivered. If you wish to stop this logging then set LOGABSTRACT=no.

Procmail's State Variables

Name	Action
PROCMAIL_OVERFLOW	If Procmail finds any lines in the Procmail script file that are longer than the buffer size while reading the file at startup, it will set the value of PROCMAIL_OVERFLOW as yes. If the line being read is a condition or action line then the action will be considered to have failed; however, if it is a variable assignment or recipe start then Procmail will stop reading the file and exit with an abnormal termination.
HOST	This holds the name of the host on which the process is running.
DELIVERED	If the mail message was delivered successfully, this is set to yes and the calling process will be informed by Procmail. If you manually set this to yes *and* the message was not delivered, it will be lost without trace but the calling process will still believe that it was successfully delivered.
LASTFOLDER	This gives the name of the last file or directory to which a message was written.
MATCH	This holds the information extracted by the last regular expression operation.
$=	This holds the result of the latest scoring recipe.
$1, $2, ...; $@; $#	Just like the standard shell this specifies the command-line arguments that Procmail was started with: $1 is the first command-line argument, and so on, $@ contains all arguments, and $# contains the number of arguments. See also the SHIFT pseudo-variable.
$$	This holds the current process ID—this can be useful for creating temporary files unique to the process.
$?	This holds the exit code of the previous shell command.

Name	Action
$_	This holds the name of the current Procmail file that is being processed.
$-	This is an alias for LASTFOLDER.
	$= and $@ can't be used directly; you have to assign the value to another variable before it can be used for anything useful.

Message Content Variables

The main use for these variables is to access data held in the appropriate section but where the recipe has a flag that restricts the processing to the other part of the message. By using HB you can access information across the whole of the message.

Name	Action
H	This holds the header information for the message being currently processed.
B	This holds the body of the message being currently processed.

Locking Variables

Name	Action
LOCKFILE	Assigning a value to this variable creates a lock file, which remains until LOCKFILE is assigned another value. This may be the name of another lock file to create or a null value to remove any lock.
LOCKEXT	Assigning a value to this allows you to override the extension used as part of the lock file name. This can be useful to aid in identifying the process that has created the lock file.
LOCKSLEEP	If Procmail wants to create a lock on a file that is already locked by another process it will go into a retry loop. The LOCKSLEEP variable specifies the number of seconds to sleep and wait before retrying to obtain the lock.
LOCKTIMEOUT	This specifies an age in seconds that the lock file must be before it will be assumed that the lock file is invalid and will be overridden. If the value is 0 then the lock file will never be overridden. The default value is 1024 seconds.

Error-Handling Variables

Name	Action
TIMEOUT	This specifies how long to wait for a child before telling the child process to terminate. The default is 960 seconds.
SUSPEND	This specifies how long to wait between NORESRETRY retries. Default is 16 seconds.
NORESRETRY	The number times Procmail will retry before giving up when a serious system resource shortage occurs such as out of disk space or the system has reached the maximum number of processes. The default value is 4 and if the number is negative then Procmail will retry forever. If the resources do not become available during the retry period then the message will be discarded and classified as undeliverable.

Miscellaneous Variables

Name	Action
LINEBUF	This sets a limit for the length of recipe lines that Procmail is ready to cope with. If you need to process very large regular expressions or store lots of data into MATCH, increase this value.
SHIFT	This is similar to the shift feature in normal shell processing. Assigning a positive number to this variable moves down Procmail's command-line arguments.
INCLUDERC	This instructs to Procmail to load another file containing Procmail recipes. This new file is loaded and processed before Procmail will continue processing the current file.
DROPPRIVS	This ensures that no root privileges are available when Procmail is executing as setuid or setgid. Setting this value to yes will make Procmail drop all its special privileges.

EXAMPLE

The following example will print out most of the environment settings in response and will provide some information that could be helpful while trying to debug problems with Procmail. It is not expected that this is included in any production files otherwise your log file could grow to be extremely large very quickly.

Create a file called rc.dump in the same directory as your other Procmail script files and place the following lines in the file. (Note that the quotes (") at the start and end—they are important to ensure that the script operates correctly.)

```
#
#   Simple Procmail Script to dump variables to a log file
#
LOG="Dump of ProcMail Variables
MAILDIR is currently :${MAILDIR}:
MSGPREFIX is currently :${MSGPREFIX}:
DEFAULT is currently :${DEFAULT}:
ORGMAIL is currently :${ORGMAIL}:
SHELL is currently :${SHELL}:
SHELLFLAGS is currently :${SHELLFLAGS}:
SENDMAIL is currently :${SENDMAIL}:
SENDMAILFLAGS is currently :${SENDMAILFLAGS}:
UMASK is currently :${UMASK}:
SHELLMETAS is currently :${SHELLMETAS}:
TRAP is currently :${TRAP}:
EXITCODE is currently :${EXITCODE}:
LOGFILE is currently :${LOGFILE}:
LOG is currently :${LOG}:
VERBOSE is currently :${VERBOSE}:
LOGABSTRACT is currently :${LOGABSTRACT}:
COMSAT is currently :${COMSAT}:
PROCMAIL_OVERFLOW is currently :${PROCMAIL_OVERFLOW}:
TODO is currently :${TODO}:
HOST is currently :${HOST}:
DELIVERED is currently :${DELIVERED}:
LASTFOLDER is currently :${LASTFOLDER}:
\$= is currently :$=:
\$1 is currently :$1:
\$2 is currently :$2:
\$$ is currently :$$:
\$? is currently :$?:
\$_ is currently :$_:
\$- is currently :$-:
LOCKFILE is currently :${LOCKFILE}:
LOCKEXT is currently :${LOCKEXT}:
LOCKSLEEP is currently :${LOCKSLEEP}:
LOCKTIMEOUT is currently :${LOCKTIMEOUT}:
TIMEOUT is currently :${TIMEOUT}:
NORESRETRY is currently :${NORESRETRY}:
SUSPEND is currently :${SUSPEND}:"
```

Run the following command:

```
# procmail ./rc.dump
<CTRL-D>
```

This will create the following output:

```
# procmail ./rc.dump
<CTRL-D>
"Dump of ProcMail Variables
MAILDIR is currently :.:
MSGPREFIX is currently :msg.:
DEFAULT is currently :/var/spool/mail/root:
ORGMAIL is currently :/var/spool/mail/root:
SHELL is currently :/bin/bash:
SHELLFLAGS is currently :-c:
SENDMAIL is currently :/usr/sbin/sendmail:
SENDMAILFLAGS is currently :-oi:
UMASK is currently ::
SHELLMETAS is currently :&|<>~;?*[:
TRAP is currently ::
EXITCODE is currently ::
LOGFILE is currently ::
LOG is currently ::
VERBOSE is currently :1:
LOGABSTRACT is currently ::
COMSAT is currently :no:
PROCMAIL_OVERFLOW is currently ::
TODO is currently ::
HOST is currently :delta.adepteo.net:
DELIVERED is currently ::
LASTFOLDER is currently ::
$= is currently :0:
$1 is currently ::
$2 is currently ::
$$ is currently :9014:
$? is currently :0:
$_ is currently :./rc.dump:
$- is currently ::
LOCKFILE is currently ::
LOCKEXT is currently :.lock:
LOCKSLEEP is currently ::
LOCKTIMEOUT is currently ::
TIMEOUT is currently ::
NORESRETRY is currently ::
SUSPEND is currently ::
```

Recipes

Procmail recipes follow a simple format; however, there are a number of ways that Procmail can be instructed to interpret or implement the instructions in the rules based on a number of flags and the way that the rules and recipes are written.

Colon Line

As we have already discovered, all rules so far have started with a :0 followed by one or more flags and instructions. Historically a number followed the : to specify the number of conditions that were present in the rule. Current versions of Procmail determine the number of conditions automatically, hence the value 0 is always used. If no 0 is provided then the rule may not function correctly in some versions of Procmail.

Locking

We have already discussed that we need to use a locking mechanism in order to stop more than one process trying to write to the same file at the same time. This requirement, of course, varies with the type of process that the filter is attempting to invoke. For example, a filter that merely changes or assigns a value has no affect on any physical file and so no locking is required. Similarly a filter that merely forwards the data on to another process or another recipient inherently does not need a lock to be applied. In most cases, automatic locking will be applied when Procmail realizes that it is writing to a file and will provide locking of the file itself. In some cases it may be necessary for the author of the filter to manual instruct the Procmail program how and when to go about providing the locking.

To give some insight into when locking is applied automatically, not required at all, or requires manual locking to be enforced, here are some examples:

Automatic Locking

Any rule that begins with :0: will apply automatic file locking. In this case Procmail will automatically determine the name of the file that the mail is being delivered to and create a lock file. If the lock file already exists then it will wait for a period of time and retry to create the lock. When it finally creates the lock file, it will continue with processing. If it is unable to create the lock file, it will report an error and continue with the next rule.

```
:0 <flags>:
```

Enforced Locking

There may be a time, especially when processing mail by an external script where enforced locking is required. In most cases Procmail will determine the name of the file that the ultimate data is being written to by examining the process command line and looking where output is directed to. However if the script takes care of choosing the output location itself, or if it relies on a file that may be altered by another Procmail process a lock file must be specifically requested as follows:

```
:0 <flags> :scriptname.lock
```

As a general rule, for most initial scripts that you are likely to write, an enforced lock file is unlikely to be needed.

No Locking

When forwarding to a pipeline that performs its own file or record-locking processes—such as storing a problem report in a database—then no record locking is required. Similarly if the message is being forwarded to another user then the final delivery will take care of the record locking. The simple rule definition is:

```
:0 <flags>
```

Flags

In the examples we have looked at so far, we have allowed the default settings of Procmail to take effect. However, there are a number of flags that may be set to control how Procmail works.

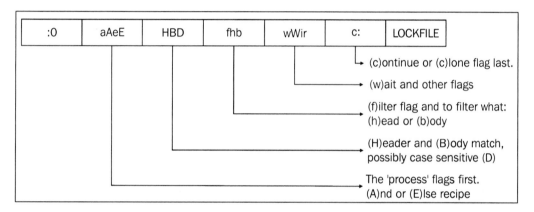

Default Flags

If no flags are stated on the colon line of the recipe, then Procmail will assume that the following flags (Hhb) have been used as default values:

Flag	Action
H	Only Mail Headers are scanned
hb	Action line is passed both headers and body of the mail data

Scope of Matching—HB

Normally matching will take place across the whole of the mail package including both the headers and the body of the mail. If the mail body could be potentially large and we know that we require the matches to be made against just the headers, it would be sensible to use the H flag to restrict the scope of the matching action to be across the headers only.

Conversely, it may sometimes be that we are looking for items of information—perhaps a repeated footer or signature that only appears in the body of the document—in which case we can use the B flag to restrict matching to the body only.

Flag	Action
H	Performs matching across only the mail headers
B	Performs matching across only the mail body
HB	Performs matching across the whole of the mail item including headers and body

Scope of Action—hb

By default, the action line processes the whole e-mail item including the headers and body. If it is required to process only one part of the mail data it is possible to specify which part is passed to the action line.

Flag	Action
h	Pass only the headers to the action line for processing.
b	Pass only the body of the message to the action line for processing.
hb	Pass both, the headers and the message body, for processing. This is the default scope.

It is important to notice the difference between "scope of matching" and "scope of action". The value of the flag in the first case determines which part of the mail—header, body, or the entire mail—has to be scanned for matching. The value of the flag in the second case determines which part of the mail needs to be processed.

Flow Control—aAeEc

This is probably the most complex set of flags to understand of all the Procmail flags. Examples later in the chapter will explain various ways of using these flags. Briefly the following may be assumed about each of the flags:

Flag	Action
A	The recipe will only be processed if the conditions of the previous recipe were met.
a	The recipe will be processed if the previous recipe's conditions were met and the operation was completed without error.
E	This is the opposite of A, in that the recipe will be processed if the previous recipe conditions were not met.

Flag	Action
e	The recipe will be processed if the previous recipe conditions were met but the processing did not complete successfully.
c	This instructs the script to create a copy or clone of the original message and process this copy with any actions in a sub-process. The parent process continues processing the original copy of the message.

The c flag should be read as Clone or Copy. It may sometimes be read as Continue but that is a confusion that is best avoided. The Clone or Copy operation creates a separate copy of the data and a separate flow of execution is created to process that data, sometimes as a totally separate child process. When this clone script has completed the parent continues execution with the original data intact.

As you get to see some scripts in action later in the chapter you will see these flags being used in a variety of ways.

Case Sensitivity—D

Die-hard Linux users have become accustomed to life being case sensitive and always view Capitals as being entirely different to capitals. The default operation of Procmail though, is to be case insensitive. That is, for Procmail Capitals and capitals are identical—*unless* it is told that case sensitivity should be applied by means of the D flag.

Execution Mode—fwWir

We can instruct Procmail how to process or execute the recipe and what actions to take if errors are encountered during the processing. Errors might not occur for smaller mail messages when the processing takes place only on the first few lines of data. However, for larger messages, the Linux shell may believe there is an error when the pipeline has only read a part of the available data.

The Filtering Mode of execution is important to understand. This terminology could be confusing since all that Procmail is designed to do is to filter mail. Think of the execution mode 'filter' in the following way: The mail message you are processing would be piped through whatever is on the action line before it is actually piped on to Procmail (or at least the rest of your script). Another way of viewing the filter mode is as a conversion mode where the data is modified in some way and returned back to the controlling Procmail script for further execution.

Flag	Action
f	Pass the message contents through the recipe to an external pipeline process for processing and then take the output of the process line ready to replace the original message contents.

Flag	Action
i	If a Linux pipeline process only reads part of its input and then terminates, the shell will send a SIGPIPE error signal to the Procmail program—the i flag instructs Procmail to ignore this signal. This should be used where it is expected that the pipeline process will return after processing only part of the message.
r	The data passed to the pipeline process should be passed just as it is without any modifications.
w	By default, the Procmail process will spawn off a sub-process and continue its own processing. The w flag instructs Procmail to wait for the sub-process pipeline to complete before continuing with its own processing.
W	This works the same as w, but also hides any error or other output messages from the pipeline process.

Conditions

There are a number of condition types that could be applied to decide if a given recipe applies to a particular mail item. The idea of applying conditions correctly is to reduce the amount of unnecessary processing that is performed.

Condition lines always begin with a * character followed by one or more spaces. It is possible to apply multiple condition lines within a recipe, but they must all be grouped together on consecutive lines. The logical operation of the grouping is to perform an AND operation such that all the conditions must be applied before the action is executed.

Apply a Rule Unconditionally

It may be required that a rule has to be applied to all messages regardless of any conditions. Such a rule could be to, say, make a backup copy of the mail message to a mail folder.

The unconditional rule is implied by the lack of a conditional line. That is, the rule will always match.

```
# Save all remaining messages to DEFAULT
:0:
$DEFAULT
```

The unconditional rule is often used at the end of a nested chain of recipes to perform a final default action if no other action has been performed.

Tests with Regular Expressions

Those of you that are familiar with the simple pattern-matching operations such as ? or * used commonly in matching of files in a file listing operation may wonder if it is possible to create similar tests to match parts of a mail header or body. The good news is that there is an excellent feature known as **Regular Expressions** or **regex** for short. These provide a mechanism for very complex pattern-matching operations to be performed. In general, this feature matches very closely with the grep command-line regular expressions; there are, however, some important differences that experienced regex users should definitely be aware of in order to understand how to write expressions tailored for Procmail operation. There is a complete section on writing regex later in this chapter.

Regular expressions may be run against the data portion of the mail message (header, body, or both) as defined by the flags or may be used to test a previously assigned variable.

Condition	Action
* regex	Tests the part of the message passed according to the flags against the regular expression. Normally this will process just the headers unless a B flag was given to indicate the scope of matching was to process the body of the message.
* variable ?? regex	This is to compare the assigned variable against the regex for comparison.

Various pseudo-variables were listed earlier in the chapter and represent ways to access information that is contained within the Procmail application. These pseudo-variables can be compared in the same way as normal variables.

EXAMPLE

The following example will make a copy of all the mail items that contain a key phrase in the message body.

```
VERBOSE=1
:0cB:
* [0-9]* Linux Rules [ok!]
${MAILDIR}/linuxrules
VERBOSE=0
```

The following is a quick explanation of the operation of the above example:

1. We specify :0cB: to make sure that we only search through the body and to make a copy so we still get the original message processed.

2. If anywhere in the body there is a phrase that has one or more numbers followed by a <SPACE>Linux Rules<SPACE> followed by either o, k, or !, then a copy will be stored in the linuxrules folder.

3. The use of the setting and unsetting the VERBOSE option before a rule is processed allows just that rule to be displayed in the log in more detail, which means less log file to search through while debugging.

Test Size of Message Part

Under some conditions, it can be assumed that very large sizes of messages will not need to be processed by a recipe. In this situation we can set a limit that the recipe will not match messages over a certain size. If you have users that use a slow data connection, perhaps using connectivity over a mobile phone connection, it can be useful to move all large items of mail into a separate folder for retrieval when the users are back at a better internet connection.

Condition	Action
* > number	Will return true if the message size is **larger** than the given number of bytes
* < number	Will return true if the message size is **smaller** than the given number of bytes

Test Exit Code of External Program

If an external program is run to provide part of the processing the exit code may need to be checked to make sure that the process completed correctly, or to perform a secondary operation to complete the overall processing.

`? /unix/command/line | another/command`

The ? instructs Procmail to pass the current message data to the Linux command line as standard input. The condition is successfully met if the command line exits with a zero exit code. Where the command line is a pipeline of several processes the exit code returned is that of the last program in the pipeline.

Any output printed to standard error by the pipeline is displayed in the log.

EXAMPLE

In this example, the action of lines between the VERBOSE=1 and the VERBOSE=0 will be logged, but all lines outside this range will not be logged. This allows you to control the amount of logging taking place and hence makes it easier to follow the log file activity.

```
VERBOSE=1
:0Bb:
* [0-9]* Linux Rules [ok!]
${MAILDIR}/linuxrules
VERBOSE=0
```

Negation

Sometimes it is useful to be able to check if a particular condition does not exist in order to continue processing in a certain way. The **Exclamation** (!) or **Bang**, as it is sometimes referred to, is used to reverse the value of the condition so that false becomes true and vice versa.

```
* ! condition
```

This tests for a negative result in the condition and returns true if the condition is *not* met.

EXAMPLE

Here we are looking for any item that was not sent directly to us and will be stored in a folder for later viewing.

```
:0:
* !^TO.*cjtaylor
${MAILDIR}/not_sent_to_me
```

Variable Substitution in Conditions

Multiple $ flags may be used to force multiple substitution passes to be applied.

```
* $ condition
```

The $ instructs Procmail to process the condition with the normal sh rules to perform variable and back tick substitution before actually evaluating the condition. The substitution process will resolve variables ($VAR) into their values rather than process them as literals. Any quoted strings will have their quotes removed and all other shell metacharacters will also be evaluated. To have any of these characters passed through this substitution process they should be escaped using the standard \ (backslash) escape mechanism.

EXAMPLE

The following example is taken from the procmailex and even there it is described as being rather exotic, but it does serve as an example. Suppose you have a file in your home directory called .urgent, and the (one) person named in that file is the sender of an incoming mail. You would like that mail to be stored in $MAILDIR/urgent instead of in any of the normal mail folders it would have been sorted in. Then this is what you could do (beware, the file length of $HOME/.urgent should be well below $LINEBUF; increase LINEBUF if necessary):

```
URGMATCH=`cat $HOME/.urgent`

:0:
* $^From.*${URGMATCH}
$MAILDIR/urgent
```

Action Line

This is the line that really does all of the processing activity. In most cases this will mean writing to a physical file or folder but can include forwarding mail to other users, passing data to a command or pipeline of commands, or in some cases, a number of successive actions to be performed as part of a compound recipe. If you want to do more than one action, you can't just stack them one after the other, you need multiple recipes (possibly unconditional, and/or grouped in a pair of braces) and a colon line (and optionally conditions, of course) for each.

Also note that flags that affect the action line are not actually taking effect until the action is actually attempted; in particular, a c flag doesn't generate a clone of the message until its conditions have all been met.

Forward to Other Addresses

Global forwarding of all messages for a user account to another user account is a process that can be handled much more efficiently by Postfix itself. However, if some logic needs to be applied to deciding what or where to send the message then Procmail can assist.

Most mail transports will allow you to pass multiple e-mail addresses for onward transmission.

```
! user1@domain2.net user2@domain1.com user3 ...
```

The above action is functionally the same as passing the message to the following pipeline:

```
| $SENDMAIL "$SENDMAILFLAGS"
```

This is a special case for forwarding mail and instructs Procmail to extract the list of recipients from the original message's actual headers:

```
! -t
```

EXAMPLE

Here we will forward mail to our support team rather than handle it ourselves. The mail includes the phrase support in the subject line.

```
:0:
* ^Subject.*support
! support@adepteo.net
```

Feed to a Shell or Command Pipeline

Procmail allows a virtually unlimited amount of freedom in what can be done to an e-mail. One of the more powerful features of working with Procmail is its ability to forward an e-mail based on given criteria to an application program or script. A possible example would be to track support requests and have the entries stored directly into a database system where they can be tracked within a dedicated application.

The pipeline process is responsible for saving its output. The recipe's flags are able to tell Procmail to expect something else. By using the >> syntax, Procmail can determine a lock file to use. It is important to always use locking when writing to a file so as to avoid two operations writing to the same file at the same time and corrupting each other's data.

```
| cmd1 param1 | cmd2 -opt param2 >>file
```

It is possible to have the output of the command pipeline stored in a variable. This by its own action makes the recipe a non-delivering recipe.

```
VAR=| cmd1 | cmd2 ...
```

Please note that this syntax is only allowed on the action line. For the same result in a plain assignment, you may use ` (back tick) operators.

```
VERBOSE=1
#Copy the data and pass the headers to the process
:0hc:
* ^Subject: Book Pipeline Example
#Copy so that the next recipe will still work
| cat - > /tmp/cjt_header.txt

#Final recipe so do not copy here, but pass the body
:0b:
| cat - > /tmp/cjt_body.txt

VERBOSE=0
```

Save to a Folder

This saves the output to a plain file. If only a filename is provided then the file will be created in the directory specified in the MAILDIR setting. Always make sure that you use some form of locking when writing to a plain file.

```
/path/to/filename
```

The /. at the end of the path name instructs Procmail to store the item in an MH formatted folder.

```
directory/.
```

If you want to store the data into several MH folders, you can list them all at the same time. The result will be that only one file will actually be written, the rest will be created as hard links.

When saving to a directory, files will be created with sequentially numbered files within the directory. The trailing slash is not strictly necessary but it aids with understanding the script's intentions when reading it again later.

```
directory/
```

Compound Recipe

If you want to perform a number of conditional processes or actions on a matched item then instead of a single action line you can specify an block of recipes to be used using the { and } (braces) characters. There must be at least one space after the { and before the } characters.

```
{
    # ... more recipes
}
```

The code between the braces can be any valid Procmail construct.

> Note that an action that is a variable assignment always has to go inside a set of braces: { VAR=value }. Using just VAR=value without the braces would result in the data being saved to a folder named VAR=value.

If you want a recipe that does not actually do any processing—perhaps as part of an if…else operation—then you can use an empty set of { } but the rules regarding the whitespace still apply and you need to ensure that there is at least one whitespace character between the two braces.

The following example takes the previous example and modifies it slightly so that only one test is performed and then a series of unconditional tests are run if the test passes:

```
VERBOSE=1
:0:
* ^Subject: Book Pipeline Example
  {
    #Copy so that the next recipe will still work
    :0hc:
    | cat - > /tmp/cjt_header.txt

    #Final recipe so do not copy here
    :0b:
    | cat - > /tmp/cjt_body.txt
  }
VERBOSE=0
```

Regular Expressions

Procmail implements a form of regular expressions that operates slightly differently to other UNIX utilities. Here we cover the basic differences and guide the new user into the powerful world of Regular Expressions, their meanings, implementations, and uses.

We have already seen that Procmail matches are case insensitive unless the D flag is used. This is also true for regular expressions. Procmail also uses multiline matches by default.

Introduction to Regular Expressions

If you are new to the world of Linux and programming in general, you could well have escaped the powerful features that Regular Expressions bring to processing data. In its simplest form, Regular Expressions can be understood as searching for a phrase or pattern anywhere in a body of data. The following simple example shows you how to match all mail items where the header and/or body contains the phrase `mystical monsters` and place the mail in a relevant folder.

```
:0 HB:
* mystical monsters
{$MAILDIR}/monsters
```

This filter would not, however, match items that contained the phrase `mystical monster` or `mystical-monsters` for example. So the real power of regular expressions can be seen in the ability to describe text or data patterns in a simplified format and then search for matches to those patterns in a body of data. Beware, however, not to be mislead by the word *simplified*. The majority of regular expressions that you will come across in real life may well be anything but simple to read if written in the native format. Take the following example, which is intended to determine if a mail item is MIME-encoded and store it in a suitable folder if it is.

```
:0:
* ^Content-Type: multipart/[^;]+;[ ]*boundary="?\/[^"]+
{$MAILDIR}/mime
```

The characters ., [, ^, ;,], +, ?, \, /, and " are special instructions rather than the literal ASCII character they normally portray. To understand these characters and their meanings we will take a whirlwind tour through the most important examples.

The Dot

This is the simplest and most common form of regular expression and simply means match any single character, (excluding a newline character, which is considered a special case). Consider the following expression:

```
:0
* Dragons ... mystical monsters
${MAILDIR}/result
```

This would match any of the following phrases:

Dragons are mystical monsters

Dragons and mystical monsters

Dragons but mystical monsters

In fact, it will match any phrase with a three-character word between Dragons and mystical. If we wanted to match any length of word with three or more characters between Dragons and Mystical, we could use the '?' or quantifier operation.

In case you want to match a literal '.' or more than one '.' you can escape any character that has special significance to a regular expression string by preceding it by a '\' so that '\.' will literally match a '.' (period) and '\\' will literally match a '\' (backslash) character.

Quantifier Operation '?'

The question mark indicates that the preceding character should be matched zero or one time only. So the following lines of code will meet our requirements:

```
:0
* Dragons ....? Mystical monsters
${MAILDIR}/result
```

This expression could be read as "Match any word consisting of three or more characters followed by nothing or any one character".

The character preceding the ? may also be a simple ASCII character in which case the expression would match as follows:

```
:0
* Dragons ..d? Mystical monsters
${MAILDIR}/result
```

Could be read as "Any two characters followed by either nothing or a letter d" and so would match both an and and but not are.

The Asterisk *

The asterisk modifier works in a similar way to the ? but means match zero or more of the preceding character except, of course, a newline. The .* is a very common sequence that you will find in a large number of recipes.

The following example will match all messages that include the word choose followed by some other words followed by the word online:

```
:0
* ^Subject: Choose.*online
${MAILDIR}/result
```

Subject: Choose discount pharmacy and expedite the service online.
Subject: Choose hassle free online shopping
Subject: Choose reliable online shopping site for reliable service and quality meds
Subject: Choose reliable service provider and save more online.
Subject: Choose the supplier for more hot offers online
Subject: Choose to shop online and choose to save

The next example will look for 'anything' (.*) followed by two (!!) or more (!*) exclamation marks:

```
:0
* ^Subject: .*!!!*
${MAILDIR}/result
```

Subject: Breathtaking New Year sale on now!!! Get ready for it!!
Subject: Hey Ya!! New Year Sale on right now!!
Subject: It Doesn't Matter!!

The Plus Sign +

The plus sign is very similar to the * except that it requires that there must be at least one instance of the character preceding the + in the regular expression.

If we consider our previous example, the next example will look for 'anything' .* followed by two !! and at least one more (!+) exclamation marks:

```
:0
* ^Subject: .*!!!*
${MAILDIR}/result
```

This would now give us a more restricted output where at least three ! in a row would be required.

Subject: Breathtaking New Year sale on now!!! Get ready for it!!

Restrictive Matches Using ( )

So far the matching patterns that we have been able to create are powerful but work in a rather unfocussed way. For example, we can easily write a rule to find any three-letter word ending in t but cannot limit the matches to only a given set of words ending in t. To overcome this we can replace the . or single character with a group of characters or sets of groups of characters in a list and then apply the quantifier operations to say exactly how many times these can be applied.

By careful use of the ( ) parentheses we can create groups of strings that we will use in the pattern matching rules. For instance, let us assume we are trying to split e-mails that are sent by a system script on a frequent basis. The script formats the subject line to have one of the following phrases in the subject line.

There is only one problem

There are 10 problems

The following regular expression will match the specific string we are looking for by matching any string that has one or more occurrences of the phrase is only one between there and problem.

```
There (is only one)* problem
```

If we wanted to filter a list of words or phrases then we would need to use the **Alternation** feature.

```
There (is only one|are)* problem
```

The | character separates lists of words that could be used to match against the pattern.

The following simple spam filter uses the alternation feature to search for text substitutions regularly used in a bid to avoid the simple word-based filters.

A Simple Spam Filter

With the growing numbers of spam messages that we receive every day I am sure that some of you reading so far will have figured out that we could start to filter some of the regular messages that we receive on a daily basis. There are a number of specific spam filters that are designed to work closely with Procmail and offer a far larger set of tests and coverage for spam filtering. One such application, **SpamAssassin**, is covered in Chapter 8.

Take for example a popular subject for spammers who encourage us to explore—Online Casinos. It is something that we are not usually interested in and so we feel happy to filter all messages that contain the words Online and Casinos into a separate folder.

Subject: Online Casino

Part of the challenge of spammers is to write subject lines that we can read while spam filters find difficult to process. A simple way of doing this is to substitute commonly mistyped characters such as Zero (0) for letter O or letter o, 1 for L or l and 4 for A or a.

So we could progress and write the rule as:

```
Subject: (o|0)n(1|l)ine casin(o|0)
```

The final iteration of this recipe is shown below where we are specifically looking for subject lines that contain both the words online and casino but to include the occasions where the word may be in different order each word is tested separately.

```
:0
* ^Subject: (o|0)n(1|l)ine
* ^Subject: casin(o|0)
${MAILDIR}/_maybespam
```

While this would work quite well, it is not really efficient to have rules that work in this way and as this sort of substitution is a common requirement for regular expressions there is a special way of expressing these terms in the **Character Classes**.

Character Classes

Any sequence of characters contained in a square brackets [ ] indicates that the listed characters are each to be checked in the expression. For common occurrences of sequences of characters such as the letters of the alphabet or a range of numbers it is possible to use [a-z] or [0-9]:

[a-e] means match all the letters a, b, c, d, e inclusive.

[1,3,5-9] means match any of the numbers 1, or 3 or 5, 6, 7, 8, or 9.

The following example will find messages that embed numbers 0 and 1 within text strings so that they look like O and L or I

```
:0
* ^Subject: [a-z]*[01]+[a-z]*
${MAILDIR}/_maybespam
```

Subject: Hot Shot St0ckInfo VCSC loadstone
Subject: M1CR0S0FT, SYMANNTEC, MACR0MEDIA, PC GAMES FROM $20 EACH
Subject: R0LEX Replica - make your first impressions count!
Subject: Small-Cap DTOI St0cks reimburse
Subject: TimelySt0ck DTOI Buy of the Week evasive

Start of Line

If we wanted to match all of a wide range of characters and not match a small number of ranges it is easier to specify the negative match using the ^ character:

```
[^0-9]
```

This means to match any string that begins with anything that is not a number between 0 and 9.

It is useful to add a start of line anchor to patterns we are searching for when we know that the pattern should start the line. For example, all headers must start on the beginning of the line so searching for the following phrase:

```
Subject: any subject message
```

Would also match headers that begin with a phrase such as:

```
Old-Subject:
```

To stop this happening we can add the **Start of Line Anchor Character** ^ and change the regular expression to:

```
^Subject: any subject message
```

End of Line

When we are planning to match strings that we know to terminate, we can add the **line termination anchor character**, $ to the pattern to ensure that we match right to the end of the string as follows:

```
^Subject:.* now$
```

This will match any subject line that ends in the word now.

Procmail Macros

As we briefly covered in the previous chapter, Procmail has a number of useful 'pre-prepared' regular expressions or Macros that provide a range of matches that are commonly used in Procmail recipes.

^TO and ^TO_

^TO was the original Procmail Macro for handling to addresses. This has been superseded by the newer ^TO_ macro that was introduced in Procmail Version 3.11pre4.

This catchall includes most headers that can include your address in them, such as To:, Apparently-To:, Cc:, Resent-To:, and so on.

In most cases you should use the ^TO_ option as it has much better coverage.

> Although it would seem logical to have a similar macro to cover the source address details, note that there is *no* corresponding ^FROM or ^FROM_ macro.

Here is the Regular Expression string from the Procmail source code:

```
"(^((Original-)?(Resent-)?(To|Cc|Bcc)|\
(X-Envelope|Apparently(-Resent)?)-To):(.*[^-a-zA-Z0-9_.])?)"
```

^FROM_MAILER

This macro caters for recognizing a wide range of mail generation programs and is a useful catchall; however, new programs are being created all the time and so additional filters will nearly always be required.

Procmail expands this short Macro into the following Regular Expression as taken from the Procmail source code.

```
"(^(Mailing-List:|Precedence:.*(junk|bulk|list)|\
To: Multiple recipients of |\
(((Resent-)?(From|Sender)|X-Envelope-From):|>?From )([^>]*[^(.%@a-z0-
9])?(\
Post(ma?(st(e?r)?|n)|office)|(send)?Mail(er)?|daemon|m(mdf|ajordomo)|
n?uucp|\
LIST(SERV|proc)|NETSERV|o(wner|ps)|r(e(quest|sponse)|oot)|b(ounce|bs\
\.smtp)|\
echo|mirror|s(erv(ices?|er)|mtp(error)?|ystem)|\
A(dmin(istrator)?|MMGR|utoanswer)\
)(([^).!:a-z0-9][-_a-z0-9]*)?[%@> ][^<)]*(\\(.*\\).*)?)?$([^>]|$)))"
```

^FROM_DAEMON

This takes a similar approach to the ^FROM_MAILER but is intended to identify messages from the more common Linux daemons and system processes.

Regular Expression string from Procmail source code.

```
"(^(((Resent-)?(From|Sender)|X-Envelope-From):|\
>?From )([^>]*[^(.%@a-z0-9])?(\
Post(ma(st(er)?|n)|office)|(send)?Mail(er)?|daemon|mmdf|n?uucp|ops|\
r(esponse|oot)|(bbs\\.)?smtp(error)?|s(erv(ices?|er)|ystem)|A(dmin(is
trator)?|\
```

```
MMGR)\
)((([^).!:a-z0-9][-_a-z0-9]*)?[%@> ][^<)]*(\\(.*\\).*)?)?$([^>]|$))"
```

EXAMPLE

The following example will store the daemon messages received in a folder that includes the year and month as part of the path. These variables ${YY} and ${MM} are assigned previously in the Procmail file and the necessary directories are also created.

```
:0:
* ^FROM_DAEMON
${YY}/${MM}/daemon
```

Advanced Recipe Examples

Here we are going to assemble the various items of Procmail capability into a couple of useful recipes that you can use as the basis for tools within your own organization. The first example is based on the traditional vacation script that informs senders of your e-mail that the message may not be read for some time. The second shows how to create the support to automatically file messages based on the date and possibly time of being processed. Finally we will complete the rule started in the previous chapter to inform the user of large mail items that have been filtered off into a separate folder.

Example 1: Vacation Auto-Reply

This example is based upon the vacation example given in man procmailex and referred to briefly earlier in this chapter.

As we have already discussed, blindly and automatically responding to an e-mail is a very bad idea and has significant ramifications. First we must decide whether to send an auto-reply. To do this we need to make sure that conditions make sense and are satisfied. If so, headers (signified by the h flag) of the current message are fed to formail, a utility program that is part of the Procmail suite of utilities. formail then checks the vacation.cache file to find out if the sender has already received an auto-reply. This is to make sure we are not sending multiple reports to a user. While this part of the processing is going on, our script will create a lock as vacation.lock.

The main reason for this is to avoid clashes when updating the cache, which could result in corruption of the cache information.

The recipe actually comprises two individual recipes. The first one provides the checks and recording of replies sent to ensure that we don't send duplicate or repetitive replies.

This recipe waits w for a return from formail. Without the c, Procmail would stop processing after completing this recipe because it is a delivery recipe. It delivers headers to formail.

There are more to the TO_ and ^FROM_DAEMON conditions than what meets the eye.

TO_ $<logname> is satisfied if the user's login name appears in any recipient header To:, Cc:, Bcc:. This avoids sending auto-replies to messages that were addressed to an alias or mail list, but not explicitly to our user.

!^FROM_DAEMON makes sure we do not auto-reply to messages from any of a wide variety of daemons.

!^X-Loop: $RECIPIENT avoids replying to our own auto-reply; notice that this X-Loop header is inserted into the auto-replies we send out.

```
:0 whc: vacation.lock
# Perform a quick check to see if the mail was addressed to us
* $^To_:.*\<$\LOGNAME\>
# Don't reply to daemons and mailinglists
* !^FROM_DAEMON
# Mail loops are evil
* !^X-Loop: $RECIPIENT
| formail -rD 8192 vacation.cache
```

The second part of the recipe takes place if the first one did not find a match in the cache. There are two reasons that the address was not found—either it has never been seen and so no reply has been sent, or it was seen so long ago that the entry has been forced out of the cache. In either case, a copy of the vacation message will be sent. The sender will never receive an automatic reply for every single message that they send—something that can really upset a prolific mail writer.

Due to e, the recipe below is executed if the preceding one returns an error status. In this case it is not really an error, it is just the signal from formail that the address didn't exist in the cache file and to go ahead with the auto-reply. Notice that if in the preceding recipe the conditions are not met causing the formail cache check to be skipped, Procmail is clever enough to skip this recipe.

The headers of the current message are fed to the formail in this recipe in order to construct the headers for the auto-reply.

The c in this recipe causes the entire current message to be processed after this recipe. Typically this means that it will be processed with no further recipes and that is how you get a copy in your mailbox. There is no need for a lock while executing this recipe so none is used.

All that is required to send back to the sender of the original message is a copy of the message, and that is held in the file .vacation_message in the user's home directory.

Storing the message information outside the Procmail script makes it easy to allow your system users to easily update the message that they send out without risk of them breaking the actual script itself.

```
:0 ehc
# if the name was not in the cache
|   (
    formail -rA"Precedence: junk" \
    -A"X-Loop: $RECIPIENT" ; \
    cat $HOME/.vacation_message \
    ) | $SENDMAIL -oi -t
```

Example 2: Organize Mail by Date

You may not want to delete mail that you feel may one day be useful. This can easily lead to gigabytes of data being stored in a variety of locations. It is possible to filter some or all of your incoming mails into folders based on a combination of the year, month, and topic so that they can be track down easily.

A generic rule that is applied to every mail process ensures that the necessary directory structure exists.

```
#Assign the name of the folder
        MONTHFOLDER=`date +%y/%m`

#Unconditional rule to create the folder
        :0 ic
        * ? test ! -d ${MONTHFOLDER}
        | mkdir -p ${MONTHFOLDER}

#Alternative way of creating the folder using an assignment operation
        DUMMY=`test -d $MONTHFOLDER || mkdir $MONTHFOLDER`

#Now store the data in an appropriate folder
        :0:
        * meeting
        ${MONTHFOLDER}/meeting
```

If you would prefer slightly more control over the output format or location, you may use these rules instead:

```
#This obtains the date formatted as YYYY MM DD
        date = `date "+%Y %m %d"`
#Now assign the Year YYYY style
        :0
        * date ?? ^^()\/
        { YYYY = $MATCH }
#Now assign the Year YY style
        :0
        * date ?? ^^..\/
        { YY = $MATCH }
#Now assign the Month MM style
        :0
        * date ?? ^^.....\/
        { MM = $MATCH }
#Now assign the Day DD style
        :0
        * date ?? ()\/..^^
        { DD = $MATCH }
```

```
#Create the various directory formats you are going to use
      DUMMY=`test -d ${YYYY}/${MM}/${DD} || mkdir -p
${YYYY}/${MM}/${DD}`
      DUMMY=`test -d ${YY}/${MM} || mkdir -p ${YY}/${MM}`

#Now store the data in an appropriate folder
      :0:
      * ^FROM_DAEMON
      ${YYYY}/${MM}/${DD}/daemon
```

Example 3: Inform Users of Large Mail

In the previous chapter we introduced a very simple rule that stored all incoming mail over 100kb in size in a largemail folder. This was useful in keeping the size of individual incoming mail folders from growing too large, but meant that a special check had to be made regularly to see if any mail had been filtered off.

In this rule we will now extract the headers and subject line plus the first few lines of the original large e-mail message and create a new message with a modified subject line. This modified message will be stored in the user's inbox at the same time as filtering the large original item into its separate largemail folder.

The main part of the test will only be applied if the size of the message is over 100,000 bytes in size so we will need a structure similar to the following recipe to do the initial testing and decide if this is a large item or not:

```
:0:
* >100000
{
MAIN PROCESS WILL GO HERE
}
```

Assuming that we do have a large item we then need to make a copy of the message using the c flag and store this copy in the largemail folder:

```
#Place a copy in the largemail folder
:0 c:
largemail
```

Extracting the first part of the body of the message comes next and this can be done using a variety of options. In this case we are going to strip off the first 1024 bytes of the message by waiting for the results of passing the body of the message only through to the system head command and telling it to return only the first 1024 bytes. The flags used here tell Procmail to wait for the results of the command-line process and to ignore any pipeline errors as the head command will only read part of the data being offered to it.

```
#Strip the body to 1kb
:0 bfwi
| /usr/bin/head -c1024
```

Now we need to rewrite the subject line, which is done using the formail program. This time we pass just the headers through to the command line and wait for the response.

In this case though, we need to obtain the current subject line so that we can pass it through to the formail program as part of the modified subject line. We do this by doing a simple match on the subject contents and then passing the $MATCH variable, which now holds the subject line contents as an argument to the formail program. For neatness we add the {* -BIG- *} wording before the original subject line to make it easy to sort and identify these messages.

```
#ReWrite the subject line
:0 fhw
* ^Subject:\/.*
| formail -I "Subject: {* -BIG- *} $MATCH"
```

Normal delivery of the message will then take place and the new shorter message will be stored in the inbox.

If we put all of this together we end up with the following complete recipe.

```
:0:
* >100000
{
#Place a copy in the largemail folder
:0 c:
largemail

#Strip the body to 1kb
:0 bfwi
| /usr/bin/head -c1024

#ReWrite the subject line
:0 fhw
* ^Subject:\/.*
| formail -I "Subject: {* -BIG- *} $MATCH"
}
```

Putting it all Together

We have covered a wide range of topics in this chapter and in an attempt to pull it all together the following example, which is based upon a simplified version of the Procmail rule files that are commonly used for e-mail processing, has been included. I hope that you find it useful in creating your own mail filtering strategy.

Creating a Structure to Base Your Own Rules Upon

Grouping related aspects of the Procmail rules and configuration will make your installation easier to maintain and less likely to create problems when making changes.

Within the main Procmail directory create individual files following a consistent naming convention such as rc.main, rc.spam, rc.lists, and so on. Then include each of these into your main .procmailrc file as follows.

```
#This obtains the date formatted as YYYY MM DD
        date = `date "+%Y %m %d"`
```

```
#Now assign the Year YYYY style
      :0
      * date ?? ^^()\/
      { YYYY = $MATCH }
#Now assign the Year YY style
      :0
      * date ?? ^^..\/
      { YY = $MATCH }
#Now assign the Month MM style
      :0
      * date ?? ^^.....\/
      { MM = $MATCH }
#Now assign the Day DD style
      :0
      * date ?? ()\/..^^
      { DD = $MATCH }
#Create the various directory formats you are going to use
      DUMMY=`test -d ${YYYY}/${MM}/${DD} || mkdir -p
${YYYY}/${MM}/${DD}`
      DUMMY=`test -d ${YY}/${MM} || mkdir -p ${YY}/${MM}`

#Make a backup copy of all incoming mail
      :0 c
      backup
#Restrict the history to just 23 mail items
      :0 ic
      | cd backup && rm -f dummy `ls -t msg.* | sed -e 1,32d`
#Make sure that all mails have a valid From value
      :0 fhw
      | formail -I "From " -a "From "
#
## Don't include this unless we need to
## INCLUDERC=${HOME}/Procmail/rc.testing
##
## Now include the various process listings
INCLUDERC=${HOME}/Procmail/rc.system
INCLUDERC=${HOME}/Procmail/rc.lists
INCLUDERC=${HOME}/Procmail/rc.killspam
INCLUDERC=${HOME}/Procmail/rc.vacation
INCLUDERC=${HOME}/Procmail/rc.largefiles
INCLUDERC=${HOME}/Procmail/rc.virusfilter
INCLUDERC=${HOME}/Procmail/rc.spamfilter
```

Now for each of the listed include files, create the file as named and include the rules related to the container in that file. It then becomes a matter of commenting out an INCLUDERC reference for temporarily isolating a section of processing for incoming mail.

Rc.system

```
#Filter system mail messages
:0:
* ^From:.*root@delta.adepteo.net
${YY}/${MM}/daemon

:0:
* ^From:.*root@ramsbottom.adepteo.net
${YY}/${MM}/daemon
```

```
:0:
* ^TO_pager@adepteo.net
${YY}/${MM}/daemon

:0:
* ^From:.*MAILER-DAEMON@delta.adepteo.net
${YY}/${MM}/daemon

:0:
* ^From:.*me@localhost.com
${YY}/${MM}/daemon
```

Rc.lists

```
#Mailing lists
#Store by date folder

:0:
* ^From:.*mapserver-users-admin@lists.gis.umn.edu
${YY}/${MM}/mapserver

:0:
* ^TO_mapserver-users@lists.gis.umn.edu
${YY}/${MM}/mapserver

:0:
* ^From:.*yourtopjob@topjobs.co.uk
${YY}/${MM}/jobs

:0:
* ^Subject: silicon Jobs-by-Email Alert
${YY}/${MM}/jobs
:0:
* ^Reply-To: Axandra Search Engine Facts <facts@Axandra.com>
${YY}/${MM}/lists

:0:
* ^Subject: A Joke A Day
${YY}/${MM}/lists

:0:
* ^List-Owner: <mailto:owner-tribune@lists.sitepoint.com>
${YY}/${MM}/lists

:0:
* ^Reply-To: newsletter@192.com
${YY}/${MM}/lists

:0:
* ^Subject: Developer Shed Weekly Update
${YY}/${MM}/lists
```

Rc.killspam

```
#Kill file for known spammers
#Store as probably known spam
```

Rc.vacation

```
#Vacation Replies
:0 whc: vacation.lock
# Perform a quick check to see if the mail was addressed to us
* $^To_:.*\<$\LOGNAME\>
# Don't reply to daemons and mailinglists
* !^FROM_DAEMON
# Mail loops are evil
* !^X-Loop: $RECIPIENT
| formail -rD 8192 vacation.cache


:0 ehc
# if the name was not in the cache
| (
    formail -rA"Precedence: junk" \
    -A"X-Loop: $RECIPIENT" ; \
    cat $HOME/.vacation_message \
    ) | $SENDMAIL -oi -t
```

Rc.largefiles

```
#Assume that files larger than 100k are not spam
    :0:
    * >100000
    {
        #Place a copy in the largemail folder
        :0 c:
        largemail

        #Strip the body to 1kb
        :0 bfwi
        | /usr/bin/head -c1024

        #ReWrite the subject line
        :0 fhw
        * ^Subject:\/.*
        | formail -I "Subject: {* -BIG- *} $MATCH"
    }
```

Rc.viruses

```
#Virus Filter
    #X-Virus-Status: Infected
    :0:
    * ^X-Virus-Status: Infected
    _virus
```

Rc.spamfilter

```
#Spam Filter
:0fw
* < 256000
| spamc
```

```
# Mails with a score of 15 or higher are almost certainly spam (with
0.05%
```

```
# false positives according to rules/STATISTICS.txt). Let's put them
in a
# different mbox. (This one is optional.)
:0:
* ^X-Spam-Level: \*\*\*\*\*\*\*\*\*\*\*\*\*\*\*\*
_almost-certainly-spam

# All mail tagged as spam (eg. with a score higher than the set
threshold)
# is moved to "probably-spam".
:0:
* ^X-Spam-Status: Yes
_probably-spam
```

Summary

In this chapter we have explored Procmail to discover a large number of services and a large amount of functionality that it can provide in getting mail under control. While we have covered a lot, there is still a lot to be learned and there are a large number of resources available on the Web dedicated to this one particular application.

Hopefully you will now have a strong grasp of the core functionality, and how to implement it, and also how to go about exploring your real-life needs and creating recipe sets that you can combine to create your own unique mail filtering strategy.

8
Busting Spam with SpamAssassin

SpamAssassin is a very popular open-source anti-spam tool. It is considered to be the best free, open-source, anti-spam tool, and better than many commercial products. In this chapter, we will learn how to download, install, and configure SpamAssassin to filter incoming e-mail. SpamAssassin can be effective in removing 80% to 95% of spam, with little effort from the system administrator.

Why Filter E-Mail?

If you don't receive any spam then there may be no need to filter spam. However, once one spam has been received, it is invariably followed by another; spammers can sometimes detect if a spam is viewed, and then know that an e-mail address is valid and vulnerable. If spam is filtered, then the initial e-mail may never get seen, and consequently the spammer may not then target the e-mail address with further spam.

Despite legal efforts against spam, it is actually on the increase. In Europe and the US, the recent legislation against spam (Directive 2002/58/EC and bill number S.877 respectively), have had little effect, and spam is still on the increase in both regions.

The main reason for this is that spam is a very good business model. It is very cheap to send spam, as little as one thousandth of a cent per e-mail, and it takes a very low 'hit rate' before a profit is made. The spammer only needs to turn one spam in a hundred thousand or so into a sale to make a profit. As a result, there are many spammers, and spam is used to promote a wide range of goods.

In contrast, the costs of spam to the recipient are remarkably high. Estimates have varied, from 10 cents per spam received, through 1,000 dollars per employee per year, up to a total cost of eight billion dollars in 2001. This cost is mainly labor—distracting people from their work by clogging up their inboxes and forcing them to deal with many extra e-mails. Spam interferes with day-to-day work, and can include material that is offensive to most people. Companies have a duty to protect their employees from such content, and spam filtering is a very cheap way of minimizing the costs and protecting the workforce.

Spam is a Moving Target

Spam isn't static. It changes on a day-to-day basis, as spammers add new methods to their arsenal, and anti-spammers develop countermeasures. Due to this, the anti-spam tools that work best are those that are updated frequently. It's a similar predicament to antivirus software: virus definitions need to be updated regularly or new viruses won't be detected.

SpamAssassin is regularly updated. In addition to new releases of the software, there is a community creating, critiquing, and testing new anti-spam rules. These rules can be downloaded, often automatically, for up-to-date protection against spam. One good place to do this is from www.rulesemporium.com.

Let's discuss some of the measures used by SpamAssassin to fight spam:

- **Open relays**: These are e-mail servers that allow spammers to send e-mails even though they are not connected to the owner of the server in any way. To counter this, the anti-spam community has developed **blocklists**, also known as **blacklists**, which can be used by anti-spam software to detect spam. Any e-mail that has passed through a server on a blocklist is treated more suspiciously than one that has not. SpamAssassin uses a number of blocklists to test e-mails.

- **Keyword filters**: These are useful tools against spam. Spammers tend to repeat the same words and phrases again and again. Rules to detect these phrases are used extensively by SpamAssassin. These make up the bulk of the tests, and the user community rules mentioned above are normally of this form. They allow specific words, phrases, or sequences of letters, numbers, and punctuation to be detected.

- **Blacklists and whitelists**: These are used to list known senders of spam, and sources of good e-mail. E-mails from an address on a blacklist are probably spam, and treated as such, while e-mails from addresses on a whitelist will be less likely to be treated as spam. SpamAssassin allows the user to enter blacklists and whitelists manually and also builds up an automatic whitelist and blacklist based on the e-mail that it processes.

- **Statistical filters**: These are automated systems that give the probability that an e-mail is spam. This filtration is based on what the filter has seen previously as both spam and non-spam. They generally work by finding words that are present in one type of e-mail but not the other, and using this knowledge to determine which type a new e-mail is. SpamAssassin has a statistical filter called the **Bayesian Filter**, which can be very effective in improving detection rates.

- **Content databases**: These are mass e-mail detection systems. Many, many e-mail servers receive e-mails, and they submit the e-mails to central servers. If the same e-mail is sent to thousands of recipients, it is probably a spam. The content databases prevent confidential e-mails from being sent to the server, by using a technique called **hashing**, which also lowers the amount of data sent to the server. SpamAssassin can integrate with several content databases, notably Razor, Pyzor, and the Distributed Checksum Clearinghouse.

- **URL Blocklists**: These are similar to open relay blocklists, but list the web sites used by spammers. In nearly all spam, a web address is given. A database of these is built up so that spam e-mails can be quickly detected. This is a very efficient and effective tool against spam. By default, SpamAssassin uses **SURBLs**, or to give them their full name **Spam URI Realtime Blocklists**, without any further configuration required.

Spam Filtering Options

Spam can be filtered on the server, or on the client. The two approaches are as explained below. In the first scenario, spam is filtered on the client:

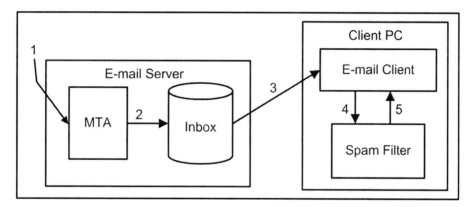

1. Incoming e-mail is processed by the MTA.
2. The e-mail is then placed in the appropriate user's inbox.
3. The e-mail client reads all new e-mail from the inbox.
4. The e-mail client then passes the e-mail to the filter.
5. When the filter returns the results the client can display the valid e-mail and either discard spam or file it in a separate folder.

In this approach, the spam filtering is always done at the client, and always when new e-mail is processed. Often when the user may be present, he or she may either experience a delay before e-mail is visible, or there may be a period where spam e-mail is present in the inbox. The amount of spam filtering that can be performed on the client may be limited; in particular, the **network tests** such as open relay blocklists or SURBLs might be too time-consuming or complex to perform on the user's PC. As spam is a moving target, updating many client PCs can become a difficult administrative task.

In the second scenario, the spam filtering is performed on the e-mail server:

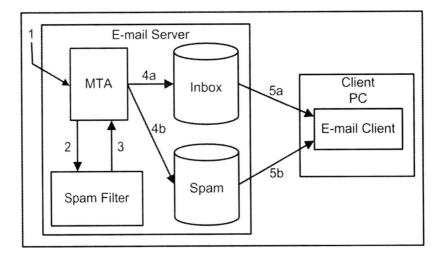

1. Incoming e-mail is received by the MTA.
2. It is then passed on to the spam filter.
3. The results are then sent back to the MTA.
4. Depending on the results, the MTA places the e-mail in the appropriate user's inbox, or in a separate inbox for spam.
5. The e-mail client accesses e-mails in the user's inbox and it can also access the spam folder if required.

This approach has several advantages:

- The spam filtering is done when the e-mail is received, which may be any time of the day. The user is less likely to be inconvenienced by delays.
- The server can specialize in spam filtering. It may use external services such as open relay blocklists, online content databases, and SURBLs.
- Configuration is centralized, which will ease setup (for example, firewalls may need to be configured to use online spam tests), and also maintenance (updating of rules or software).

SpamAssassin in Detail

Spam filtering actually involves two phases—detecting the spam and then doing something with it. SpamAssassin is a spam detector and it modifies the e-mail it processes by putting in headers to mark whether it is spam or not. It is up to the MTA or something else in the e-mail system to react to the headers that SpamAssassin creates in an e-mail, to filter it out.

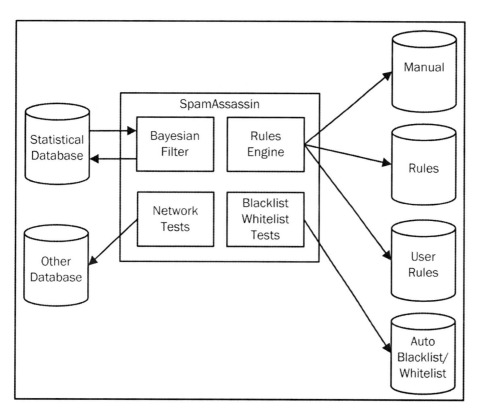

A schematic of SpamAssassin is shown above. At the heart of SpamAssassin is its rules engine. This determines which rules are called. Rules trigger whether the various tests are used, including the Bayesian Filter, the network tests, and the auto-whitelists.

SpamAssassin uses various databases to do its work, and these are shown too. The rules and scores are text files—default rules and scores are included in the SpamAssassin distribution, and, as we will see, both system administrators and users can add rules or change the scores of existing rules by adding them to files in specific locations. The Bayesian filter (which is a major part of SpamAssassin, and will be covered later) uses a database of statistical data based on previous spam and non-spam e-mails. The auto-blacklist/whitelist also creates its own database.

Getting SpamAssassin

SpamAssassin is slightly different to most of the software that is used in this book. It is written in a language called **Perl**, which has its own distribution method called **CPAN (Comprehensive Perl Archive Network)**. CPAN is a large web site of Perl software (normally, Perl *modules*), and the term CPAN also covers software to download those modules and install them. Though SpamAssassin is provided as a package by many Linux distributions, we recommend that you install it from source rather than use a package.

Most Perl users will build Perl modules using CPAN and experience no difficulties. CPAN can automatically locate and install any dependencies (other components that are required to make the desired component work properly). From a Perl point of view, using CPAN to install Perl modules is like using the rpm command in Linux. The basics are very simple, and once a system is configured, it generally works every time.

However, some people may be put off learning and configuring a new way of installing software. SpamAssassin is available via the **RedHat Package Manager (RPM)** for many distributions, and is also offered as an RPM from the SpamAssassin web site. The SpamAssassin team members themselves advise that the latest version should be installed, and now provide a method of installing SpamAssassin on an RPM-based system. We strongly advise you to install via CPAN or using the rpmbuild command as described below, in preference to using an RPM provided by a manufacturer.

As SpamAssassin is a Perl Module, it appears on CPAN first—in fact, it is only released when it arrives at CPAN. Users of CPAN can download the latest version of SpamAssassin literally minutes after it has been released.

Support is also easier to obtain if SpamAssassin is built from source. Some distributors make unusual decisions when creating their RPM of SpamAssassin, or may modify certain default values. These make obtaining support more difficult.

RPMs also take time to be delivered. For example, SpamAssassin 3.0 was released on September 22, 2004, but the RPM for Fedora Core Linux was not created until October 19, 2004. Some distributors may be quicker, but this cannot be relied on.

Using CPAN

The prerequisites for installing SpamAssassin 3.0 using CPAN are as follows:

- **Perl version 5.6.1 or later**: Most modern Linux distributions will include this as part of the base package.

- **C compiler**: This may not be installed by default and may have to be added using the rpm command. The compiler used will normally be called gcc.

- **Internet connection**: CPAN will attempt to download the modules using HTTP or FTP, so the network should be configured to allow this.

Configuring CPAN

If you've used CPAN before, you can skip to the next section, *Installing SpamAssassin Using CPAN*.

If a proxy server is required for internet traffic, CPAN (and other Perl modules and scripts) will use the HTTP_proxy environment variable. If the proxy requires a user name and password, these need to be specified using environment variables. As CPAN is normally run as root, these commands should be entered as root:

```
# HTTP_proxy=http://proxy.name:80
# export HTTP_proxy
# HTTP_proxy_user=username
# export HTTP_proxy_user
# HTTP_proxy_pass=password
# export HTTP_proxy_pass
```

Next, enter this command:

```
# perl -MCPAN -e shell
```

If the output is similar to the following, the CPAN module is already installed and configured and you can skip to the next section, *Installing SpamAssassin Using CPAN*.

```
cpan shell -- CPAN exploration and modules installation (v1.7601)
ReadLine support enabled
```

If the output is similar to the following, the CPAN module is installed but not configured.

```
/root/.cpan/CPAN/MyConfig.pm initialized.

CPAN is the world-wide archive of perl resources. It consists of
about 100 sites that all replicate the same contents all around the
globe. Many countries have at least one CPAN site already. The
resources found on CPAN are easily accessible with the CPAN.pm
module. If you want to use CPAN.pm, you have to configure it
properly.

If you do not want to enter a dialog now, you can answer 'no' to this
question and I'll try to autoconfigure. (Note: you can revisit this
dialog anytime later by typing 'o conf init' at the cpan prompt.)

Are you ready for manual configuration? [yes]
```

During configuration, the CPAN Perl module prompts for answers to around 30 questions. For most of the questions, selecting the default value is the best response. This initial configuration must be completed before the CPAN Perl module can be used. The questions are mainly about the location of various utilities, and the defaults can be chosen by pressing *Enter*. The only question for which we should change the default is the one about building prerequisite modules. If we configure CPAN to follow dependencies, it will install required modules without prompting.

```
Policy on building prerequisites (follow, ask or ignore)? [ask]
follow
```

Once CPAN is configured, exit the shell by typing exit and pressing *Enter*. We are now ready to use CPAN to install SpamAssassin.

Installing SpamAssassin Using CPAN

To install SpamAssassin, enter the CPAN shell by typing:

```
# perl -MCPAN -e shell
```

If the CPAN module is correctly configured, the following output (or something similar) will appear:

```
cpan shell -- CPAN exploration and modules installation (v1.7601)
ReadLine support enabled
```

Now, at the cpan prompt, enter the following command:

```
cpan> install Mail::SpamAssassin
```

The CPAN module will query an online database to find the latest version of SpamAssassin and its dependencies, and then install them. Dependencies will be installed before SpamAssassin. The sample output is shown below:

```
cpan> install Mail::SpamAssassin
Running install for module Mail::SpamAssassin
Running make for F/FE/FELICITY/Mail-SpamAssassin-3.00.tar.gz
Fetching with LWP:
    ftp://cpan.etla.org/pub/CPAN/authors/id/F/FE/FELICITY/Mail-
SpamAssassin-3.00.tar.gz
CPAN: Digest::MD5 loaded ok
Fetching with LWP:

ftp://cpan.etla.org/pub/CPAN/authors/id/F/FE/FELICITY/CHECKSUMS
Checksum for /root/.cpan/sources/authors/id/F/FE/FELICITY/Mail-
SpamAssassin-3.00.tar.gz ok
Mail-SpamAssassin-3.00/
Mail-SpamAssassin-3.00/ninjabutton.png
Mail-SpamAssassin-3.00/masses/
....
    CPAN.pm: Going to build F/FE/FELICITY/Mail-SpamAssassin-
3.00.tar.gz
```

SpamAssassin may require the user to respond to a few questions. The responses provided might affect the module configuration or only be part of the testing performed before installation.

```
What e-mail address or URL should be used in the suspected-spam
report
text for users who want more information on your filter
installation?
(In particular, ISPs should change this to a local Postmaster
contact)

default text: [the administrator of that system] user@domain.com
Check network rules during 'make test' (test scripts may fail due to
```

```
network problems)? (y/n) [n] n
Run SQL-based Auto-whitelist tests during 'make test' (additional

information required) (y/n) [n] n
Run Bayes SQL storage tests during 'make test' (additional

information required)? (y/n) [n] n

Writing Makefile for Mail::SpamAssassin
Makefile written by ExtUtils::MakeMaker 6.17
```

The build process tests the capabilities of the C compiler, configures and builds the module, creates documentation, and tests SpamAssassin. At the end of the build, the output should be similar to the following:

```
chmod 755 /usr/share/spamassassin
    /usr/bin/make install    -- OK

cpan>
```

This indicates that SpamAssassin has been installed correctly. If SpamAssassin installation was successful, then you can skip to the *Testing the Installation* section.

If the installation failed, then the output may look like this:

```
Failed 17/68 test scripts, 75.00% okay. 50/1482 subtests
failed, 96.63% okay.
make: *** [test_dynamic] Error 29
/usr/bin/make test -- NOT OK
Running make install
make test had returned bad status, won't install without force
cpan>
```

If the output does not end with the /usr/bin/make install -- OK message, then an error has occurred. Firstly, you should examine all the output for possible warnings and error messages, especially for prerequisite packages. If this does not assist, then avenues for support are described in the section *Testing the Installation.*

Using the rpmbuild Utility

If a version of Linux based on the **RedHat Package Manager (RPM)** format is used, then SpamAssassin can be installed using the rpmbuild command. Download the SpamAssassin source from http://www.cpan.org/modules/01modules.index.html into a working directory.

Then issue the following command to build SpamAssassin:

```
$ su - - rpmbuild -tb Mail-SpamAssassin-3.0.4.tar.gz
Password: (enter root password)
Executing(%prep): /bin/sh -e /var/tmp/rpm-tmp.48734
+ umask 022
+ cd /usr/src/redhat/BUILD
+ cd /usr/src/redhat/BUILD
+ rm -rf Mail-SpamAssassin-3.0.4
+ /bin/gzip -dc /var/download/Mail-SpamAssassin-3.0.4.tar.gz
+ tar -xf -
... (output continues)
Wrote: /usr/src/redhat/RPMS/i386/spamassassin-3.0.4-1.i386.rpm
Wrote: /usr/src/redhat/RPMS/i386/spamassassin-tools-3.0.4-
1.i386.rpm
Wrote: /usr/src/redhat/RPMS/i386/perl-Mail-SpamAssassin-3.0.4-
1.i386.rpm
Executing(%clean): /bin/sh -e /var/tmp/rpm-tmp.65065
+ umask 022
+ cd /usr/src/redhat/BUILD
+ cd Mail-SpamAssassin-3.0.4
+ '[' /var/tmp/spamassassin-root '!=' / ']'
+ rm -rf /var/tmp/spamassassin-root
+ exit 0
$
```

It is possible that the installation will fail due to missing dependencies. These are Perl modules that SpamAssassin uses, that are installed separately. Error messages often hint at the name of the dependency, as in the following installation:

```
$ su - - rpmbuild -tb Mail-SpamAssassin-3.0.4.tar.gz
Password: (enter root password)
rpmbuild -tb Mail-SpamAssassin-3.0.4.tar.gz
error: Failed build dependencies:
perl(Digest::SHA1) is needed by spamassassin-3.0.4-1
```

In this case, the Perl package Digest::SHA1 is needed. The solution is to install it using CPAN. In some cases, SpamAssassin may require particular versions of packages, which may require the installed versions to be upgraded.

When installing SpamAssassin using CPAN all the dependencies are installed automatically, but while using rpmbuild command the dependencies need to be installed manually. Using CPAN is generally less trouble than rpmbuild.

Using Pre-Built RPMs

SpamAssassin is packaged with many Linux distributions, and packages of new releases of SpamAssassin are often made available from other sources. As mentioned earlier,

RPMs are not the recommended method of installing SpamAssassin but are more reliable than building from source on unusual platforms.

To install an RPM, simply download or locate it on the distribution CD, and install it and use the `rpm` command. The following command can be used to install the RPM for SpamAssassin:

```
# rpm -ivh /path/to/rpmfile-9.99.rpm
```

Graphical installers can also be used to install SpamAssassin RPMs. The RPMs listed on the SpamAssassin web site are usually the latest version of SpamAssassin and are complete. If these cannot be installed, the RPM provided by the Linux distribution should be installed.

Testing the Installation

It is worth performing a few tests to ensure that SpamAssassin is installed correctly, and the environment is complete. If you want to test a particular user account, you should log in to that account to perform the test.

SpamAssassin includes a sample spam e-mail and a sample non-spam e-mail. It can be tested by processing the sample e-mails. These e-mails are in the root of the SpamAssassin distribution directory. If you used CPAN to install SpamAssassin, using the root user, then the path to this directory may be similar to ~root/.cpan/build/ Mail-SpamAssassin-3.01/, where 3.01 is the version of SpamAssassin installed. If the files cannot be located, then download the SpamAssassin source from http://www.cpan.org/modules/01modules.index.html and unpack the source into a temporary directory. The sample e-mails are in the root of the unpacked source.

To test SpamAssassin, change to the directory containing `sample-spam.txt` and use the following commands. Example results are shown after each command:

```
$ spamassassin -t < sample-nonspam.txt | grep X-Spam
X-Spam-Checker-Version: SpamAssassin 3.0 (2004-07-16) on
X-Spam-Level:
X-Spam-Status: No, score=0.4 required=5.0 tests=LINES_OF_YELLING
autolearn=no


$ spamassassin -t < sample-spam.txt | grep X-Spam
X-Spam-Flag: YES
X-Spam-Checker-Version: SpamAssassin 3.0.0-pre2-r22977 (2004-07-16)
on
X-Spam-Level: **************************************************
X-Spam-Status: Yes, score=1002.6 required=5.0
tests=ALL_TRUSTED,DCC_CHECK,
```

The output from the command using `sample-nonspam.txt` should have X-Spam-Status: No, and that using `sample-spam.txt` should have X-Spam-Flag: YES and X-Spam-Status: Yes.

SpamAssassin can verify its configuration files with the `--lint` flag and report any errors. In the following example, a `score` entry does not match a rule:

```
$ spamassassin --lint
warning: score set for non-existent rule RULE_NAME
lint: 1 issues detected. please run with debug enabled for more
information
```

If the output includes warnings, then something has gone wrong. It's worth fixing SpamAssassin before going on and using it. The best places to visit are the SpamAssassin Wiki (`http://wiki.apache.org/spamassassin/`), the archives of the SpamAssassin mailing lists (`http://wiki.apache.org/spamassassin/MailingLists`), and your favorite search engine. As with most open-source projects, the developers are volunteers and appreciate users who search for the solution to their problem before posting a plea for help, as most problems have been encountered many times before.

Modified E-Mails

In addition to the e-mail headers mentioned above, SpamAssassin will modify an e-mail if it is thought to be spam. It takes the original e-mail, and converts it to an e-mail attachment, with a simple e-mail around it. SpamAssassin always wraps an e-mail if it detects a potential virus or other dangerous content. In its default configuration, it will add an envelope e-mail around the spam, but this can be turned off if desired—consult the SpamAssassin documentation regarding the `report_safe` directive. The envelope e-mail looks like this:

```
Spam detection software, running on the system "host.domain.com", has
identified this incoming e-mail as possible spam. The original
message has been attached to this so you can view it (if it isn't
spam) or label similar future e-mail. If you have any questions, see
postmaster@domain.com for details.

Content preview:  Heya, Do you want a rolex watch? In our online
store you can buy replicas of Rolex watches. They look and feel
exactly like the real thing. [...]

Content analysis details:   (23.8 points, 4.0 required)

 pts rule name                description
---- --------------------- -----------------------------------------
---------
 1.9 BAYES_99              BODY: Bayesian spam probability is 99 to
100%
                          [score: 1.0000]
 1.0 URIBL_SBL             Contains a URL listed in the SBL
blocklist
                          [URIs: roiex.com]
 0.4 URIBL_AB_SURBL        Contains a URL listed in the AB SURBL
blocklist
                          [URIs: roiex.com]
 ....
```

Using SpamAssassin

Now that SpamAssassin is installed, we need to configure the system to use it. SpamAssassin can be used in many ways. It can be integrated into the MTA for maximum performance, it can run as a daemon, or run as a simple script to avoid complexity. It can use separate settings for each user or use a single set of settings for all users, and it can be used for all accounts or just for chosen ones. In this book, we will discuss using SpamAssassin in three ways.

The first method is with Procmail. This is the simplest method to configure and is suitable for low-volume sites, for example, less than 10,000 e-mails a day.

The second method is to use SpamAssassin as a daemon. This is more efficient, and can still be used with Procmail, if desired.

The third method is to integrate SpamAssassin with a content filter, such as amavis-d. This offers performance advantages, but occasionally the content filter will not work with the latest release of SpamAssassin. Problems, if any, are usually resolved quickly.

> To help you get the most out of SpamAssassin, Packt Publishing has published *SpamAssassin: A practical guide to integration and configuration* by Alistair McDonald, ISBN 1-904811-12-4.

Using SpamAssassin with Procmail

Procmail was covered in Chapters 6 and 7. If you have at least a basic understanding of Procmail, then what follows here should be easy to understand. If you jumped to this chapter and you don't know about Procmail then it would probably be worthwhile reading Chapter 6 on Procmail basics before continuing here.

Before we configure the system to use SpamAssassin, let's consider what SpamAssassin does: SpamAssassin is *not* an e-mail filter. A filter is something that changes the destination of an e-mail. SpamAssassin adds e-mail headers to an e-mail message to indicate if it is spam or not.

Consider an e-mail with headers like this:

```
Return-Path: <user@domain.com>
X-Original-To: jdoe@localhost
Delivered-To: jdoe@host.domain.com
Received: from localhost (localhost [127.0.0.1])
    by domain.com (Postfix) with ESMTP id 52A2CF2948
    for <jdoe@localhost>; Thu, 11 Nov 2004 03:39:42 +0000 (GMT)
Received: from pop.ntlworld.com [62.253.162.50]
    by localhost with POP3 (fetchmail-6.2.5)
    for jdoe@localhost (single-drop); Thu, 11 Nov 2004 03:39:42
+0000 (GMT)
Message-ID: <D8F7B41C.4DDAFE7@anotherdomain.com>
Date: Wed, 10 Nov 2004 17:54:14 -0800
From: "stephen mellors" <gregory@anotherdomain.com>
```

```
User-Agent: MIME-tools 5.503 (Entity 5.501)
X-Accept-Language: en-us
MIME-Version: 1.0
To: "beau oquinn" <jdoe@domain.com>
Subject: nearest pharmacy online
Content-Type: text/plain;
        charset="us-ascii"
Content-Transfer-Encoding: 7bit
```

SpamAssassin will add a header lines:

```
X-Spam-Flag: YES
X-Spam-Checker-Version: SpamAssassin 3.1.0-r54722 (2004-10-13) on
        host.domain.com
X-Spam-Level: *****
X-Spam-Status: Yes, score=5.8 required=5.0 tests=BAYES_05,HTML_00_10,
        HTML_MESSAGE,MPART_ALT_DIFF autolearn=no
        version=3.1.0-r54722
```

SpamAssassin doesn't change the destination of the e-mail, all it does is add headers that enable something else to change the destination of the e-mail.

The best indication that an e-mail is spam is the X-Spam-Flag—if this is YES, then SpamAssassin considers the mail to be spam and it can be filtered by Procmail.

SpamAssassin also assigns a **score** to an e-mail—the higher the score, the more likely that the e-mail is spam. The threshold that determines if an e-mail is spam can be configured on a system-wide or per-user basis. The default of 5.0 is a sensible default if you are using an unmodified installation of SpamAssassin without any custom rulesets.

Global procmailrc File

Let's suppose that we want to check all incoming e-mail for spam using SpamAssassin. Commands in the /etc/procmailrc file are run for all users, so executing SpamAssassin here is ideal.

The following simple recipe will run SpamAssassin for all users, when placed in /etc/procmailrc:

```
:0fw
| /usr/bin/spamassassin
```

To place all spam in an individual spam folder, ensure that the global/etc/procmailrc file has a line specifying a default destination, for example:

```
DEFAULT=$HOME/.maildir/
```

If not, then add a line specifying DEFAULT. To filter spam into a folder, add a recipe similar to the following:

```
* ^X-Spam-Flag: Yes
.SPAM/new
```

This assumes that each user has a folder called SPAM already configured.

To place all the spam in a single, central folder, use an absolute path to the destination in the recipe:

```
* ^X-Spam-Flag: Yes
/var/spool/poss_spam
```

This will place all spam in a single folder, which can be reviewed by the system administrator. As regular e-mail may occasionally be wrongly detected as spam, the folder should not be world-readable, which leads to a more generalized statement:

> SpamAssassin will be run under the system account used for Postfix. This means that the Bayesian database and the auto-whitelists and blacklists will be shared by all users. From a security point of view, it's important that the various databases that SpamAssassin creates are not world-writable.

SpamAssassin stores user-specific files in the ~/.spamassassin/ directory. Here is a list of files that *may* be present for a user:

Files	Contents

`auto-whitelist`
`auto-whitelist.db`
`auto-whitelist.dir`
`auto-whitelist.pag`
	SpamAssassin creates a database of users who send ham and uses it to predict whether an e-mail from a particular sender is spam or ham. These files are used to track users.

`bayes_journal`
`bayes_seen`
`bayes_toks`
	SpamAssassin uses a statistical technique called Bayesian analysis. These files are used for this feature.

`user_prefs`	This file allows global settings to be overridden for a particular user. This file can contain configuration settings, rules, and scores.

Some of them may contain confidential data, for example regular contacts will appear in the auto-whitelist files. Careful use of permissions will ensure that the files are not readable by regular user accounts.

Using SpamAssassin on a Per-User Basis

Perhaps some users don't receive spam, or there may be issues with users sharing whitelists and Bayesian databases. SpamAssassin can be run on an individual basis by moving the recipes above to the ~/.procmailrc of specific users. This should increase the filtering performance for each user, but increases disk space usage for each user, and requires setting up each individual user account by modifying its ~/.procmailrc.

A typical user's `.procmailrc` might look like this:

```
MAILDIR=$HOME/.maildir
:0fw
| /usr/bin/spamassassin
:0
* ^X-Spam-Flag: Yes
.SPAM/cur
```

As suggested above, e-mail may sometimes be wrongly detected as spam. It's worthwhile reviewing spam to ensure that legitimate e-mails have not been wrongly classified. If the user receives a lot of spam, then wading through it all is time-consuming, tedious, and error prone. Spam e-mail can be filtered by Procmail depending on its spam score. The low-scoring spam (for example, scoring up to 9) can be placed in one folder called `Probable_Spam`, while higher scoring e-mails (which are more likely to be spam) are placed a folder called `Certain_Spam`.

To do this, we use the `X-Spam-Level` header, which SpamAssassin creates. This is simply a number of asterisks, related to the `X-Spam-Level` value. By moving e-mail with more than a certain number of asterisks to the `Certain_Spam` folder, the remaining spam is "Probable Spam". E-mail that is marked with `X-Spam-Flag: NO`, is, of course, non-spam.

The following `.procmailrc` file will filter high scoring spam separately from low-scoring spam and non-spam:

```
MAILDIR=$HOME/.maildir
:0fw
| /usr/bin/spamassassin
:0
* ^X-Spam-Level: \*\*\*\*\*\*\*\*\*\*\*\*\*\*\*
.Certain_Spam/cur
:0
* ^X-Spam-FLAG: YES
.Probable_Spam/cur
```

Using SpamAssassin as a Daemon with Postfix

A daemon is a background process; one that waits for work, processes it, and then waits for more work. Using this approach actually improves performance (as long as there is sufficient memory) because responsiveness is improved—the program is always ready and waiting, and does not have to be loaded each time spam tagging is required.

To use SpamAssassin as a daemon, a user account should be added—it's dangerous to run any service as `root`. As root, enter the following commands to make a user and a group called spam:

```
# groupadd spam
# useradd -m -d /home/spam -g spam -s /bin/false spam
# chmod 0700 /home/spam
```

To configure Postfix to run SpamAssassin, use SpamAssassin as a daemon. The Postfix `master.cf` file must be changed. Edit the file and locate the line that begins with 'smtp inet'. Amend the line to add `-o content_filter=spamd` to the end:

```
smtp      inet n    -    n    -    -    smtpd -o
  content_filter=spamd
```

Add the following lines to the end of the file:

```
spamd unix -    n    n    -    -    pipe
  user=spam argv=/usr/bin/spamc -f
  -e /usr/sbin/sendmail -oi -f ${sender} ${recipient}
```

If the text is spread across several lines then any continuing line must begin with spaces as shown. The changes to the file define a filter called spamd that runs the spamc client for each message and also specify that the filter should be run whenever an e-mail is received via SMTP.

On this line, spamd is the name of the filter and matches the name used in the `content_filter` line. The `user=` portion specifies the user context that should be used to run the command. The `argv=` portion describes the program that should be run. The other flags are used by Procmail and their presence is important.

Using SpamAssassin with amavisd-new

amavisd-new is an interface between MTAs and content checkers. Content-checkers scan e-mail for viruses and/or spam. amavisd-new is written in Perl and runs as a daemon. Instead of accessing SpamAssassin via the spamc or spamassassin clients, it loads SpamAssassin into memory and accesses the SpamAssassin functions directly. It is therefore closely coupled to SpamAssassin, and may need to be upgraded at the same time as SpamAssassin.

amavisd-new is available in source form, RPMs are available for SuSE and Mandrake Linux, and third-party RPMs are available for RedHat Linux. Details of versions available are listed on `http://www.ijs.si/software/amavisd/#download`. If an RPM is available, use it.

Installation from Package

To install amavisd-new from package, use the `rpm` command for RPM-based distributions. amavisd-new has many dependencies, all of which are Perl modules. Each version may have different dependencies, which are listed in the install file that is part of the package. The prerequisites for version 40040701 are:

```
Archive::Tar
Archive::Zip
Compress::Zlib
Convert::TNEF
Convert::UUlib
MIME::Base64
MIME::Parser
```

```
Mail::Internet
Net::Server
Net::SMTP
Digest::MD5
IO::Stringy
Time::HiRes
Unix::Syslog
BerkeleyDB
```

To view the prerequisites for a particular version of amavisd-new, download the source and unpack it, as shown here, and read the install file:

```
$ cd /some/dir
$ wget http://www.ijs.si/software/amavisd/amavisd-new-20040701.tar.gz
http://www.ijs.si/software/amavisd/amavisd-new-20040701.tar.gz
$ gunzip -c amavisd-new-20040701.tar.gz
$ cd amavisd-new-20040701
$ vi install
```

Several of the dependencies may be installed already, as they are used by SpamAssassin.

Installing Prerequisites

Some RPM-based Linux distributions may automatically install the prerequisites as dependencies. For other distributions, all the prerequisites must be downloaded from CPAN and installed. This is easiest to accomplish with the cpan command. An alternative method is to download the source code for each prerequisite individually and install it with the following commands:

```
$ cd /some/directory
$ gunzip -c source-nn.tar.gz | tar xf -
$ cd source-nn
$ perl Makefile.pl
$ make test
$ su
# make install
```

Installing from Source

amavisd-new has no makefile, configuration script, or installation routine. To install it, the sole executable script is copied to /usr/local/bin, and its attributes modified to ensure it cannot be modified by non-root users:

```
# cp amavisd /usr/local/sbin/
# chown root /usr/local/sbin/amavisd
# chmod 755 /usr/local/sbin/amavisd
```

The sample amavisd.conf file should be copied to /etc and its attributes should also be modified:

```
# cp amavisd.conf /etc/
# chown root /etc/amavisd.conf
# chmod 644 /etc/amavisd.conf
```

amavisd-new must be configured to run as a daemon, and so the sample `init` script should be copied to the appropriate directory:

```
# cp amavisd_init.sh /etc/init.d/amavisd-new
```

The `init` script should also be added to the system startup. Most Linux distributions use the `chkconfig` command to do this:

```
# chkconfig --add amavisd-new
```

Create a User Account for amavisd-new

To create a user account, first create a dedicated group using the `groupadd` command and then use the `useradd` command to add the user.

```
# groupadd amavis
# useradd -m -d /home/amavis -g amavis -s /bin/false amavis
```

Configuring amavisd-new

Several changes need to be made to the `/etc/amavisd.conf` file. This file will be parsed as Perl source and syntax is important. Each line should end in a semicolon, and the casing is important. The following variable declaration lines should be changed to contain the following values:

```
$MYHOME = '/home/amavis';
$mydomain = 'domain.com';
$daemon_user = 'amavis';
$daemon_group = 'amavis';
$max_servers  = 5;      # number of pre-forked children  (default 2)
$max_requests = 10;     # retire a child after that many accepts
                        # (default 10)
$child_timeout=60;      # abort child if it does not complete each
                        # task in n sec
```

Ensure that the correct domain is specified for $mydomain. The number 5 specified for $max_servers is the number of daemons that will be run.

In `/etc/amavisd.conf`, one line needs to be uncommented as virus scanning is not going to be used. amavisd-new will not start if this step is omitted. This line begins with:

```
# @bypass_virus_checks_acl
```

The initial # and space characters need to be removed.

```
@bypass_virus_checks_acl = qw( . );   # uncomment to DISABLE
                                       # anti-virus code
```

Within `/etc/amavisd.conf`, there is a section on SpamAssassin-related configuration settings:

```
$sa_tag_level_deflt  = 3.0;
$sa_tag2_level_deflt = 6.3;
$sa_kill_level_deflt = 12;
```

These three settings are used with the SpamAssassin score level associated with e-mail being processed. The $sa_tag_level_deflt setting is the threshold at which ham is separated from spam and the X-Spam-Status and X-Spam-Level headers are added to an e-mail.

E-mails that score below this threshold do not receive the headers, while e-mails above the threshold receive the headers. The $sa_kill_level_deflt setting is the threshold at which spam e-mail is rejected.

The default configuration is to reject spam. To forward spam to another e-mail address, locate the line specifying $final_spam_destiny and change it as follows:

```
$final_spam_destiny        = D_PASS;  # (defaults to D_REJECT)
```

The recipient of the spam has to be defined. Locate the line that specifies $spam_quarantine_to, and alter it to contain an e-mail address. The $mydomain variable, which was configured earlier in this step, can be used to refer to the domain, and the @ symbol must be prefixed with a backslash:

```
$spam_quarantine_to = "spam-quarantine\@$mydomain";
```

Now, amavisd-new should be started. Most Linux distributions use the following command:

```
# /etc/init.d/amavisd-new start
```

Configuring Postfix to Run amavisd-new

Edit /etc/postfix/master.cf and locate this line:

```
smtp          inet  n       -         n        -         -        smtpd
```

Add these lines after it:

```
smtp-amavis unix   y  -              5                         smtp
    -o smtp_data_done_timeout=1200
    -o disable_dns_lookups=yes

127.0.0.1:10025 inet n            y--                          smtpd
    -o content_filter=
    -o local_recipient_maps=
    -o relay_recipient_maps=
    -o smtpd_restriction_classes=
    -o smtpd_recipient_restrictions=permit_mynetworks,reject
    -o mynetworks=127.0.0.0/8
    -o strict_rfc821_envelopes=yes
```

In the smtp-amavis line, the number 5 specifies the number of instances that can be used at once. This should correspond to the $max_servers entry specified in the amavisd.conf file.

Edit /etc/postfix/main.cf and add the following line near the end of the file:

```
content_filter = smtp-amavis:[localhost]:10024
```

Restart Postfix with the postfix reload command:

```
# postfix reload
```

Configuring E-Mail Clients

Instead of placing spam in a separate folder by using Procmail, this can be performed by the e-mail client. Most e-mail clients allow rules or filters to be created. These typically come into action when new e-mail is read, or a folder is opened.

Rules in an e-mail client run on the value of an e-mail header. It is best to use the X-Spam-Flag and search for the value YES. The procedure to move tagged messages to a separate folder is outlined below:

1. Create a folder or mailbox for holding spam e-mail. The folder name should be intuitive, for example Spam.

2. Create a rule to be run when e-mails arrive. The rule should look for the text X-Spam-Flag in the message headers.

3. The action on the rule should be to move the e-mail to the Spam folder created in the first step.

4. Once the filter is created, send test messages—both spam and non-spam—to check that the filter works properly.

Microsoft Outlook

Microsoft Outlook is popular in large organizations. It integrates well with IMAP servers. Follow the following steps to configure Outlook to filter spam, based on the X-Spam-Flag in e-mail headers:

> These instructions are based on Outlook as shipped with Microsoft Office 2002; other versions have similar configuration details.

1. Create a folder to store the spam. Click on the Inbox in the folder list to select it, right-click, and select New Folder from the menu. Choose Spam or another meaningful name, then click OK.

2. Click on the Tools menu and select Rules Wizard. Click on New to create a new rule.

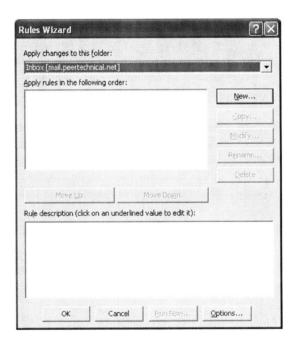

3. Select Start from a blank rule. Ensure that Check messages when they arrive is selected. Press Next.

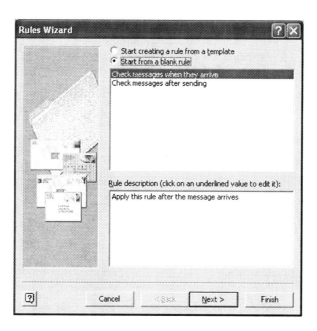

4. Check with specific words in the message header. This will allow Outlook to check the x-spam-Flag e-mail header. Click on specific words to select the correct phrase.

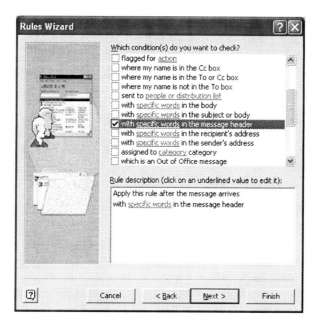

5. In the next dialog, carefully enter X-Spam-Flag: Yes and click Add, then press OK, then press Next.

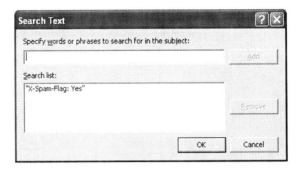

6. The next window offers a choice of actions. Choose move it to the specified folder, and click on specified, which will display a list of folders.

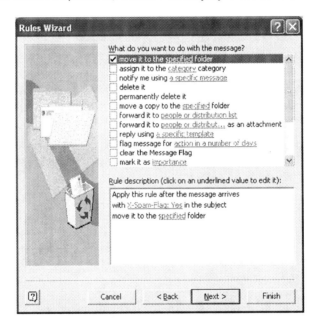

7. Choose the folder created earlier and press OK. Click Next. There are no exceptions, so click Next again.

8. The Rules Wizard allows the rule to be run immediately on any existing messages in the Inbox. To do this, make sure that the checkbox next to Turn on this rule is checked.

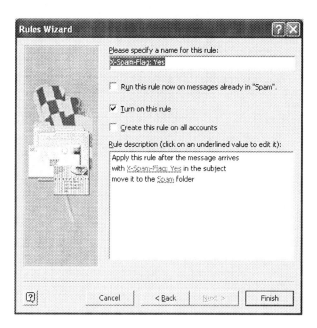

9. Finally, click Finish, and the rule is created and run on all messages in the Inbox.

Microsoft Outlook Express

Outlook Express is shipped with most versions of Windows. It provides POP3 connectivity and many features, such as HTML e-mail. Some e-mail clients, including Outlook Express, do not allow filtering on every e-mail header, but only on certain specific headers, such as the `From:` and `Subject:` headers. SpamAssassin by default only writes additional headers, but it can be configured to alter the `Subject`, `From`, or `To` headers of an e-mail. To do this, the `/etc/spamassassin/local.cf` file should be altered. (This change can also be made on a per-user basis by editing `~user/.spamassassin/user_prefs`).

Add the following line to the file:

```
rewrite_header Subject *****SPAM*****
```

This will change the header of the e-mail to `*****SPAM*****`. The tag can be altered if desired.

Now that SpamAssassin configuration is complete, Outlook Express can be configured to act on the modified message subject. Follow these steps:

1. Create a folder for the Spam. To do this, select the File menu, click on Folder, and then on New. Type in Spam, or another descriptive name, as the folder name, and then click OK.

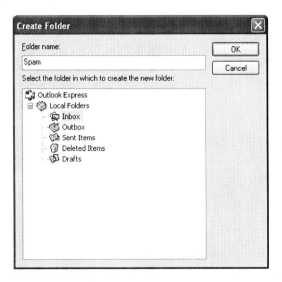

2. Select the Tools menu, and then select Message Rules. On the next window, ensure that the conditions include Where the Subject line contains specific words, and the actions include Move it to the specified folder.

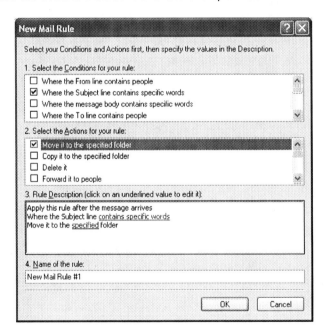

3. Click on **specific words**, and enter *****SPAM*****, or the alternative phrase chosen when configuring SpamAssassin. Click OK.

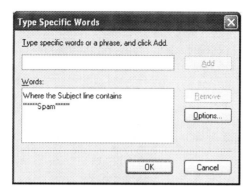

4. Click on **specified** in the next line of the Rule Description. Select the folder created above and click OK.

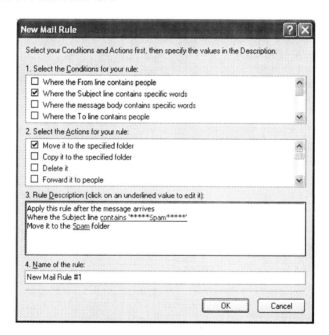

5. The rule is summarized. Click OK to save it.

Mozilla Thunderbird

Mozilla Thunderbird is a free, open-source e-mail client with most of the features of Microsoft Outlook. It is available free from www.mozilla.org/products/thunderbird/. It has full filtering capabilities. To configure it, follow these steps:

1. Create a folder to store the spam. Click on the File menu and select New, then Folder. Choose a location (the inbox should be fine) and a name, such as Spam. Click OK.

2. Click on the Tools menu and select Message Filters. Click on the New button to create a new filter.

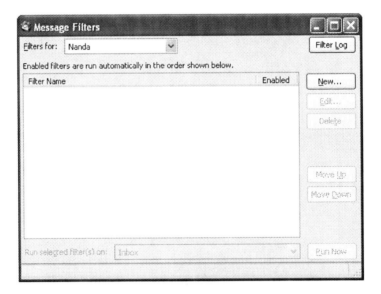

3. In the next dialog, choose a name for the filter, such as Spam. Then select the Match all of the following button. In the left list, type X-Spam-Flag, in the middle list select is, and in the right select Yes. In the box below, click on Move to folder, and select the folder created in the first step.

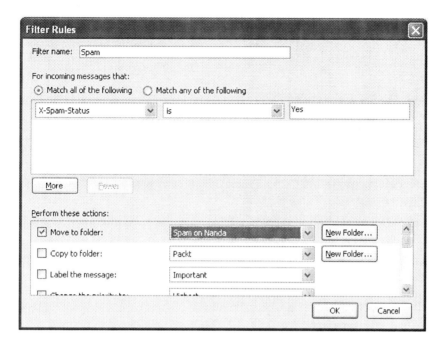

4. Click OK and the rule summary will show the rule. Press Run Now to test the rule.

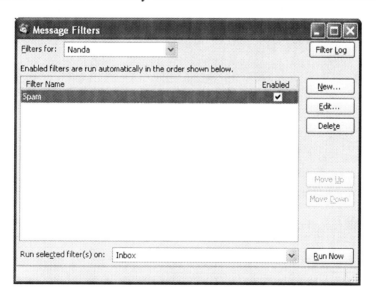

Customization

SpamAssassin is very configurable. Almost every setting can be configured on a system-wide or user-specific basis.

Reasons to Customize

If SpamAssassin is so good, then why configure it? Well, there are several good reasons why it's worth improving spam filtering with SpamAssassin:

- SpamAssassin by default (i.e. when installed but not customized) typically manages to detect over 80% of spam. After adding a few customizations, the detection rate can be greater than 95%.

- Everyone's spam is different and one user's spam is another user's ham. By trying to be general, SpamAssassin may fail to filter someone's spam.

- Some of the features of SpamAssassin are disabled by default. By enabling them, the spam recognition rate is increased.

The following configuration options are discussed in this chapter:

- **Altering the scores for rules**: This allows rules to be disabled, poor rules to be given less weight, and better rules to be given a greater weight

- **Obtaining and using new rules**: This can improve spam detection

- **Adding e-mail addresses to white and blacklists**: This allows the e-mail from specified senders to always be treated as ham, no matter the content, or the opposite

- **Enabling SpamAssassin's Bayesian filter**: This can increase filtering from 80% accuracy to 95% or more

Rules and Scores

The configuration files for standard, site-wide, and user-specific settings are saved in different directories as follows:

- Standard configuration settings are stored in /usr/share/spamassassin.

- Site-wide customizations and settings are stored in /etc/mail/spamassassin/. All files matching *.cf are examined by SpamAssassin.

- User-specific settings are stored in ~/.spamassassin/local.cf.

The bulk of the standard configuration files is devoted to simple rules and their scores.

A rule is typically a match for letters, numbers, or other printing **characters**. Rules are written using a technique called **regular expressions**, or **regex** for short. This is a shorthand method of specifying that certain combinations of characters will trigger the rule. A rule might try to detect a particular word, such as 'Viagra', or it might look for particular words in certain orders, such as 'buy viagra online'. The rules are stored in text files.

Default files are stored in /usr/share/spamassassin. These are files that are shipped with SpamAssassin and may change with each release. It's best not to modify these files, or place new files in this directory, as an upgrade to SpamAssassin will overwrite these files. Most of the rules that SpamAssassin uses, and the scores applied to each rule, are defined within files in this directory.

Site-wide configuration files should be placed in /etc/mail/spamassassin. SpamAssassin will read all files matching *.cf in this directory. Settings made here can overrule those in the default files. They can include defining new rules and new rule scores.

User-specific customizations can be placed in the file ~/.spamassassin/local.cf. Settings made here can override site-wide settings defined in /etc/mail/spamassassin, and default settings in /usr/share/spamassassin/. New rules may be defined here, and scores for existing rules can be overridden.

SpamAssassin first reads all the files in /usr/share/spamassassin in alphanumerical order; 10_misc.cf will be read before 23_bayes.cf. SpamAssassin then reads all the .cf files in /etc/mail/spamassassin/, again in alphanumeric order. Finally, SpamAssassin reads ~user/.spamassassin/user_prefs. If a rule or score is defined in two files, then the setting in the last file read is used. This allows the administrator to override the defaults, and a user to override the site-wide settings.

Each line in a rules file can be blank or contain a comment or a command. The hash or pound (#) symbol is used for comments. Rules generally have three parts, the rule definition, a textual description, and the score or series of scores. Convention dictates that all rule scores for rules provided by SpamAssassin should be located together in a separate file. That file is /usr/share/spamassassin/50_scores.cf.

Altering Rule Scores

The simplest configuration change is to change a rule score. There are two reasons why this might be done:

1. A rule is very good at detecting spam, but the rule has a low score. E-mails that fire the rule are not being detected as spam.
2. A rule is acting on non-spam. As a result, e-mails that fire the rule are wrongly being detected as spam.

The rules that fire when SpamAssassin is run are listed in the X-Spam-Status: header of the e-mail:

```
X-Spam-Status: Yes, score=5.8 required=5.0 tests=BAYES_05,HTML_00_10,
    HTML_MESSAGE,MPART_ALT_DIFF autolearn=no
    version=3.1.0-r54722
```

241

The rules that applied to the e-mail are listed after `tests=`. If one continually appears in e-mail that should be marked as spam, but isn't, then the score for the rule should be increased. If a rule often fires in e-mail that is wrongly classified as spam, then the score should be decreased.

To find the current score, use the `grep` utility in all the locations that a score can be defined:

```
grep score.*RULE_NAME
$ grep score.*BAYES /usr/share/spamassassin/*
/etc/mail/spamassassin/* ~/.spamassassin/local.cf

/etc/mail/spamassassin/local_scores.cf:score RULE_NAME 0 0 1.665
2.599
/etc/mail/spamassassin/local_scores.cf: 4.34
```

In the above example, the rule has a default score that is overridden in `/etc/mail/spamassassin/local_scores.cf`.

The original score for the rule had four values. SpamAssassin changes the scores it uses depending on whether network tests (those that test open relays, for example) are in use, and whether the Bayesian Filter is in use or not. Four scores are listed, which are used in the following circumstances:

	Bayesian filter not in use	Bayesian filter in use
External tests not in use	1st score	3rd score
External tests in use	2nd score	4th score

If only one score is given, as overridden in `/etc/mail/spamassassin/local_scores.cf`, then it is used in all circumstances.

In the example above, the system administrator has overridden the default score in `/etc/mail/spamassassin/local_scores.cf` with a single value in `/etc/mail/spamassassin/local_scores.cf`. To change this value for a particular user, their `~/.spamassassin/local.cf` might read:

```
score RULE_NAME  1.2
```

This changes the score used from `4.34`, set in `/etc/mail/spamassassin/local_scores.cf` to `1.2`. To disable the rule entirely, the score can be set to zero:

```
score RULE_NAME  0
```

Endless hours can be spent configuring rule scores. SpamAssassin includes tools to recalculate optimal rule scores, by examining existing e-mails, both spam and non-spam. They are covered in detail in the SpamAssassin book published by Packt.

Using other Rulesets

SpamAssassin has a large following, and the design of SpamAssassin has made it easy to add new rulesets. There are many different rulesets available. Most are based on a particular theme, for example finding the names of drugs often sold with spam, or telephone numbers found in spam e-mails. Most custom rulesets are listed on the Custom Rulesets page of the SpamAssassin Wiki at http://wiki.apache.org/spamassassin/ CustomRulesets. The Wiki page gives a general description of each ruleset, and a URL to download it. Once a ruleset has been chosen, we install it as follows:

1. In a browser, follow the link on the SpamAssassin Wiki page. In most cases, the link will be to a file with a name matching *.cf, and a browser will open it as a text file.

2. Save the file using the browser (normally, the File menu has a Save as option).

3. Copy the file to /etc/mail/spamassassin—the rules will be automatically run if the file is placed in this location.

4. Check that the file has scores in it—otherwise the rules will not be used.

5. Monitor spam performance to ensure that legitimate e-mail is not being detected as spam.

Adding rules to SpamAssassin will increase the memory used by SpamAssassin, and will also increase the time that it takes to process e-mails. It is best to be cautious and add new rulesets gradually, to ensure that the effect on the machine is understood.

Whitelists and Blacklists

SpamAssassin works very well at detecting spam, but there is always a risk of errors. By using a list of e-mail addresses that are known spam producers (a blacklist), e-mail from spammers who consistently use the same e-mail addresses or domains can be filtered out. With a list of e-mail addresses that are legitimate e-mail senders (a whitelist), e-mails from regular or important correspondents are guaranteed to be filtered as ham. This prevents the delay or nondelivery of important e-mails that may otherwise be marked as spam.

Blacklists that list individual e-mail addresses have limited use—spammers normally use different or random e-mail addresses for each spam run. However, some spammers use the same domain for multiple runs. As SpamAssassin allows wildcards in its blacklisting, entire domains can be blacklisted. This is more useful for filtering out spam.

Manual whitelisting and blacklisting involves adding configuration directives to the global configuration file /etc/mail/spamassassin/local.cf and/or in ~/.spamassassin/user_prefs.

The whitelist and blacklist entries allow the ? and * characters to be used to match a single character or many characters respectively. So, if a whitelist entry read

*@domain.com, then joe@domain.com and bill@domain.com would both match. For an entry that read *@yahoo?.com, joe@yahoo1.com, and bill@yahoo2.com would match but billy@yahoo22.com would not match. *@yahoo*.com would match all three examples.

The whitelist and blacklists rules do not immediately cause an e-mail to be tagged as spam or ham, even though the scores are heavily weighted—the default score for the USER_IN_WHITELIST rule is -100.0. It is technically possible that an e-mail may match a whitelist entry and still trigger enough other tests to result in it being marked it as spam. In practice, this is unlikely to occur, unless the scores have been changed from the defaults.

To blacklist an e-mail address or whole domain, use the blacklist_from directive:

```
blacklist_from    user@spammer.com
blacklist_from    *@spamdomain.com
```

To whitelist an e-mail address or domain, use the whitelist_from directive:

```
whitelist_from    user@mycompany.com
whitelist_from    *@mytradingpartner.com
```

SpamAssassin has more complex rules for managing white and blacklists, as well as an automatic whitelist/blacklist. Both blacklists and whitelists can be specified as discrete items (blacklist joe@domain.com and bill@another.com) or as wildcards (blacklist every joe, and blacklist everyone from domain.com). The wildcards are particularly powerful, and care should be taken to ensure that legitimate e-mail is not rejected.

Bayesian Filtering

This uses a statistical technique to determine if an e-mail is spam or not, based on previous e-mails of both types. Before it will work, it needs to be trained with e-mail that is known spam, and also e-mail that is known non-spam. It is important that the e-mail is correctly categorized; otherwise the effectiveness of the filter will be reduced. The learning process is done on the e-mail server, and the sample e-mails should be stored in an accessible location.

The sa-learn command is used to train the Bayesian filter with e-mail messages that are known ham or spam. The SpamAssassin installation routine will have placed sa-learn in the path, normally in /usr/bin/sa-learn.

It is used on the command-line, and is passed a directory, file, or series of files. For this to work, the e-mail has to be stored on the server, or exported from the client in a suitable format. SpamAssassin recognizes mbox format, and many e-mail clients use a compatible format. To use sa-learn, a directory or series of directories can be passed in to the command:

```
$ sa-learn --ham ~/.maildir/.Trash/cur/ ~/.maildir/cur
Learned from 75 message(s) (175 message(s) examined).
```

If the mbox format is used, then the mbox flag should be used, so that SpamAssassin searches the file for more than one e-mail:

```
$ sa-learn -mbox --spam ~/mbox/spam ~/mbox/bad-spam
Learned from 75 message(s) (175 message(s) examined).
```

If SpamAssassin has already learned from an e-mail, sa-learn detects this and will not process it twice. In the example above, 100 of the 175 e-mails had been processed already and were ignored on this run. The remaining 75 e-mails had not been processed before.

If sa-learn is passed a number of messages, then there may be no feedback for some time. The --showdots flag provides feedback in the form of dots (.) whenever an e-mail is processed:

```
$ sa-learn --spam --showdots ~/.SPAM/cur ~/.SPAM/new
........................
Learned from 20 message(s) (25 message(s) examined).
```

Once SpamAssassin has learned enough e-mails, it will begin to use the Bayesian filter automatically. It can be kept up-to-date by using the auto-learn feature.

Auto-learning should not be used without additional user input. There are two reasons for doing this:

- SpamAssassin occasionally gets spam detection wrong, and e-mail that is spam may be learned as an example of non-spam. Auto-learning would confuse the Bayesian filter and decrease its effectiveness.

- The score threshold that an e-mail is auto-learned at is higher than that for detection as spam. In other words, an e-mail may be detected as spam, but not auto-learned. In this case, the rest of SpamAssassin is doing a fairly good job of detecting border-line spam (those with scores close to the threshold for spam), but the Bayesian filter is not being taught the e-mails.

To use automatic learning, set the bayes_auto_learn flag to 1. This can be configured site-wide in the /etc/mail/spamassassin/local.cf file, or can be overridden in a user's ~/.spamassassin/user_prefs file. Two other configuration flags also affect auto-learning, and are the thresholds for learning ham and spam. These values are in the same units as SpamAssassin's score for each e-mail.

```
bayes_auto_learn           1
bayes_auto_learn_threshold_nonspam        0.1
bayes_auto_learn_threshold_spam           12.0
```

When auto-learning is enabled, any e-mail that is assigned a score of less than bayes_auto_learn_threshold_nonspam is learned as ham. Any e-mail that is assigned a value of greater than bayes_auto_learn_threshold_spam is learned as spam.

It is recommended that the bayes_auto_learn_threshold_nonspam threshold is kept low (close to or below zero). This will avoid the situation where a spam e-mail that escapes detection is used as an example to train the Bayesian filter. Keeping the `bayes_auto_learn_threshold_spam` threshold high is to some extent a matter of choice, although it should be above the scores of any e-mails that have been wrongly classified as spam in the past. This may occur up to a score of 10 for the default spam threshold of 5. Thus, using an auto-learn threshold of less than 10 for spam may cause non-spam to be accidentally learned as spam. If this happens, the Bayesian database will begin to lose effectiveness, and future Bayesian results will be compromised.

SpamAssassin keeps the Bayesian database in three files in the `.spamassassin` directory within a user's home directory. The format used is usually Berkeley DB format, and the files are named as follows:

```
bayes_journal
bayes_seen
bayes_toks
```

The `bayes_journal` file is used as a temporary storage area. Sometimes it is not present. This file is generally relatively small, with a size of around 10 KB. The `bayes_seen` and `bayes_toks` files can each be several megabytes in size.

Other SpamAssassin Features

This chapter has only scratched the surface of SpamAssassin's capabilities. If spam is a problem for an organization, then SpamAssassin will reward further study. Some of the other features that it contains are:

- **Network Tests**: SpamAssassin can integrate with Open Relay Databases. (The 3.x distribution contains tests for over 30 databases, although not all of them are enabled by default.) Open Relay tests do not require a fast machine or lots of RAM, and so are relatively 'cheap' tests to use. They have a fairly successful detection rate.

- **External content databases**: SpamAssassin can integrate with external content databases. These work in a participating network—all the participants send details of all the e-mails they receive to central servers. If the e-mails have been sent many times before, then the e-mail is probably a spam that has been sent to many users. The services are designed so that no confidential data is sent.

- **Whitelist and blacklist**: SpamAssassin includes an automatic whitelist and blacklist, which work in a similar way to the manual lists described earlier. This is particularly effective at preventing regular correspondents from having their e-mail wrongly detected as spam.

- **Creating new rules**: New rules can be written and developed. Creating rules is not particularly difficult, with a little imagination and a suitable source of spam. System Administrators can rid their users of any persistent spam that fails to be detected with the default SpamAssassin rules.

- **Customizable headers**: The headers that SpamAssassin adds to e-mails can be customized, and new headers can be written. SpamAssassin will also attempt to detect viruses and Trojan software, and will wrap an e-mail address like that in a special envelope e-mail.

- **Multiple installations**: SpamAssassin can be installed on multiple machines, serving one or more e-mail servers. In very high volume e-mail systems, many 'spam servers' may be run, each only processing spam. This leads to a high-throughput, high-availability service.

- **Customizable rule scores**: SpamAssassin includes tools to customize rule scores, based on samples of the spam and legitimate e-mail received at an organization. This helps to improve the filtering rate. With SpamAssasin 3.0, the tools were improved significantly, and the procedure to perform this is much less time-consuming than it was.

Summary

In this chapter, you have seen how SpamAssassin can be obtained and installed. Three different methods of using SpamAssassin were presented, with suggestions on which option to choose for a particular installation.

Configuration of popular e-mail clients was also covered, namely Microsoft Outlook, Microsoft Outlook Express, and Mozilla Thunderbird.

9

Antivirus Protection

One of the many options for filtering with Procmail is to remove executable attachments from e-mails in order to protect your system from possible virus attacks. This will be, at best, a crude operation; at worst, it will remove files that do not contain viruses and possibly leave other infected documents such as scripts that are not executables. These can have an equally devastating effect.

It is also possible to scan e-mails on the client side but in a company environment, it is not always possible to rely on every individual having their machines up to date and correctly installed with suitable virus checking software. The obvious solution is to run an efficient process on the server to ensure that all e-mail sent or received by the organization is correctly scanned for viruses.

There are a number of antivirus solutions available for Linux-based systems. We have chosen to focus on the ClamAV software. This is open-source software and regular updates to the database of viruses checked for are available for download.

Introduction to ClamAV

Clam Antivirus is an open-source antivirus toolkit for Linux. The main design feature of ClamAV was to integrate it with mail servers to perform attachment scanning and help filter out known viruses. The package provides a flexible and scalable multi-threaded daemon, a command-line scanner, and a tool for automatic updating via the Internet. The programs are based on a shared library distributed with the Clam Antivirus package, which you can use with your own software.

The version of ClamAV that we are going to use in this chapter is version 0.8, which has an up-to-date virus database and signatures to enable detection of over 20,000 viruses, worms, and Trojans including Microsoft Office and MacOffice macro viruses. Although not covered in this book, it is also able to perform on access scanning under Linux with suitable installation into the Linux Kernel.

Document Types Supported

A wide range of document types can contain or spread viruses and ClamAV provides protection from the majority of them:

- Portable executable files compressed with UPX, FSG, and Petite: This is the standard format for Microsoft Windows Executables and one of the most common transports for viruses.
- Many forms of Microsoft documents can contain scripts or executables. The following document and archive types can be processed by ClamAV:
  - MS OLE2
  - MS Cabinet files
  - MS CHM (Compressed HTML)
  - MS SZDD
- Other common archive formats that may contain any form of document and that ClamAV can process include:
  - RAR (2.0)
  - Zip
  - Gzip
  - Bzip2
  - Tar

Scanning of archives also includes the scanning of supported document formats held within the archives.

Downloading and Installing ClamAV

As viruses are being discovered on an almost daily basis it is well worth installing the latest stable version of ClamAV software. If your system is lucky enough to already have ClamAV installed it is possible that the installation may be based on an out of date installation package. It is highly recommended that you download and install the latest version from the ClamAV web site to ensure the highest level of security against viruses on your systems.

Requirements

It is necessary to install the GNU MP package to be able to verify digital signatures on the virus updates. This allows freshclam to verify the digital signatures of the virus databases. If freshclam was compiled without GMP support, it will display SECURITY WARNING: NO SUPPORT FOR DIGITAL SIGNATURES on every update. You can download GNU MP from http://www.swox.com/gmp/index.orig.html#DOWNLOAD.

Adding a New System User and Group

You will have to add a new user and group to your system for the ClamAV system to use

```
# groupadd clamav
# useradd -g clamav -s /bin/false -c "Clam AntiVirus" clamav
```

ClamAV

There are a number of installation packages available for ClamAV and details can be found on the ClamAV web site at http://www.clamav.net/binary.html#pagestart.

If you are using the RedHat Fedora package, the installation may be performed using either of the following options:

```
# yum update clamav
```

or

```
# up2date -u clamav
```

If your system does not have yum or up2date installed then you can install the software manually using the following procedure:

1. Follow one of the appropriate links for your system from the ClamAV web site http://www.clamav.net/binary.html#pagestart.

2. Download the appropriate RPM files from the repository you have chosen. You will need to download and install the latest version of clamav-0.xxxx.i386.rpm.

```
# wget http://crash.fce.vutbr.cz/crash-hat/1/clamav/clamav-0.85.1-
1.i386.rpm
# rpm -install clamav-0.85.1-1.i386.rpm
```

> Make sure you are installing version **0.81** or higher as there are significant enhancements over previous versions. In general, you should always install the latest stable version available.

Post Installation Testing

When you have installed the software, you will end up with two configuration files and several key binary files that will need editing to match your server configuration and your geographical location.

To verify that the software is correctly installed, try the following test to scan the source directory recursively:

```
$ clamscan -r -l scan.txt clamav-x.yz
```

It should find some test files in the `clamav-x.yz/test` directory. The scan result will be saved in the `scan.txt` log file. To test `clamd`, start it and use `clamdscan` (or connect directly to its socket and run the SCAN command instead):

```
$ clamdscan -l scan.txt clamav-x.yz
```

Editing the Config Files

After installation of the software, two configuration files need to be edited. The first file (`/etc/clamd.conf`) is for the actual virus scanning software itself. Most of the important configuration options for this file are discussed in the following sections. The second configuration file (`/etc/freshclam.conf`) is covered later in this chapter; this is where we add the configuration for the automatic virus database updates.

clamd

You have to edit the configuration file if you are going to use the daemon, otherwise `clamd` won't run:

```
$ clamd
ERROR: Please edit the example config file /etc/clamd.conf.
```

This shows the location of the default configuration file. The format and options of this file are fully described in the `clamd.conf(5)` manual. The `config` file is well commented and configuration should be straightforward.

Closest Mirrors

A number of mirror servers are available on the Internet from which you can download the latest antivirus database. To avoid overloading any one server, the configuration file should be setup to make sure that the download is being taken from the nearest available server. The included `update` utility makes use of the DNS system to locate a suitable server based upon the country code you are requesting.

The configuration file entry that you need to modify is `DatabaseMirror`. You may also specify the `MaxAttempts` times to download the database from the server.

The default database mirror is `clamav.database.net` but you are able to apply multiple entries in the configuration file. The configuration entry should be made using the following format `db.xx.clamav.net` where `xx` represents your normal two-letter ISO country code. For example, if your server is in Ascension Island you should add the following lines to `freshclam.conf`: The full list of two-letters country codes is available at `http://www.iana.org/cctld/cctld-whois.htm`.

```
DatabaseMirror db.ac.clamav.net
DatabaseMirror db.local.clamav.net
```

If the connection to the first entry fails for any reason then an attempt will be made to download from the second mirror entry. You should not use the default entry as you may find that your server or IP address becomes blacklisted and you are not able to obtain any updates at all.

Sample Config File

The sample `config` file that is provided is very well documented with comments at every significant configuration value. Here are some key values that you may wish to modify.

```
##
## Example config file for the Clam AV daemon
## Please read the clamd.conf(5) manual before editing this file.
##

# Comment or remove the line below.
Example
```

The `Example` line will cause the program to halt with a configuration error and is a deliberate inclusion to force you to edit the file before the software will operate correctly. Placing a # at the beginning of the line will be enough to resolve this problem.

```
# Uncomment this option to enable logging.
# LogFile must be writable for the user running daemon.
# A full path is required.
# Default: disabled
LogFile /var/log/clamd.log
```

It is well worth setting up a log file to enable you to check for errors and monitor correct operation over the first few weeks of operation. Thereafter you can of course decide whether to stop the logging or leave it operational.

```
# Log time with each message.
# Default: disabled
LogTime
```

Enabling time stamping in the log files ensures that you can of course track down the time of the event being logged to aid in debugging problems and matching events to entries in other log files.

```
# Path to the database directory.
# Default: hardcoded (depends on installation options)
#DatabaseDirectory /var/lib/clamav
DatabaseDirectory /usr/local/share/clamav
```

Make sure that the database directory is correctly configured so that everything knows exactly where the virus signature information is being stored.

```
# The daemon works in a local OR a network mode. Due to security
# reasons we
# recommend the local mode.

# Path to a local socket file the daemon will listen on.
# Default: disabled
```

```
LocalSocket /var/run/clam/clamd.sock
```

This is an important configuration change and is required to ensure the security of the system on which ClamAV is installed.

```
# Remove stale socket after unclean shutdown.
# Default: disabled
FixStaleSocket
```

Enabling the local socket ensures that the system continues to operate after a machine crash or shutdown.

```
# TCP address.
# By default we bind to INADDR_ANY, probably not wise.
# Enable the following to provide some degree of protection
# from the outside world.
# Default: disabled
TCPAddr 127.0.0.1
```

Another security-related configuration item to ensure that only local processes can gain access to the service.

```
# Execute a command when virus is found. In the command string %v
# will
# be replaced by a virus name.
# Default: disabled
#VirusEvent /usr/local/bin/send_sms 123456789 "VIRUS ALERT: %v"
```

This could be a useful feature to consider in some situations. However, with the wide range and frequency of virus delivery, this could prove to be a significant annoyance to have messages arriving throughout the night or day.

```
# Run as a selected user (clamd must be started by root).
# Default: disabled
User clamav
```

By creating a user especially for ClamAV we can assign ownership of files and processes to this user ID and help improve security of the files by restricting access to only this user ID. Also when running processes are listed on the system, it is easy to identify those that are owned by the ClamAV system.

Downloading, Building, and Installing ClamSMTP

A software interface is required between Postfix and ClamAV. The interface we are going to use is **ClamSMTP**. Postfix is designed to allow external filters to be called to process mail messages and to return the processed data back to postfix for onward delivery. ClamSMTP has been designed to work directly between Postfix and ClamAV to ensure a simple and reliable implementation.

ClamSMTP

ClamSMTP is an SMTP filter for Postfix and other mail servers that check for viruses using the ClamAV antivirus software. It is lightweight, reliable, and simple, without a myriad of options. It is written in C without major dependencies.

- **Homepage**: `http://memberwebs.com/nielsen/software/clamsmtp/`
- **Supports**: `clamd`

Follow the instructions that follow to integrate ClamSMTP into Postfix.

Download Source Code

The latest source code may be downloaded from `http://memberwebs.com/nielsen/software/clamsmtp/` directly onto your Linux system using the `wget` command. Change to a suitable location to download and build the software. The command option for the current version (1.4) would be `wget <url>`.

```
# wget http://memberwebs.com/nielsen/software/clamsmtp/clamsmtp-1.4.1
.tar.gz
```

You should check on the web site for the latest version that you can download. After you have downloaded the file, unpack the contents of the file using the `tar` command:

```
# tar xvfz clamsmtp-1.4.1.tar.gz
```

This will create a directory structure with all the relevant files contained below the current directory.

Build and Install

Before starting to build and install the software, it is well worthwhile to read through the `INSTALL` and `README` documents.

For most Linux systems, the simplest installation method can be reduced by following steps listed here:

1. Run the `configure` utility to create the right build environment by running the `configure` command:

```
# ./configure
```

2. After the configuration script is completed, you can run the `make` command to build the software executables:

```
# make
```

3. The final step is to copy the executables into the correct position for operation on the system:

make install

At all stages you should check the processes output for any significant errors or warnings.

Configure into Postfix

Postfix provides support for mail filtering by passing mail items through external processes. This operation can be performed either before or after the mail has been queued. The way communication between Postfix and clamsmtp works is by pretending that clamsmtp is itself an SMTP server. This simple approach provides an easy way to create a distributed architecture whereby different processes could be working on different machines to spread the load in very busy networks. For our use, we will assume that we are only using the one machine with all software running on that machine.

The clamsmtp filter interface was designed specifically to provide an interface between ClamAV and the Postfix mail system. The filter is implemented as an after-queue filter for antivirus scanning.

The first configuration option requires adding lines to the Postfix main.cf file:

```
content_filter = scan:127.0.0.1:10025
receive_override_options = no_address_mappings
```

The content_filter instruction forces Postfix to send all mail through the service named scan on port 10025. The scan service will be one that we set up using clamsmtpd. The instruction for receive_override_options is for Postfix to perform no_address_mappings, which stops Postfix from expanding any e-mail aliases or groups resulting in duplicate e-mails being received.

The second configuration change needs to be made to the Postfix master.cf file:

```
# AV scan filter (used by content_filter)
scan    unix  -  - n  -   16      smtp
        -o smtp_send_xforward_command=yes

# For injecting mail back into postfix from the filter
127.0.0.1:10026 inet  n - n  -   16 smtpd
        -o content_filter=
        -o receive_override_options=no_unknown_recipient_checks,
no_header_body_checks,no_address_mappings
        -o smtpd_helo_restrictions=
        -o smtpd_client_restrictions=
        -o smtpd_sender_restrictions=
        -o smtpd_recipient_restrictions=permit_mynetworks,reject
        -o mynetworks_style=host
        -o smtpd_authorized_xforward_hosts=127.0.0.0/8
```

> The formatting of the files is very important. You should ensure that there are no spaces around the = (equal) signs or , (commas) in the text you added.

The first two lines added do the actual creation of the scan service. The remaining lines set up a service for accepting mail back into Postfix for onward delivery. The rest of the options are there to prevent a mail loop occurring as well as to relax address checking.

As we are using just one machine in this configuration, we should specify the OutAddress option in clamsmtpd.conf as 127.0.0.1:10026. It is important to make sure that the processes are run as the same user as you use to run clamd or you may find that each process has problems accessing the other's temporary files. To set the user ID that a process runs as you can use the User configuration option.

We are now ready to perform the start up of the clamsmtpd process. You should start this as root and make sure that you provide the location of the clamsmtpd configuration file on the command line so that the correct configuration is being used:

```
# clamsmtpd -f /path/to/clamsmtpd.conf
```

If you have problems with starting the service make sure that the clamd (the ClamAV daemon) is running, and that it is listening on the socket you specified. You can set this in clamav.conf using the LocalSocket or TCPSocket directives (be sure that you only uncomment one). You should also make sure that the ScanMail directive is set to on.

Testing Filtering

Viruses, by definition, are things that we would prefer to avoid having any contact with at all; but in order to be certain that our filtering and detection processes are working correctly and that we are fully protected we need to have access to a virus for testing purposes. Using real viruses for testing in the real world is rather like setting fire to the wastebin in your office to see whether the smoke detector is working. Such a test will give meaningful results, but with possibly unappealing and unacceptable risks. What we need is a file that can safely be passed around and which is obviously non-viral, but which your antivirus software will react to as if it were a virus.

EICAR Test Virus

A number of antivirus researchers have already worked together to produce a file that their (and many other) products 'detect' as if it were a virus. Agreeing on one file for such purposes simplifies matters for users.

This test file is known as the **EICAR (European Institute for Computer Anti-virus Research) Standard Anti-Virus Test File**. This file itself is not a virus, does not contain any program code at all, and is therefore safe to pass on to other people. However most antivirus products will react to the file as though it really is a virus, which can make it a rather tricky file to manipulate or send via e-mail if you or the recipient has good virus protection systems in place.

The file is a simple text file consisting entirely of printable ASCII characters, so that it can easily be created with a regular text editor. Any antivirus product that supports the EICAR test file should detect it in any file that starts with the following 68 characters:

X5O!P%@AP[4\PZX54(P^)7CC)7}$EICAR-STANDARD-ANTIVIRUS-TEST-FILE!$H+H*

When you are creating this file you should take care of the following facts. The file uses only upper case letters, digits, and punctuation marks and does not include spaces. There are a couple of common mistakes that can be made when re-creating this file and these include ensuring that the third character is the capital letter O, not the digit zero (0), and that all 68 characters must be on one line, which must be the very first line in the file.

Example: Test from the Command Line

The first test we need to do is to make sure that the virus scanner is installed and that the virus definitions database is downloaded and included correctly.

The simplest way to do this is to create a copy of the EICAR test file on your server and then run the clamscan program with the −i flag so that only infected files will be shown and the −r flag so it will scan directories recursively. You should get output like this:

```
# clamscan -i -r
/var/local/src/clamav-0.81/test/clam.cab: ClamAV-Test-File FOUND
/var/local/src/clamav-0.81/test/clam.exe: ClamAV-Test-File FOUND
/var/local/src/clamav-0.81/test/clam.rar: ClamAV-Test-File FOUND
/var/local/src/clamav-0.81/test/clam.zip: ClamAV-Test-File FOUND
/var/local/src/clamav-0.81/contrib/clamdwatch/clamdwatch.tar.gz:
Eicar-Test-Signature FOUND
/var/local/src/clamav-0.81/test_virus: Eicar-Test-Signature FOUND
----------- SCAN SUMMARY -----------
Known viruses: 30279
Scanned directories: 42
Scanned files: 663
Infected files: 6
Data scanned: 13.09 MB
I/O buffer size: 131072 bytes
Time: 10.893 sec (0 m 10 s)
```

Testing CLAMD

By using the clamdscan process, we can again scan the current directory but do this by instructing the clamd process to do the scanning. This is an excellent test to make sure that the clamd daemon process is running.

The expected output should look something like the following:

```
# clamdscan
/var/local/src/clamav-0.81/test/clam.cab: ClamAV-Test-File FOUND
/var/local/src/clamav-0.81/test/clam.exe: ClamAV-Test-File FOUND
/var/local/src/clamav-0.81/test/clam.zip: ClamAV-Test-File FOUND
/var/local/src/clamav-0.81/contrib/clamdwatch/clamdwatch.tar.gz:
Eicar-Test-Signature FOUND
/var/local/src/clamav-0.81/scan.txt: Unable to open file or
directory ERROR
/var/local/src/clamav-0.81/test_virus: Eicar-Test-Signature FOUND
----------- SCAN SUMMARY -----------
Infected files: 5
Time: 6.996 sec (0 m 6 s)
```

Testing Mail-Borne Virus Filtering

The first simple test of scanning for mail-borne viruses can be performed by simply sending yourself a copy of the EICAR virus as an e-mail attachment.

The sample EICAR virus file must be created as an attachment to an e-mail. The following command chain from the Linux command prompt will send a very simple uuencoded attachment copy of the virus-infected file.

```
uuencode test_virus test_virus | mail virus@adepteo.net
```

This proves the simple case of a straightforward attachment containing a virus, but of course, in the real world viruses are slightly more clever than your average e-mail attachment. So more thorough testing is required to be sure that the filtering is set up correctly. Luckily, there is a web site set up to send out e-mails to you that contain the EICAR virus encoded within e-mails in a wide range of ways. Currently it supports 26 individual tests.

Thorough E-Mail-Borne Testing

The http://www.webmail.us/testvirus site requires you to register the e-mail address you wish to test and sends a confirmation e-mail to that address. In this e-mail is a link to follow that confirms that you are the valid user in control of that e-mail address. You are then able to send any or all of the 26 virus tests to this e-mail address. If any of the e-mail ends up unfiltered in your inbox then the installation has failed.

There are, however, two test messages on the site that are not strictly viruses and so are not detected by the ClamAV process. This is because the messages do not themselves contain viruses and so there is nothing to find and therefore nothing to stop.

> By definition, ClamAV only traps malicious code. Both gfi
> (`http://www.gfi.com/emailsecuritytest/`) and testvirus
> (`http://www.webmail.us/testvirus`) send this type of test messages. The
> nature of these messages is that they have some malformed MIME tags that can fool
> Outlook clients. It is not the job of an antivirus program to detect such messages.

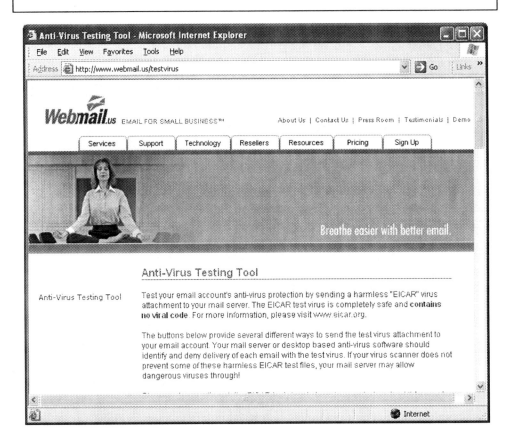

Automating Startup and Shutdown

One of the contributed scripts that are available in the ClamAV sources is a script to be
used for automatically starting and stopping the operating daemons when the system is
booted. For RedHat or Fedora, the following command from the root of the ClamAV
sources can be used.

```
# cp contrib/init/RedHat/clamd /etc/init.d/clamd
```

After copying the file make sure that the script has execute permissions and is not
modifiable by anyone other than the system root user:

```
# ls -al /etc/init.d/clamd
-rwxr-xr-x    1 root      root         1290 Nov 23 15:54
/etc/init.d/clamd
```

Automating Update of Virus Data

ClamAV is provided by volunteers and the servers and bandwidth that are used to enable the software and virus database to be distributed are voluntarily funded. As such, it is important to ensure that there is a balance between the frequency of checking for updates to maintain an up to date database and overloading the various servers.

> ClamAV group recommends the following: If you are running ClamAV 0.8x or higher, you can check for database update even 4 times per hour *provided* that you have the following option in `freshclam.conf`:
> `DNSDatabaseInfo current.cvd.clamav.net`.
> If you don't have that option, then you must stick with one check per hour.

Setting Up Auto-Updating

The Virus database files for ClamAV can be downloaded from the ClamAV servers in a variety of ways. This includes using manual or automated tools such as `wget`. This is not the preferred way of doing the updates.

A utility called **freshclam** is installed with ClamAV. Its function is to download the latest antivirus database automatically on a regular basis. It can either be setup to work automatically from a `cron` entry or from the command line or it can run as a daemon process and handle its own scheduling. When `freshclam` is started by a user with root privileges, it drops the special privileges and switches user ID to the `clamav` user.

`freshclam` uses the capabilities of the DNS system to obtain details of the latest version of virus database that is ready to be downloaded and where it can be obtained from. This can significantly reduce the load on your own as well as remote systems as in most cases the only action performed is a check with the DNS server. Only if a newer version is available will it attempt to perform a download.

Quick Test

In order to make sure that everything is configured correctly, run an interactive copy of `freshclam` from the command line whilst logged in as a root level user. Check the output for any error messages that may occur and rectify the configuration appropriately.

If everything works correctly, you are ready to create the empty log file in the /var/log directory and set the log file ownership and permissions to the user ID that freshclam will be running as:

```
# touch /var/log/clam-update.log
# chmod 600 /var/log/clam-update.log
# chown clamav /var/log/clam-update.log
```

The final configuration option required is to instruct freshclam to use the log file just created. To do this you should edit the freshclam.conf configuration file and set the UpdateLogFile instruction to point to the log file as shown.

```
# Path to the log file (make sure it has proper permissions)
# Default: disabled
UpdateLogFile /var/log/clam-update.log
```

We are now ready to start the freshclam process. If you have decided to run it as a daemon process then simply execute the command

```
# freshclam -d
```

Then check that the process is running and that the log file is being updated correctly.

The other method available is to use the cron daemon to schedule the freshclam process to run at a regular period. To do this you will need to add the following entry to the crontab file for either the root or the clamav user.

```
N * * * * /usr/local/bin/freshclam -quiet
```

> N can be any number of your choice between 1 and 59. Please don't choose any multiple of 10, because there are already too many servers using those time slots.

Proxy settings are only configurable via the configuration file and freshclam will require strict permissions on the config file when HTTPProxyPassword is enabled.

```
HTTPProxyServer myproxyserver.com
HTTPProxyPort 1234
HTTPProxyUsername myusername
HTTPProxyPassword mypass
```

Freshclam Configuration

A sample freshclam configuration file is also included in the source distribution. This well-documented file needs to be edited as well before the freshclam software will operate correctly.

```
##
## Example config file for freshclam
## Please read the freshclam.conf(5) manual before editing this file.
```

```
## This file may be optionally merged with clamd.conf.
##

# Comment or remove the line below.
Example
```

Make sure that this line is commented to allow the daemon to operate.

```
# Path to the log file (make sure it has proper permissions)
# Default: disabled
UpdateLogFile /var/log/clam-update.log
```

Enabling the log file is useful to track the ongoing updates that are being applied and to monitor the correct operation of the system during early testing stages.

```
# Enable verbose logging.
# Default: disabled
LogVerbose
```

The above option enables more detailed error messages to be included in the update log file.

```
# Use DNS to verify virus database version. Freshclam uses DNS TXT
# records to verify database and software versions. We highly
# recommend enabling this option.
# Default: disabled
DNSDatabaseInfo current.cvd.clamav.net
# Uncomment the following line and replace XY with your country
# code. See http://www.iana.org/cctld/cctld-whois.htm for the full
# list.
# Default: There is no default, which results in an error when
running freshclam
DatabaseMirror db.uk.clamav.net
```

This is an important configuration to get right to reduce network traffic overheads and ensure that you are obtaining updates from a geographically close server.

```
# database.clamav.net is a round-robin record which points to our
# most
# reliable mirrors. It's used as a fall back in case db.XY.clamav.net
# is not working. DO NOT TOUCH the following line unless you know
# what you are doing.
DatabaseMirror database.clamav.net
```

As the instruction says—leave this line alone.

```
# Number of database checks per day.
# Default: 12 (every two hours)
Checks 24
```

For busy servers with lots of traffic, it is worthwhile updating the virus database at a more frequent interval. However, this is recommended only for systems running version 0.8 or higher of the ClamAV software.

```
# Run command after successful database update.
# Default: disabled
#OnUpdateExecute command

# Run command when database update process fails.
```

```
# Default: disabled
#OnErrorExecute command
```

To aid monitoring of the updates to configuration files, the above options are available to apply suitable actions if updates do or do not occur correctly.

Monitoring Log Files

It is important to monitor the log file on a regular basis. Here you will be able to track the regular updating of virus database information and to make sure that your system is as well protected as possible.

Regular update messages should appear similar to the following

```
Received signal 14, wake up
ClamAV update process started at Wed Jan 26 19:45:07 2005
main.cvd is up to date (version: 29, sigs: 29086, f-level: 3, builder:
tomek)
daily.cvd is up to date (version: 685, sigs: 727, f-level: 3, builder:
diego)
-------------------------------------
```

Occasionally new software will be released and will need to be updated. Then you may get warning messages such as the following:

```
Received signal 14, wake up
ClamAV update process started at Wed Jan 26 20:45:07 2005
WARNING: Your ClamAV installation is OUTDATED - please update
immediately!
WARNING: Local version: 0.80 Recommended version: 0.81
main.cvd is up to date (version: 29, sigs: 29086, f-level: 3, builder:
tomek)
daily.cvd is up to date (version: 685, sigs: 727, f-level: 3, builder:
diego)
```

In cases when there are internet problems or the remote files themselves are being updated, the process may log error messages. No action needs to be taken provided that these errors are later overcome.

Disinfecting Files

A common request is for files to be disinfected automatically before being forwarded on to the final recipient. In the current version (0.81), ClamAV cannot disinfect files. The following information is available from the ClamAV documentation.

"We will add support for disinfecting OLE2 files in one of the next stable releases. There are no plans for disinfecting other types of files. There are many reasons for it: cleaning viruses from files is virtually pointless these days. It is very seldom that there is anything useful left after cleaning, and even if there is, would you trust it?"

Summary

We have now installed a very efficient system for checking all incoming e-mails for infected attachments and have significantly secured our systems—both, the server and the workstation—against attack. Constant vigilance is still required to make sure that software and files are always kept totally up-to-date in this ongoing battle.

10

Backing Up Your System

In order to prevent catastrophic loss of service in case of a major hardware (or even software!) malfunction you absolutely need to have a backup. The backup is supposed to let you restore the software (or rather: the software's configuration) and other data that you need to re-establish your service. This includes the users' mails, the system's mail queue, and their authentication data among other things.

This chapter will guide you through the process of backing up and restoring your server's precious data. It shows why to back up, what data to back up, and the different backup and restore methods.

What to Back Up

The big question with backups always is "What should we back up?"

There are many reasons that contribute to your final decision. Of course, you want to back up your server's configuration because it is essential to your server's functionality. But you also want to back up the users' data because it is your business' valuable assets. Is there a company policy that says people may use e-mail for private communication? If there is, will you back up those messages as well?

You should only back up what you need to restore your system to a functional state. This saves space on your backup media and shortens the time required to perform a backup.

After all, the space on your backup media is limited and thus precious. It is more important to back up all the users' mail than to have a complete backup of your /tmp directory. Also, the less data you back up, the less time is required to perform the backup, thus returning your system's resources (CPU cycles, I/O bandwidth) faster to their main purpose—handling users' mail.

Over time, we have developed the following list of items we back up:

To get a working system you need to:

- Install the software that your services require
- Configure that software

- Restore the users' mailboxes
- Restore the users' credentials
- Restore the logs (for billing purposes and end-user requests)
- Restore the mail queue

This leads us to this list of data that needs to be backed up:

- **Authentication data**: Users cannot authenticate themselves using their username and password combination without this. The data that needs to be backed up depends on the way the authentication is done and would include:
  - The three files /etc/passwd, /etc/shadow, and /etc/group
  - A MySQL database (if your users' credentials are stored in that database)
- **Configuration files regarding mail**: The server will not perform its expected duties without these. Some of the configuration files that need to be backed up are:
  - /etc/courier: This directory holds Courier-IMAP's configuration data. Backing this up is not needed if you store your courier config in a separate subversion repository.
  - /etc/postfix: This directory holds Postfix's configuration data. Backing this up is not needed if you store your Postfix config in a separate subversion repository.
  - **Remaining system configuration (the rest of** /etc**)**: This directory tree includes stuff like network settings, routings, and much more, which you'd otherwise need to memorize.
- **The users' mailboxes**: This is where the users' mails are stored. This includes the whole directory tree of /home and below. This is the bulk of your backup—vast amounts of data.
- **The mail queue**: If your server is very busy, you may have quite a bit of deferred mail in there. This includes the directory tree /var/spool/postfix and below.
- **Logfiles**: You should at least store the logs generated by Postfix and Courier. You need those to process user requests like "Where did my mail go?". If you do billing based on mail volume sent and/or received, you definitely need a backup of Postfix's logs.
  Since Postfix's and Courier's logs are normally written by your system's syslogd, you need to check the /etc/syslog.conf file to see where these logs go. Both programs log their messages with the syslog "mail" facility.
- **Store the files** /var/log/mail*: To be on the safe side, go for the whole directory tree of /var/log.

- **A list of installed software**: In order to restore your installed software you need to have a list of software currently installed.
  - o In Debian, this is given by the following command. The `installed_software` file contains the current state of which software on your system is installed/not installed:

    `% dpkg --get-selections > installed_software`

  - o With an RPM-based distribution, that would be:

    `% rpm -qa > installed_software`

  - o This file can later be used to install the same set of software:

    `% dpkg --set-selections < installed_software`
    `% dselect`

  - o In the `dselect` utility select 'i' for 'install' and then confirm the installation.

- An option similar to the one offered by Debian is not available with RPM-based distributions (at least we don't know any).

What not to Back Up

You do not need to back up all of the installed binaries since these can simply be reinstalled using the aforementioned "list of installed software". This, of course, assumes that you have the installation media around when you need to reconstruct your system. As a security conscious administrator you should keep your system up-to-date by installing the vendors' patches. Over the course of time, the versions of the installed and subsequently patched software will differ significantly from the versions that came on your installation media. If you can install these via the net (RedHat's **up2date** or Debian **apt-get**), you're lucky and you don't have to keep them on-site.

So you don't simply need the installation media, but also a complete set of updates since the configuration of your installed software may only work with the latest, greatest patched version.

E-Mail

It may or may not make sense to back up the Postfix queue of a working system depending on the situation.

With Postfix, e-mail messages hit your disk at least twice:

- The first time that the e-mail messages hit your drive is when they are being accepted by Postfix; they are written to Postfix's `queue_directory` before delivery continues.

> More disk I/O may be generated by a virus scanner or a program that detects spam (for example, amavisd-new).

- If it's mail for your domains, then your server is the final destination for these mails and their lifespan in the queue_directory is extremely short. They hit the queue, just to be delivered to the user's mailbox immediately afterwards. That's the second time they hit your disk.

- If it's mail that goes to other domains (because your server acts as a relay), then Postfix will immediately contact the recipient's mailserver and try to deliver the message there—only in case of problems will the queue ever contain a significant number of e-mails not yet delivered. These problems are:

  o **The content_filter is slow or not operational**: For example, amavisd-new or any other product.
  o **Remote sites have problems**: Large free e-mail providers often have problems and thus may not be able to accept your e-mails immediately.

In both these cases, the deferred queue will fill up with mail that's still to be delivered and that should obviously be backed up in case of a failure.

Maildir and Backup

Both Courier and Postfix use the Maildir format for users' mailboxes. It considers every mail as a single file allowing easy backup and restore operations even for single mails.

Backup operations are very easy with the Maildir format:

- "Back up an e-mail" corresponds to "back up a file to the backup media"

- "Restore an e-mail" corresponds to "restore a file from the backup media"

- "Back up a Mailbox" corresponds to "back up a Maildir and all its subdirectories to the backup media"

- "Restore a Mailbox" corresponds to "restore a Maildir and all its subdirectories from the backup media"

Incremental and Full Backups for the Mailboxes

There are basically two approaches to backing up your data: The simple method stores all your data, whenever you perform a backup. This is called a **full backup**. Its advantage is the simplicity, and its main disadvantage is the sheer amount of data that needs to be stored on the backup media. This problem is addressed by the concept of the **incremental backup**. An incremental backup only saves the changes since the last incremental (or full) backup.

If the space on your backup media allows for a full backup everyday, then do that for the sake of simplicity. That way you only need to look at the last intact backup to restore all the data.

Incremental backups are simple: The backup software only needs to back up files and directories that were not there or have changed since the last backup. Professional backup software and on-board utilities like tar, dump/restore (which are available for the XFS, ext2, ext3, and ReiserFS filesystems), and even rsync can handle this without problems.

If the space doesn't allow for that simple solution, you could use this instead:

- Perform a full backup every week.
- Do six incremental backups, one each day.

If you need to restore from scratch, restore the last full backup, then restore up to six incremental backups. That way you lose at most one day of mail—which is as close as you can get with a daily backup interval.

Storage Considerations

We recommend putting the mailboxes (/home) on a separate partition for many reasons:

- You can perform file system maintenance independently from other parts of your system (simply unmount /home, perform an fsck, mount it again).
- You could easily put that partition on a separate disk or on a RAID, thus separating the users' I/O (on that partition) from the system's I/O (logs, mail queue, virus scanner).
- You can use another file system that's better suited for the users' data. The root file system could be on an ext3 file system for reliability, while the mailboxes could be on a ReiserFS or XFS file system for better performance

Most important of all:

- If you choose dump/restore, you can only dump whole partitions (OK, that's not entirely true, but a dump/restore is done easily only with whole partitions).
- An overfull partition containing the mailboxes will not negatively influence the system's ability to write logfiles or other important system information. If all the data (logs, mailboxes, the system files) were on a single partition, filling this partition would cause logging to stop.

Backing Up E-Mail

Now for the actual task of backing up the mailboxes we'll use dump/restore (or xfsdump/xfsrestore in the case of an XFS file system) to dump the whole partition containing our mailboxes.

Some of the reasons for using it are:

- It is incredibly fast (in my tests, the network is the bottleneck).

- It is simple (one command suffices).

- It can run unattended (for example, as `cron` job).

- It does not need any additional software to be installed.

- It does not need a GUI.

Full Backup

We're now about to perform a full backup of the partition containing our users' Maildirs. In this example, this partition will be /dev/hda1 (the first partition of the primary IDE disk). So, we will want to back up /dev/hda1.

To find out which partition you'd need to back up on your system, examine the output of the `mount` command:

```
# mount
/dev/cciss/c0d0p6 on / type ext3 (rw,errors=remount-ro)
proc on /proc type proc (rw)
sysfs on /sys type sysfs (rw)
devpts on /dev/pts type devpts (rw,gid=5,mode=620)
tmpfs on /dev/shm type tmpfs (rw)
/dev/cciss/c0d0p5 on /boot type ext3 (rw)
/dev/hda1 on /home type ext3 (rw,noatime,quota)
```

As you can seen, /home is the partition /dev/hda1.

Out plan is to use the dump tool to create the backup for this partition. This backup data needs to go to our backup medium, which could be another disk, a tape, or a disk in the backup server.

There are various methods to get data across the network, one of them being `ssh`.

To get our backup data across the network onto another disk in the backup server, we use to power of Linux to marry the dump and `ssh` programs:

The output of the dump program will be fed into `ssh`, which in turn spawns another program on the backup server to finally write that data onto its disk.

The following lines of code give a full dump of the ext2 or ext3 partition containing the mailboxes to a file on a remote box. We assume that the mailboxes are on the partition /dev/hda1.

As root, run:

```
# dump -b 1024 -0 -u -f - /dev/hda1 | ssh -c arcfour user@backup-
host.domain.com \
  dd of=/backupdirectory/subdir/fulldump bs=20M
```

dump -b 1024 -0 -u -f - performs a level 0 (full) dump to a file ("-" in this case, being stdout, the standard output) of the partition /dev/hda1 (which contains /home in our example) using a block size of 1024 (for maximum performance) and updates the file /var/lib/dumpdates after the dump had been successful.

See man dump (your manual page for the dump command) for details.

So, how will the two tools be chained?

Since the dump data goes to standard output (stdout), we can pipe that stdout into ssh, which in turn executes dd of=/backupdirectory/subdir/fulldump bs=20M and runs as user on the backup server at backup-host.domain.com. This causes the dump data to be written into the /backupdirectory/subdir/fulldump file, using a block size of 20 MB.

The -c arcfour option chooses the fastest cipher in OpenSSH. We recommend the use of the key-based authentication scheme that SSH offers—that way the backup can run unattended, since nobody has to enter the password needed to log in as user on backup-host.domain.com.

The output looks like this:

```
# dump -b 1024 -0 -u -f - /dev/hda1 | ssh -c arcfour user@backup-
host.domain.com \
   dd of=/backupdirectory/subdir/fulldump bs=20M

DUMP: Date of this level 0 dump: Wed Dec 22 11:37:39 2004
DUMP: Dumping /dev/hda1 (/home) to standard output
DUMP: Label: none
DUMP: Writing 10 Kilobyte records
DUMP: mapping (Pass I) [regular files]
DUMP: mapping (Pass II) [directories]
DUMP: estimated 14295582 blocks.
DUMP: Volume 1 started with block 1 at: Wed Dec 22 11:38:36 2004
DUMP: dumping (Pass III) [directories]
DUMP: dumping (Pass IV) [regular files]
DUMP: 10.45% done at 4978 kB/s, finished in 0:42
DUMP: 26.81% done at 6387 kB/s, finished in 0:27
DUMP: 44.53% done at 7072 kB/s, finished in 0:18
DUMP: 56.03% done at 6674 kB/s, finished in 0:15
DUMP: 68.94% done at 6570 kB/s, finished in 0:11
DUMP: 83.68% done at 6645 kB/s, finished in 0:05
DUMP: Volume 1 completed at: Wed Dec 22 12:14:33 2004
DUMP: Volume 1 14290100 blocks (13955.18MB)
DUMP: Volume 1 took 0:35:57
DUMP: Volume 1 transfer rate: 6624 kB/s
DUMP: 14290100 blocks (13955.18MB)
DUMP: finished in 2157 seconds, throughput 6624 kBytes/sec
DUMP: Date of this level 0 dump: Wed Dec 22 11:37:39 2004
DUMP: Date this dump completed:  Wed Dec 22 12:14:33 2004
DUMP: Average transfer rate: 6624 kB/s
DUMP: DUMP IS DONE
28580200+0 records in
28580200+0 records out
14633062400 bytes transferred in 2210.683475 seconds (6619248
bytes/sec)
```

This next example will simply write the backup data to a directory—no `stdout` wizardry this time!

The following lines of code give a full dump of the `ext3` or `ext2` partition containing the mailboxes to a file on a separate disk to hold the backups:

```
% dump -0 -u -f /backupdirectory/subdir/fulldump /dev/hda1
```

This is, of course, much faster and simpler than sending all the data across the network via `ssh` with the data encryption and decryption carried out during the transit (which takes a lot of time and CPU power).

But if your server is burnt to cinders, then a backup on a build-in hard drive won't help you a bit there...

Keep in mind that `/backupdirectory/subdir/fulldump` can also be an NFS mount or an SMB mount. This would give you both, the advantage of a simple command line, and an offsite backup. So make sure you do have an offsite backup. It's easy enough either way.

In both cases you can compress the backup (also called "the dump") using `gzip` (or `bzip2`) to save space.

```
% gzip -1 /backupdirectory/subdir/fulldump
```

Incremental Dumps

The first incremental dump is done like this:

```
% dump -1 -u -f /backupdirectory/subdir/fulldump /dev/hda1
```

This saves everything that has changed since the last dump with a lower level.

Likewise, the second incremental dump uses the following code to dump everything since the dump with the level 1. And so on...

```
% dump -2 -u -f /backupdirectory/subdir/fulldump /dev/hda1
```

Checking the backup is not possible. "Why is that?" you may ask. The reason for this is that data we were just backing up is constantly in flux.

Remember that each file represents an e-mail. Whenever a user gets new mail or deletes old mail the state of the file system changes. Users constantly get mail, read mail, and delete mail, even when you're about to perform a backup.

Restore

All the data that has been backed up needs to be restored before it can be used. This can be done in two ways, interactively or non-interactively.

Interactive Restore

To restore data from a dump interactively, you need to copy the dump from your backup media onto your system or perform the selection of files to restore on the computer you stored the dump on. You may require additional space like a spare drive (unless you use an SMB or NFS mount) to do this.

For an interactive restore run:

```
$ /sbin/restore -i -f /backupdirectory/subdir/fulldump
>
```

The > is the prompt of the interactive interface to restore. It is Spartan. It allows you to navigate through the dump as if you were on a live file system. Use ls and cd to show directory contents or change directories. Issue ? to get a list of supported commands.

Once you've found the data you want to restore, type the following command:

```
> add directory
> add file
```

This adds the particular directory and all data below it or the file (only the file itself) to the set of files that need to be restored.

Once you're done with adding all the data that needs to be recovered, you issue the extract command:

```
> extract
```

You have not read any volumes of the backup (which dump organizes as "volumes") yet. Start with the last volume and work towards the first one unless you know on which volume your file(s) are placed. Specify next volume # (none if no more volumes): none

```
...
> quit
```

Do this with the last full dump and each incremental dump up to the last incremental dump available. This makes sure that you restore all changes since the last full backup.

> If the data you are restoring hasn't changed between two dumps, then you won't find it in the second incremental dump at all.

Non-Interactive Restore Across the Network

The manual approach makes sense if your want to restore just a few mailboxes. If you want a complete recovery of all mailboxes, you need to use the non-interactive scheme. This doesn't need additional storage space on the target system since the dump data is being piped across the network.

Recreate the file system on your newly installed, pristine hard disk (which needs to be partitioned, though!) and mount it:

```
% mke2fs -j /dev/hda1
% mount /dev/hda1 /home
```

Now there's a ext3 journaling file system on /dev/hda1 again and it's mounted as /home.

Please note that you need to recreate the data using the same file system you used when creating the backup!

Let the restore begin:

```
% cd /home
% ssh -c arcfour user@backup-host.domain.com \
  dd if=/backupdirectory/subdir/fulldump | restore -r -f -
```

Just like when we performed the backup across the network, we now do the same with the restore.

```
ssh -c arcfour user@backup-host.domain.com
```

The above line executes the following command as the user on the backup-host.domain.com host.

```
dd if=/backupdirectory/subdir/fulldump
```

The output is piped across the network and fed into restore -r -f -, which restores the whole dump's contents to their original locations using the original permissions and ownerships.

Configurations

There are two approaches to the backup of configuration data:

- **Store the data on your backup media**: This approach will be described here first.

- **Store the data in a repository on a remote machine**: This approach (using Subversion) will be described later in the chapter.

Backing Up Configurations on Backup Media

To keep it simple, we just use the tar tool to create an archive of the whole directory tree, /etc, and store it in the same directory as the full dump or incremental dumps on the backup server:

```
% tar cfj /etc /backupdirectory/subdir/etc.tar.bz2
```

If /backupdirectory/subdir/ is not mounted using NFS or SMB, we need to create the tar-Archive locally and scp it over:

```
% tar cfj /etc /tmp/etc.tar.bz2
% scp /tmp/etc.tar.bz2 user@backup-host.domain.com
/backupdirectory/subdir
```

Restoring the Configuration

```
% cd /
% tar xfj /backupdirectory/subdir/etc.tar.bz2
```

If /backupdirectory/subdir/ is not mounted using NFS or SMB:

```
% scp /backupdirectory/subdir/etc.tar.bz2 /tmp
% cd /
% tar xfj /tmp/etc.tar.bz2
```

Subversion

Configuration files are easy to break. "But I made only one little change!"—and afterwards it takes two colleagues one hour each to find out that:

- It was not one little change
- It was the wrong change
- The correct settings take ages to find

Needless to say, this is a royal pain!

Enter the **Revision Control System**. A revision control system can keep track of changes and it can help to restore older versions of a configuration file quickly. Here's a list of all the things it can do for you:

- Store different versions of the same file
- Keep track of who made changes
- Keep track of what has been changed
- Restore an older version of a file
- Store configurations on a different host with its own backup

There are a few open-source revision control systems out there starting from the ancient RCS or the widespread CVS and ending at Subversion, which we will use here.

We've chosen Subversion because it is well documented, so we can get additional information easily, and is easy to set up and use—just what we want on an average day working with computers.

We don't want to spend a lot of time doing manual backups because we might ignore the importance of backups if doing them becomes too complicated.

> If you never have dealt with a revisions control system before, you can refer chapters 1 and 2 from the book, *Version Control with Subversion* (`http://svnbook.red-bean.com/en/1.0/index.html`). This will give you a good start to understand what we will do in the following sections.

Before we start, let's do some thinking. What exactly do we want from our revision control system and what is it we don't want it to do?

We should want to store all configuration data from Postfix, Courier IMAP, and Cyrus SASL in such a way that changes to Courier or a restore from a Postfix configuration file do not affect any of the other applications. Speaking in revision control system terminology, we will have to create separate repositories for Postfix, Courier IMAP, and Cyrus SASL.

We also want to add some metadata to the files we put under revision control. A line at the start of each file should indicate the version we are dealing with and who did the last changes in case we need get additional information from that person.

Additionally we want to have a ChangeLog in each application's configuration directory that gives us a global overview of all the changes that have been done to the application. This history of all the changes made will make it easier to track down a problem to the version where it was introduced to our system. It might also make us aware of dependencies that would break if we changed something.

Among the files we don't want to put under revision control are sockets and especially databases. Sockets will be created any time we start the applications so we don't need to put them under version control.

Databases can be rebuilt easily, but are hard to back up since they are constantly undergoing changes.

That's it for our requirements. In the following examples we presume that the revision control system will be installed on a different host than the one that runs the mail server. Of course you can also install it on the same host, but then if the disks crash you will loose the revision system as well—maybe not the best security strategy. Let's see how can bring such a system to life.

Installing Subversion

Installing Subversion should not take you long time. Almost all distributions include it as a package. To find out if Subversion is already installed on a Fedora Redhat system, type:

```
$ rpm -q subversion
subversion-1.0.9-1
```

If the query echoes a line like the one above you have subversion installed. If your package manager does not report an installed Subversion, get it online from `http://subversion.tigris.org/project_packages.html` or from a CD and install it.

Configuring Basic Subversion Functionality

Once you have installed Subversion you need to make it available to remote hosts. This requires you to go through the following steps:

1. Create a directory where repositories will be stored.
2. Create a configuration for `xinetd` that invokes `svnserve` whenever needed.

Creating the Repositories Directory

Subversion needs to know where it should put files that we check into the revision control system. Later when different users check their files into the repositories they need read and write permission. This, however, collides with the default permissions that are set when a user checks a file into the repository; it will be writable only to this user, but not to the others by default.

To get around this we will not write to the repository via the file system, but use `svnserve`, the Subversion server, to access the repository. It will be the only one accessing the repository via the file system and handle write or read request on behalf of all other users. This will eliminate problems with access permissions.

The user and group `svnserve` will run as will be 'nobody'. To lay the foundation for `svnserve` we must make the top repository directory fully accessible to `nobody`.

In order to find the right location for our repository directory, we consult the **Filesystem Hierarchy Standard**, version 2.3 (`http://www.pathname.com/fhs/pub/` SRVDATAFORSERVICESPROVIDEDBYSYSTEM). It tells us that data for services provided by this system must go into `/srv`. Thus we create the following directories and set correct permissions for `nobody` as `root`:

```
# mkdir /srv
# mkdir /srv/subversion
# chown nobody:nobody /srv/subversion
# chmod 770 /srv/subversion/
```

That does it for the repository directory preparation. Next we will build the configuration that runs `svnserve`.

Creating a Configuration for svnserve

The Subversion server can be run as a standalone server or it may be invoked by a super-daemon such as `xinetd`. We prefer to start it only when there is need for revision control to spare resources on our host for other processes. When we are done with the configuration and a request for revision control comes in, `xinetd` will start `svnserve` just in time to get the job done.

The default port for Subversion to listen to incoming connections is port 3690. You might want to check that your /etc/services contains entries to identify the kind of service that runs on this port. If you can't find any entry for port 3690, simply add the following to the /etc/services file:

```
/etc/services:
svn                3690/tcp                      # Subversion
svn                3690/udp                      # Subversion
```

Then you need to tell xinetd what it should do if a connection on port 3690 comes in. There are two ways to do this and which way you need to go depends on your system. Either you need to add additional configuration to /etc/xinetd.conf or you need to create a separate file in /etc/xinet.d holding the configuration. The following example deals with the later case where you need to create a separate file called svn in /etc/xinet.d:

```
# default: on
# Subversion server
service svn
{
        port            = 3690
        socket_type     = stream
        protocol        = tcp
        wait            = no
        user            = nobody
        disable         = no
        server          = /usr/bin/svnserve
        server_args     = -i -r /srv/subversion
}
```

Most of the parameters will speak for themselves. If you are unsure what they mean consult xinetd(8) for further details. Take care that the user you define in the xinetd configuration matches the one that you have given access to the repository directory. Also keep an eye on the server_args parameter.

The -i option tells svnserve to cooperate with xinetd and the -r option /srv/subversion tells svnserve where it will find the repository directory.

Once you have created the configuration, restart xinetd to make it read the new configuration and run the following Telnet test to see if xinetd works the way we need it to:

```
$ telnet localhost 3690
( success ( 1 2 ( ANONYMOUS ) ( edit-pipeline ) ) ) QUIT
```

If you see this output, you have successfully reached svnserve. A QUIT will end the Telnet session.

Repositories

Now that we have a top directory for our repositories and svnserve is ready to serve our users it's time to create the separate repositories for Postfix, Courier IMAP, and Cyrus

SASL. This will be created in the following sections using Postfix as an example. Once you've gone through the steps to put Postfix under revision control, simply iterate over the steps to get Courier IMAP and Cyrus SASL under control as well.

Creation

Your first step will be to create the repository. It takes a few steps to do that. First you will need to create the repository itself and then you will need to accommodate the read and write permissions so that it can be used by the user nobody.

> If you don't want to go through these steps over and over again you can download the add_repository script from http://postfix.state-of-mind.de/add_repository/. It will do everything described in the following by a single keystroke.

In order to create the repository run the following command as root:

```
# svnadmin create /srv/subversion/postfix
```

This created the repository, but now all files are owned by root. We need to change permissions to have the user and group nobody get full access like this:

```
# chown -R nobody:nobody /srv/subversion/postfix
# chmod -R g+w /srv/subversion/postfix
# chmod g+s /srv/subversion/postfix/db
```

Once you've set these permissions your next step is to configure the repository.

Configuration

Configuring the repository is fairly easy. We will need to specify who will have access to the repository and we need to create an authentication realm. The entire configuration we need to do happens in /srv/subversion/postfix/conf/. That's why we first change to that directory:

```
# cd /srv/subversion/postfix/conf/
```

In this directory you should find a file called config. It already contains the parameters we will now simply fit to suit our needs. If you don't have the file, create it, and add the following lines:

```
[general]
anon-access = none
auth-access = write
password-db = passwd
realm = Postfix Configuration
```

These settings will deny access to anonymous users and will give write and read permissions to authenticated users. The list of users, including their passwords, will be stored in the same directory as config; its name will be passwd. The authentication realm will be Postfix Configuration.

Use your favorite editor to create the passwd file and add as many users as you need. To begin the section of users and passwords you need to start with [users] like this:

```
[users]
patrick = patrick_secret
ralf = ralf_secret
```

As you can see passwords are stored in plaintext. To protect them from curious eyes you should change its permissions like this:

```
# chown nobody:nobody passwd
# chmod 400 passwd
```

This way only the user and group nobody will have access to the file.

Hooks

As a last, but optional step, you can configure Subversion to do something for you automatically when a certain event takes place. You can, for example, configure Subversion to send a mail to a list of users that contains the commit log message and a **diff** (a diff is a representation of the differences between the two versions, thus the name "diff") of the changes that took place.

This is very useful, because it will not only automatically notify all your administrators that a change has taken place, but also what exactly has been changed. Another administrator might find a problem reading the mail and you could fix it before it becomes a real big problem.

The mechanisms that trigger the execution of scripts in Subversion are called hooks. If you change to /srv/subversion/postfix/hooks you will find a set of templates, each containing a set of sample lines to show you how you might invoke a script.

The template we are looking for is called post-commit.tmpl. Open the template and edit it like this:

```
REPOS="$1"
REV="$2"

/usr/bin/commit-email.pl --from admins@example.com "$REPOS" "$REV" \
admins@example.com
```

In the example above you can see that /usr/bin/commit-email.pl will send a mail to admins@example.com. Of course you can use any other recipient address that suits your needs as long as it is a valid recipient. It could, for example, be a list of recipients you defined in /etc/postfix/aliases.

The command line above also sets the From: header to admins@example.com. This enables readers to reply easily and informs all other mail recipients of the admins@example.com list.

Finally you must put `commit-email.pl` into place. The script comes with the Subversion docs and it might not be located in /usr/bin by default. Locate it and copy it to /usr/bin/commit-email.pl. Then check the permissions to verify that the user nobody will be allowed to execute it.

Once this is done, admins@example.com should receive status reports of repository changes automatically.

Preparing the svn Client

As a last step before we will add our Postfix configuration files to the repository we will configure the svn client. We will tell it which editor we want to use when writing **commit** messages (these are the messages the editor assigns to the changes he or she checks into the repository, so people know what was changed) and to ignore some files that should not go into the repository. We will also take a security measure and specify that our files will have UNIX-style end-of-line markers. This will ensure that no matter what platform any of the files have been edited on they will always be readable on our Linux system.

Change to $HOME/.subversion to configure the svn client settings. This is the location where your svn client keeps its configuration. Open the config file and search for the section called [helpers]. If you prefer vim, for example, you would configure this:

```
[helpers]
editor-cmd = vim
```

Next you will have to tell your Subversion client to ignore some files. It should especially ignore all the .db files. There's no need to add them to the repository, since it is always better to create them anew from their original text files using postalias or postmap.

Scroll down until you find the [miscellany] section and add *.db to the global-ignores parameter it like this:

```
[miscellany]
global-ignores = *.o *.lo *.la #*# .*.rej *.rej .*~ *~ .#* .DS_Store
*.db
```

The Subversion client will now happily ignore all files with a suffix of db.

Also, while you are at it, uncomment the enable-auto-props parameter to read like this:

```
enable-auto-props = yes
```

This enables setting properties automatically, which we will need to control the end-of-line markers in the auto-props section you will find at the bottom of the file.

Uncomment the [auto-props] section and as many rules as you have files that should be in UNIX end-of-line style. The following rules should take care of the most important Postfix configuration files:

```
[auto-props]
```

```
*.cf = svn:eol-style=LF
aliases = svn:eol-style=LF
virtual = svn:eol-style=LF
transport = svn:eol-style=LF
canonical = svn:eol-style=LF
relocated = svn:eol-style=LF
access = svn:eol-style=LF
```

> Be aware that Subversion currently has no mechanism to provide all your users with this client configuration automatically. All your administrators will have to configure their Subversion client manually.

Importing Configuration

After all the preparations have been done you are finally ready to add the Postfix configuration directory to your repository. Since the Postfix configuration directory is already there, all you need to do is import it. The following example presumes that the machine hosting the Subversion server is backup.example.com:

```
# svn import -m "Initial import" /etc/postfix/
svn://backup.example.com/postfix
```

The command imported the current configuration files to the repository, but still the original files are not under version control. To get a copy of the files under version control you need to check them out of the repository, replacing the unversioned files.

Move the directory containing the original files to a safe location:

```
# mv /etc/postfix/ /etc/postfix.orig
```

Then change to the /etc directory and check a copy of the Postfix repository out:

```
# cd /etc
# svn co svn://localhost/postfix
```

Now you have a fully functional Postfix configuration directory that is under version control. Let's do some refinement.

Setting Properties

One of the nifty features of Subversion is to maintain metadata of the files under version control. While it can hold almost any metadata you may provide we will only go for the most basic, which will give us a comprehensive overview of the files' history.

The particular meta-information we will go for is Id, part of Subversion's default set of keywords. It will tell us the revision number that was used when it was added, the date the commit took place, and the name of the user who did the commit. Subversion will automatically update it any time we commit a new version to the repository or get an update from it.

To tell Subversion which files it should maintain the Id property for we need to run the following command:

```
# svn propset svn:keywords "Id" aliases main.cf master.cf virtual
property 'svn:keywords' set on 'aliases'
property 'svn:keywords' set on 'main.cf'
property 'svn:keywords' set on 'master.cf'
property 'svn:keywords' set on 'virtual'
```

As you can see in this example, you can use a list of files when you set a special property.

Now that you have told Subversion to keep track of the Id property, you need to edit each file that you've assigned the property to and provide the property as keyword. Subversion will search for the keyword upon a commit in the file and will replace it with the appropriate information.

The keyword notation requires you to put a '$' (dollar) sign before and after the keyword. In addition, you need to prepend a valid comment sign to the keyword, for example, '#' (hash or pound). Otherwise the application reading the line will try to interpret it as configuration parameter.

An initial addition of the Id keyword to main.cf at its beginning would look like this:

```
# $Id: 10_Backing_Up_Your_System.txt 43 2004-12-29 00:51:46Z patrick
$
# Global Postfix configuration file. This file lists only a subset
# of all 300+ parameters. See the postconf(5) manual page for a
# complete list.
```

Go through all the files that you have assigned the keyword to and edit them as in the example above. Once you are done with this you are ready to do your first commit.

Committing Changes

A **commit** is done to put an altered file that is under version control back into the repository. During the commit you will be asked to write a commit message; at its best you will describe what you have done in a way that others understand as well.

Make sure that you are in the directory that is under version control—for example, /etc/postfix—and type the following command to add all the files you changed at once:

```
# svn ci
Adding          aliases
Sending         main.cf
Sending         master.cf
Sending         virtual
Transmitting file data ....
Committed revision 2.
```

The output above tells that aliases was added to the repository, in this particular case main.cf had had the aliases_maps parameter pointing to /etc/aliases, which was changed to /etc/postfix/aliases after the import to have it in the repository.

The remaining messages simply tell you that the versioned files that had been changed were sent to the repository.

Maintaining a ChangeLog

We have set properties to keep track of single files, but if something were to go wrong and we needed a quick overview of all the changes that have been done to the files in the repository, we'd be lost.

This is where a ChangeLog comes in handy. Arthur de Jong wrote a conversion style sheet that uses Subversion's log entries to create a UNIX-style ChangeLog. Download it at http://freshmeat.net/projects/svn2cl/, unpack it, and copy svn2cl.xsl to /usr/local/share/svn/ to make it available to all users on your machine.

Then change into the directory that holds your configuration, for example /etc/postfix, and run the following command:

```
# svn log --xml --verbose | xsltproc /usr/local/share/svn/svn2cl.xsl - >
ChangeLog
```

After the command has run you will find a new ChangeLog file in the directory. It gives you a complete overview from the initial import up to the last change that has been done.

Rollback

If you followed all the steps until here you should be able to restore your Postfix configuration easily. Looking at the ChangeLog file you can easily detect which version to fall back to. All you need to do then is call the following command and Subversion will restore the corresponding file:

```
# svn update -r 27
```

In the example above, Subversion would restore all files to match version 27 of the ChangeLog.

However at the current state of Subversion development you still need to manually set the file and directory permissions, because Subversion currently does not account these. The following Makefile will do that for a Vanilla Postfix install:

```
all:    perms maps
# to make all, make the perms first and then the maps

perms:
        cd /etc/postfix
        chown root:root *
        chmod 755 post-install postfix-script postfix-chroot.sh
        chmod 640 access aliases canonical postfix-files relocated \
          transport virtual
        chmod 644 LICENSE main.cf master.cf

maps:   aliases.db virtual.db
# to generate the target maps, generate aliases.db virtual.db first
```

```
aliases.db:     aliases
        /usr/sbin/postalias aliases
# special rule for aliases, they need postalias instead of postmap!

%.db:   %
        /usr/sbin/postmap -w $*
# generic rule for all *.db files
# *.db is being generated from *.proto, which needs to contain the
# ascii form of the map
```

Simply run the following command as root and you will get correct permissions and your aliases and virtual databases will be recreated:

```
# make all
cd /etc/postfix
chown root:root *
chmod 755 post-install postfix-script postfix-chroot.sh
chmod 640 access aliases canonical postfix-files relocated \
   transport virtual
chmod 644 LICENSE main.cf master.cf
/usr/sbin/postalias aliases
/usr/sbin/postmap -w virtual
```

If you only want to fix the permissions simply run:

```
# make perms
cd /etc/postfix
chown root:root *
chmod 755 post-install postfix-script postfix-chroot.sh
chmod 640 access aliases canonical postfix-files relocated \
   transport virtual
chmod 644 LICENSE main.cf master.cf
```

Summary

In this chapter we showed you how to back up e-mail and mailserver configuration. We started off with an introduction on what you should consider worth backing up and ended with a sophisticated solution using a software repository. In particular we had a look at the following topics:

- What to back up
- Incremental and full backups for the mailboxes
- Storage considerations
- Restore
- Server configuration backup
- Installing and configuring Subversion
- Maintaining a ChangeLog

When you've set up everything we've shown you in this chapter you will sleep a lot better and, in any case, your users will love the range and functionality your system can offer.

Index

default flags, 185
execution mode, 187
flow control, 186
matching, 185
rule flags, 172
Formail utility program, 173
FROM_DAEMON, Procmail macro, 200
FROM_MAILER, Procmail macro, 200
full backup, 272

G

G/PGP Encryption plug-in, SquirrelMail, 112
getpwent method, SASL, 123
groupadd tool, Postfix, 21

H

hook, script execution mechanism, 282
HTML Mail plug-in, SquirrelMail, 111
HTTP Auth plug-in, SquirrelMail, 111

I

IMAP protocol, 10
chkconfig command, 87
configuring Courier-IMAP, 83
configuring Courier-IMAP, configuration
    directives, 84
e-mail, retrieving with Mozilla Thunderbird,
    87
IMAP server as authentication backend, 132
IMAP service, auto-start, 87
IMAP service, testing, 86
imapd file, 84
imapd file, sample configuration file, 86
imapd file, 84
incremental backup, 274
indirect mail delivery, 27

K

kerberos method, SASL, 123

L

ldap method, SASL, 123
local aliases, 53
locking, 184
lookup tables, 24, 25

M

macros, Procmail
^FROM_DAEMON, 200
^FROM_MAILER, 200
^TO_, 200
mail exchanger record type, 13
MAIL FROM command, SMTP transaction,
    10
mail tranfer agent, 15
mail transfer agent. *See* **Postfix**
maildir, backup, 270
maildir, message format, 29
mail-filtering system. *See also* **Procmail**
about, 149
file locking, 153
mail, forwarding, 152
uses, 151
main.cf file, Postfix configuration
about, 23
alias_maps parameter, 29
always_bcc parameter, 30
default_privs parameter, 54
defer_transports parameter, 30
delay_warning_time parameter, 30
home_mailbox parameter, 29
hostname settings, 26
inet_interfaces parameter, 22, 28
mailbox_size_limit parameter, 31
maximal_queue_lifetime parameter, 31
message_size_limit parameter, 31
mydestination parameter, 26
mydomain parameter, domain settings, 25
myhostname parameter, 26
mynetworks_style parameter, relay rules, 119
myorigin parameter, domain settings, 26
notify_classes parameter, 30
parameters for checking content, 43
proxy_interfaces parameter, 31
relay rules, 119
relayhost parameter, 27
structure, 23
master daemon, MTA, 16
master.cf file, Postfix master configuration, 24
mbox message format, 28
mechanisms, SASL layer, 122
methods, SASL layer, 123
Mozilla Thunderbird, retrieving e-mail via
    IMAP, 87
MTA, 15, *See* **Postfix**
MX record, 12

Thank you for buying Linux Email: Set Up and Run a Small Office Email Server

Packt Open Source Project Royalties

When we sell a book written on an Open Source project, we pay a royalty directly to that project. In the long term, we see you and ourselves—customers and readers of our books—as part of the Open Source ecosystem, providing sustainable revenue for the projects we publish on. Our aim at Packt is to establish publishing royalties as an essential part of the service and support a business model that sustains Open Source.

If you're working with an Open Source project that you would like us to publish on, and subsequently pay royalties to, please get in touch with us.

Writing for Packt

We welcome all inquiries from people who are interested in authoring. Book proposals should be sent to authors@packtpub.com. If your book idea is still at an early stage and you would like to discuss it first before writing a formal book proposal, contact us: one of our commissioning editors will get in touch with you.

We're not just looking for published authors; if you have strong technical skills but no writing experience, our experienced editors can help you develop a writing career, or simply get some additional reward for your expertise.

About Packt Publishing

Packt, pronounced 'packed,' published its first book "*Mastering phpMyAdmin for Effective MySQL Management*" in April 2004 and subsequently continued to specialize in publishing highly focused books on specific technologies and solutions.

Our books and publications share the experiences of your fellow IT professionals in adapting and customizing today's systems, applications, and frameworks. Our solution-based books give you the knowledge and power to customize the software and technologies you're using to get the job done. Packt books are more specific and less general than the IT books you have seen in the past. Our unique business model allows us to bring you more focused information, giving you more of what you need to know, and less of what you don't.

Packt is a modern, yet unique publishing company, which focuses on producing quality, cutting-edge books for communities of developers, administrators, and newbies alike. For more information, please visit our website: www.PacktPub.com.

Printed in the United States
131747LV00003B/38/A

9 781904 811374